THE HOUSE ON G STREET

The House on G Street

A CUBAN FAMILY SAGA

LISANDRO PÉREZ

NEW YORK UNIVERSITY PRESS

New York

NEW YORK UNIVERSITY PRESS
New York
www.nyupress.org

Library of Congress Cataloging-in-Publication Data

Names: Pérez, Lisandro, author.
Title: The house on G Street : a Cuban family saga / Lisandro Pérez.
Other titles: Cuban family saga
Description: New York : New York University Press, [2023] | Includes bibliographical references
and index. | Summary: "Through the intimate lens of one family, the dramatic history that led to
the Cuban Revolution is brought to life in this highly personal and moving story that combines
memoir, oral history, family papers, and archival research"—Provided by publisher.
Identifiers: LCCN 2023005979 | ISBN 9781479824625 (hardback) | ISBN 9781479824632 (ebook) |
ISBN 9781479824656 (ebook other)
Subjects: LCSH: Pérez, Lisandro—Family. | Perez family. | Havana (Cuba)—Biography. | Havana
(Cuba)—Social life and customs. | Havana (Cuba)—History. | Miramar (Havana, Cuba)—
Biography. | Cuba—History—Revolution, 1959.
Classification: LCC F1799.H353 A296 2023 | DDC 972.91/23063092 [B]—dc23/eng/20230425
LC record available at https://lccn.loc.gov/2023005979

Maps by Raúl Hernández.

This book is printed on acid-free paper, and its binding materials are chosen for strength and
durability. We strive to use environmentally responsible suppliers and materials to the greatest
extent possible in publishing our books.

Manufactured in the United States of America

1 3 5 7 9 8 6 4 2

Also available as an e-book

In memory of those who are always with me, lighting my path.

And dedicated to their many descendants, especially

Lisandro José Pérez-Rey, Julián Gabriel Pérez Rey,

Gabriela Pérez, and Paula Pérez.

CONTENTS

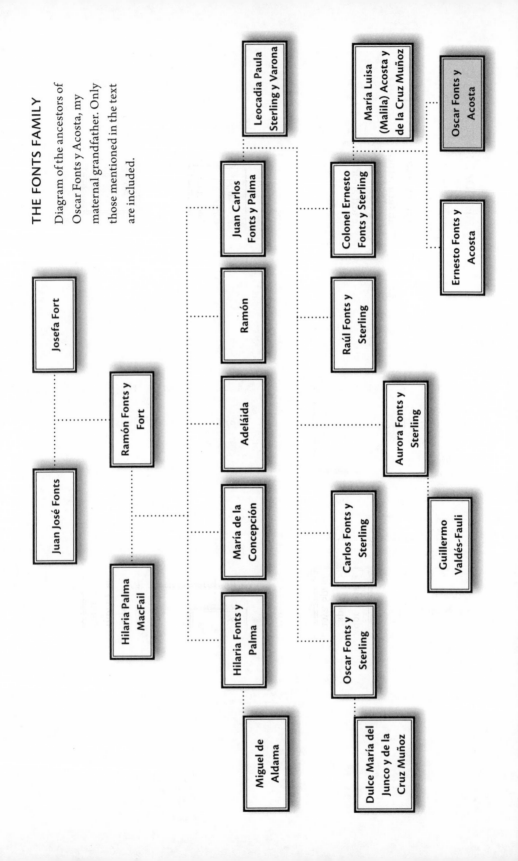

THE FONTS FAMILY

Diagram of the ancestors of Oscar Fonts y Acosta, my maternal grandfather. Only those mentioned in the text are included.

Josefa Fort

Juan José Fonts

Ramón Fonts y Fort

Hilaria Palma MacFail

Juan Carlos Fonts y Palma

Ramón

Adeláida

María de la Concepción

Hilaria Fonts y Palma

Miguel de Aldama

Leocadia Paula Sterling y Varona

Colonel Ernesto Fonts y Sterling

Raúl Fonts y Sterling

Aurora Fonts y Sterling

Carlos Fonts y Sterling

Oscar Fonts y Sterling

Guillermo Valdés-Fauli

Dulce María del Junco y de la Cruz Muñoz

María Luisa (Malila) Acosta y de la Cruz Muñoz

Oscar Fonts y Acosta

Ernesto Fonts y Acosta

THE VIDAL CARO FAMILY

Diagram of the Spanish/Cuban family of Amparo Rodríguez Vidal, my paternal grandmother, with their respective places of birth. Only those mentioned in the text are included.

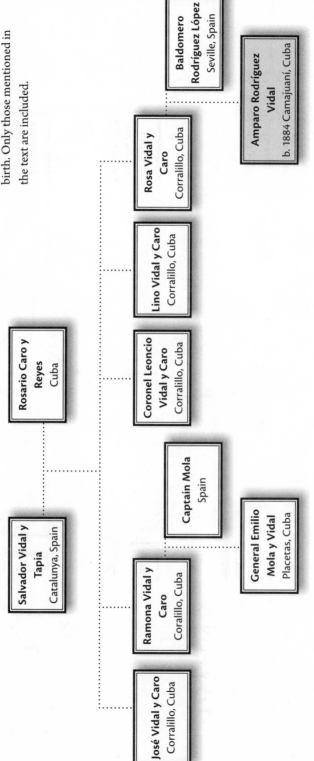

Baldomero Rodríguez López
Seville, Spain

Amparo Rodríguez Vidal
b. 1884 Camajuaní, Cuba

Rosa Vidal y Caro
Corralillo, Cuba

Lino Vidal y Caro
Corralillo, Cuba

Coronel Leoncio Vidal y Caro
Corralillo, Cuba

Rosario Caro y Reyes
Cuba

Salvador Vidal y Tapia
Catalunya, Spain

Captain Mola
Spain

General Emilio Mola y Vidal
Placetas, Cuba

Ramona Vidal y Caro
Corralillo, Cuba

José Vidal y Caro
Corralillo, Cuba

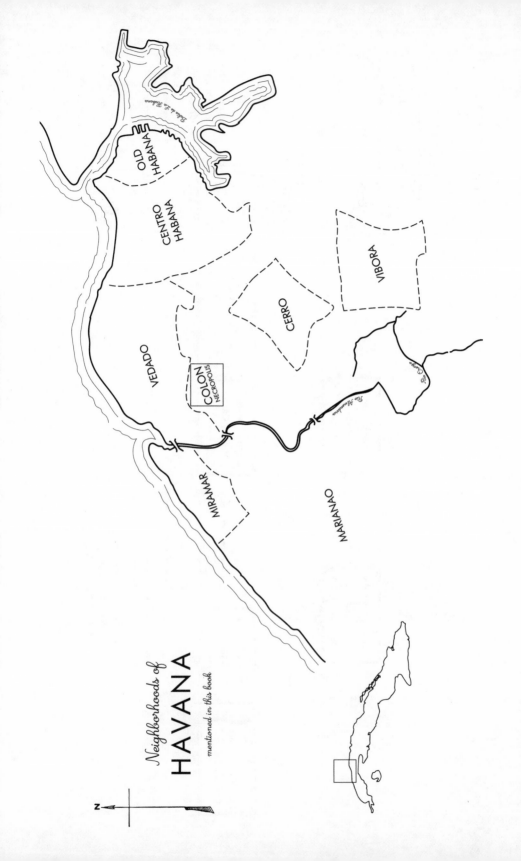

Neighborhoods of
HAVANA
mentioned in this book

OLD HABANA

CENTRO HABANA

VEDADO

COLON NECROPOLIS

CERRO

VIBORA

MIRAMAR

MARIANAO

Bahía de la Habana

Río Almendares

Río Orengo

N

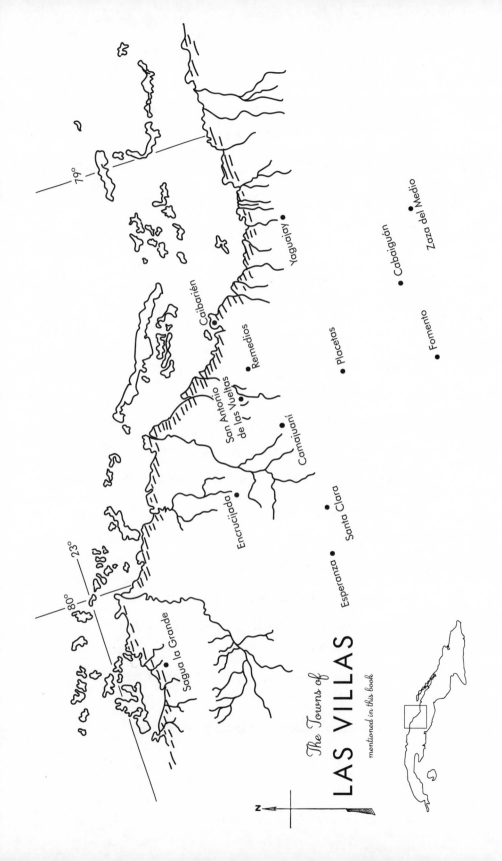

79°

Yaguajay

Zaza del Medio

Cabaiguán

Caibarién

Fomento

Remedios

Placetas

San Antonio
de las Vueltas

Camajuaní

Encrucijada

23°

80°

Santa Clara

Esperanza

Sagua la Grande

N

The Towns of

LAS VILLAS

mentioned in this book.

FIGURES

The house on G Street, circa 1930. Author's collection.

PROLOGUE

I sit once more on the bench directly across from the house on G Street. It's October 2015. There are many benches on the promenade that runs along the median of the street, but during my visits to Havana I always sit on this bench, the one facing the house.

I sat here with my father in the year 2000, on the day of his eightieth birthday, during his only trip back to Cuba since he left the island forty years before. We both sat on the bench for a long time, gazing at the house and saying almost nothing. We can't go in and visit the house, I told him, because it's a day care center full of toddlers and we can't just walk in unannounced. We would not be welcomed. He did not question that, and I was glad he did not. At this distance, from the bench, the house did not look too different from when he lived there for eighteen years, from the time he was ten years old to the moment he left the house in a tuxedo with tails to marry my mother. The house's exterior still had the reddish-brown color of unpainted stone, just as when it was first built. The tall iron fence that encloses the property was intact, as was the colonnade that frames the front portico. As seen from the bench, one of the columns even mercifully covered the sign near the front door that proclaimed the day care center's name: *Vietnam Heroico.*

Had my father gone in, however, the illusion that the years had not passed would have quickly and sadly faded. His heart would have sunk at the deterioration of the interior and the many unattractive ways it had been modified to serve little children. I think he knew that. I knew it because I had been inside during previous trips, on afternoons when I waited on the bench until all the children had left for the day to walk up to the door and give the administrators or the watchman some pretext to go inside and walk around. It did not always work, but a few times it did, and I would enter and try to see as much as I could before I was asked to leave. The sharp contrast between what I was seeing and my memories of how the house looked when I was a child was jarring. But I also felt grateful that the house had not met the fate of other stately Havana homes: abandoned, or turned into a tenement, or perhaps even put out of its misery with a total demolition. The house was minimally maintained, and I felt gratified that it had served to care for generations of children since the days of, well, Heroic Vietnam.

But now, in 2015, everything about the house has changed since my father last saw it fifteen years before. Someone decided that for the first time in its nearly ninety-year history, the exterior of the house needed to be painted. The dignified terra-cotta look gave way to a bright white with mustard accents. But the worst thing that happened was that *Vietnam Heroico* was no more. The day care center closed, and the house was shuttered. From the bench I can see the heavy rusted chain that wraps through and around the iron lattice of the tall double doors of the front entrance, the ends of the chain secured by a huge lock.

I made inquiries when I first learned of the closure. Cuba's birth rate is so low that perhaps they need fewer day care centers and there is nothing wrong with the house. But no; I found out that the roof leaks everywhere. I was told that the day care closed suddenly after a large chunk of plaster, weakened by water seepage, came crashing down from the kitchen's ceiling. Fortunately, no one was around when it happened. My aunt Leticia, the only one of my father's nine siblings who was still alive at that time, suspected as much. "The roof had always been the house's weakness," she declared.

There are no plans to repair the house. The Ministry of Education would have to do it, and they presumably have no money. With each passing day the house moves inexorably toward abandonment and, eventually, demolition. The idea seems inconceivable.

The closure made me realize the depth of my emotional connection with the house on G Street, a connection I still do not quite understand. I never lived there. When my parents married, they went to live in an apartment in Miramar, a new suburb at the time. I lived in that apartment until 1960, when I was eleven years old and my parents decided we would leave the country. But every Sunday, my parents, my brother, and I would join my uncles and aunts and their children for lunch at the house on G Street. Perhaps it was the sense of belonging that came with those weekly lunches, with uncles and aunts doting over every niece and nephew, and with all those cousins as playmates. The house gave my life a sense of stability, with its spaciousness and solidness. I knew my grandfather had built it and that my father and his siblings had grown up in it. I imagined what it must have been like to live there at the time my father was a child and how the house and its occupants shaped my life in many ways. The house was the physical representation of my family legacy, and once I no longer lived in Cuba it became in my mind the reference point for everything that had been and would never be again. The house on G Street became Cuba for me.

As I sit on the bench and look at the house, I can easily imagine the many events that took place there that marked my life and, even more, determined my very existence. None were probably more important than the get-acquainted dinner between my two sets of grandparents. It must have taken place sometime in 1947. After more than two years of courtship, my father finally proposed to my mother, who he had met when she was still a teenager, not long after her graduation from the Sacred Heart of Jesus School. Lisandro Pérez Moreno and Amparo Rodríguez Vidal decided it was time to formally meet the parents of the woman their son was marrying, so they invited the Fonts to their home. It was an intimate occasion with just the two couples. Their children did not attend.

That evening, Oscar Fonts y Acosta drove his Cadillac to the house on G Street and entered the driveway that flanked the house on its left (north) side. The iron gates to the driveway had been left open, awaiting the guests. Oscar stopped the car below the wide staircase that led up from the street level to the portico. A servant opened the door on the passenger side and my grandmother, Nancy Boullosa, slowly emerged from the car. She was a timid woman and was nervous about this important occasion. My grandfather Oscar bounded out of the car and turned it over to César, Lisandro's chauffer, who would park it at the end of the driveway near the rear of the house. Aware of his wife's timidity, Oscar quickly took Nancy's hand and placed it on the inside of his bent elbow and led her up the dozen or so steps of the terrazzo staircase. Lisandro and Amparo were waiting at the top to greet them.

In the somewhat intimate world of Havana's upper classes, referred to by its own members as *gente conocida* (literally "known people"), it is likely that the two families were at least aware of each other and may have had occasion to meet informally. But they were not well acquainted. They socialized in different circles, reflecting the very dissimilar paths they had taken to become *gente conocida*, with entries in the Havana Social Register. The Fonts were not among the oldest of old money in Havana, but they were old enough, dating back to their arrival in Cuba in the early nineteenth century from the seaside town of Torredembarra, just south of Barcelona. They were not as wildly successful as other Spaniards who arrived during the island's sugar boom, but both the men and the women were fair, tall, and handsome *catalanes* who managed to marry into some of the most prominent and wealthy Havana families. That wealth, however, did not survive intact into the twentieth century, and Oscar and Nancy were not heirs to any fortune, living primarily on Oscar's salary as the administrator of Havana's largest printing company. But Oscar had attended high school in the United States, he was the son of a veteran of the Cuban war for independence, and bearing and family name still added up to important social capital in twentieth-century Cuba.

Lisandro and Amparo, in contrast, were from small towns far from Havana. Lisandro was an orphan raised by his older sisters. Never finishing school, he developed an unrelenting work ethic and a sharp entrepreneurial sense that eventually led him to establish a very profitable business exporting leaf tobacco to the United States. By the time the two families formally met on that day in 1947, the Pérezes were far wealthier than the Fonts family. The house on G Street, built by Lisandro in 1929 in the desirable neighborhood of Vedado, was a stately residence, considerably larger than Oscar and Nancy's house in the Miramar suburb.

The two couples also differed from each other in a very evident way. In 1947 Lisandro and Amparo were seventy-six and sixty-three, respectively, while Oscar was forty-four and Nancy was forty-three. Oscar's father, long deceased, was born only two years before Lisandro.

My grandfather Oscar was no doubt curious about Lisandro, his family, and his house. Vedado was a fashionable neighborhood dotted with mansions that rapidly sprouted during the first three decades of the twentieth century. They were built with fortunes made once the Cubans were finally granted a government to run under the tutelage of the United States. The Platt Amendment, imposed on Cubans in 1901 by the US Congress, was designed to create a stable political and economic environment for American investments.[1] Cuba was open for business. Enterprising Cubans were able to rise from the poverty created by the independence wars and build fortunes on the rising tide of US trade, capital, and investments that flowed into Cuba during the early years of the Cuban Republic.

Many long-standing Havana elite families rode that tide of prosperity. But Lisandro's rise in Havana society was not typical. Born into a rural family totally "unknown" in Havana, the family he created would become *gente conocida* of the capital, with a house in Vedado and membership in the top-tier Habana Yacht Club. Most Vedado mansions tended to ooze new money with their ostentation: gilded finishes, baroque cornices, indoor statuary, monumental columns and winding staircases, stained glass windows, and the inevitable giant oil painting of the family hanging over a fireplace that was purely decorative given Cuba's climate. Oscar Fonts, with the inevitable conceit of old money families, was curious to see if the house on G Street was typical of the style of the newly rich.

The portico where Oscar and Nancy were received was part of a long and wide terrace enclosed by a colonnade that ran all along the front and Fifteenth Street sides of the house. Upon entering the house through the iron and glass front doors, Oscar and Nancy found themselves in a long foyer. On the left was the entrance to Lisandro's library and office, paneled in dark wood and lined by bookcases with glass doors. On the right of the foyer were two living rooms: one an enclosed and sparsely furnished room that featured a grand piano, and the other an open sitting room with wood and wicker sofas and chairs in the traditional Cuban style.

But the eyes of the visitor were invariably drawn past the foyer to the wide, high-ceilinged central hallway that ran almost the entire length of the house. On the right side of the hallway were two large bedrooms and a bathroom, and on the left side were four bedrooms and two bathrooms. Rows of windows near the ceiling in the hallway allowed for light and ventilation to enter the center of the house. The off-white color of the hallway and its pale marble floor reflected the light that streamed in, giving the central artery of the house an airy, illuminated feeling. The hallway ended in a paneled dining room, the largest room in the house, with a table large enough to comfortably seat a family of twelve and a few guests. Off the dining room, in the left back corner of the house, was the kitchen.

It was an eminently practical house, designed for a family with ten children. Its floor plan had more in common with a dormitory than with an upscale mansion. There was no grand staircase because the house did not have a second floor, except in the back of the house, where a steep and concealed stairway led to a modest apartment with two bedrooms and a bathroom. The house had no flourishes or frills, no baroque touches, no gold finishes, no cherubic faces protruding from the corners, no statuary, and no monumental oil paintings of the family. The exterior columns had plain Doric capitals, not the more ornate Corinthians found throughout Vedado. It was a solid, functional house, built by a man who had moved his family to Havana when he was nearing fifty years of age, too mature for the cosmopolitan capital to dazzle him into abandoning the simplicity and austerity of the small-town lifestyle that had taken him far in life.

To build the house, Lisandro did not contract the Havana architectural firms that were in vogue among the newly rich in Vedado. Instead, he went with an American engineering firm, Frederick Snare Corporation, that had built some of the largest public works projects in Cuba and in upstate New York. Lisandro valued functionality in design and wanted to hire a construction firm with experience in building solid, utilitarian structures. After the family moved from central Cuba in 1919, they lived for ten years in several rented houses in Havana, giving Lisandro a definite sense of the floor plan that would work for his family.

Before being called to the dining room for dinner, the two couples had drinks and some canapés in the sitting room. My father may have tipped off Lisandro that Oscar was faithful to Pinch Scotch. Oscar immediately asked for permission to smoke, which was, of course, granted. I do not remember my grandfather Oscar without a cigarette in his hand. Lisandro smoked cigars, but only after meals.

The platters that came out of the kitchen that night were filled with hearty Cuban food. A soup, two meat dishes, rice, beans, plantains, and starchy vegetables such as yuca and malanga. Despite the capital's growing interest in continental cuisine, Amparo knew no other fare than what she grew up eating in central Cuba. She now had someone to cook and serve for her, but she drew up the menus and closely supervised her kitchen. The family's new wealth did not make her forget that feeding her family was still, as it had been in leaner times, one of her principal duties. She rarely entrusted to the cooks her specialty, the desserts: rich sugary concoctions, especially flans and homemade tropical fruit preserves with cheeses.

Amparo presided over a large kitchen that had retained the original charcoal hearth that was used when the family moved into the new house on the Feast of the Epiphany, January 6, of the year 1930. Eventually, a gas stove was added to the kitchen, but the hearth was never dismantled, a reminder perhaps that back in central Cuba Amparo would probably still be cooking with charcoal. Even after the installation of the gas stove, Amparo would periodically return to that hearth to cook. She remained apprehensive about the gas stove, especially after it malfunctioned and singed the hair of one of the servants.

In a prominent spot in the kitchen was a huge freestanding manual coffee grinder. Mounted on its right side was a large iron wheel with a handle that ground the coffee beans very fine with just a few revolutions of the wheel, depositing the grounds in a wooden box. My grandfather had purchased the grinder from the kitchen of an abandoned sugar mill in central Cuba. With the grinder and the charcoal hearth, the kitchen had a traditional country look to it, something that was no doubt intentional.

The grounds from the grinder were used to make the strong coffee that, served in demitasse cups, signaled the end of the dinner. Oscar had already lit up a cigarette, and Lisandro had sent for his box of H. Upmanns. The man who made a living from tobacco kept his cigars not in a fancy humidor but on one of the shelves of an open linen nook in the bathroom. The humidity in the bathroom was apparently just right.

Oscar Fonts left the house on G Street that evening impressed that his future in-laws did not display the ostentatiousness and affectations so rampant among Havana's newly rich. But he was perhaps more impressed by the fact that the house had some truly fine art hanging on the walls; nothing gauche. He never attended college, but Oscar prided himself on being a broadly educated man with a special interest in art. He immediately recognized, as he walked through the central hallway, the works of some of the most prominent painters of Cuba's romantic period, even though the paintings, all pastoral scenes, were unknown works that must have been acquired directly from the artists' studios. Lisandro knew little about art, but he had the good sense to get some expert buying advice when he furnished the new house he had built. After all, he had to hang something on the walls of that wide central hallway, and he might as well make a sound investment in the process. His preference was clearly for romantic depictions of the Cuban countryside.

The artworks featured prominently in the favorable debriefing on the dinner that Oscar gave his daughter when he and Nancy returned that night to the Fonts house in the suburb of Miramar. "The most impressive ones are the two Menocals," he said, referring to two paintings by the last of the Cuban romantic painters, Armando Menocal. "They are the most valuable things in that house."

My father was the oldest male of the ten Pérez offspring and was named after his father, Lisandro, as I was also named. My mother was the oldest of Oscar and Nancy's four children, and she was named after her mother.

Lisandro and Nancy, my parents, were married on Valentine's Day 1948 in the Church of Santa Rita, on Fifth Avenue in Miramar.

* * *

Even as a child, I asked to be told stories about my family, so I have been hearing them, many repeatedly, throughout my lifetime. I have always thought that someday I would put the stories in writing and pass them on to my descendants, but I never anticipated waiting until the twilight of my seventh decade to do it. There were always more pressing writing projects, especially my most significant and time-consuming work, *Sugar, Cigars, and Revolution: The Making of Cuban New York*, published by New York University Press in 2018, a book that took me more than a decade to research and write.[2] And of course, there were also classes to teach and academic departments and research institutes to establish and manage.

As of this writing, there are more than eighty living descendants of my grandparents, including my two sons, my granddaughter, and my twenty-one cousins. I know that none of those descendants has accumulated the trove of family histories, lore, and anecdotes that I have managed to store in my memory, record in my notebooks, and acquire through my research. I therefore have a keen sense of obligation to leave behind the result of my lifelong curiosity about those who preceded me and who shaped who I am. In *Sugar, Cigars, and Revolution*, I wrote about Cuban families who had lived in New York during the nineteenth century. I subsequently felt a sense of urgency to write about my own family, whose story is no less interesting nor less important than the stories of those Cuban New Yorkers.

But I could not limit myself to a simple recounting of inherited family lore. If I wanted to fully understand the lives of my ancestors, and hence understand my own life, I had to place my family's story within the changing forces that shaped Cuban colonial society, the Cuban Republic, and the advent of the Cuban Revolution. That contextualization is important for any family history, but it is especially critical in the Cuban case, where turbulent social change so dramatically impacted the lives of generations of Cubans.

I did not need to look beyond my own experience to see the need to contextualize my family's story within the broader sweep of Cuban history. Growing up in the tempestuous Havana of the 1950s, I developed early in life what C. Wright Mills called "the sociological imagination"—that is, the ability to see the connection between history and biography, to appreciate that the course of our lives can only be fully understood within the social, economic, political, and cultural contexts in which we live those lives. Even a child could not fail to realize that the winds of revolution that were swirling around us in that place and time would have a lasting effect on the world as I knew it, culminating in what has remained to this day my most important life-changing event: the decision that my parents and most of my relatives made to leave the island in 1960, nearly two years after the rise of the revolutionary order on January 1, 1959. I was eleven years old when we left.

In *Freedom Papers: An Atlantic Odyssey in the Age of Emancipation*, Rebecca J. Scott and Jean M. Hébrard demonstrate the extraordinary utility of "microhistory," the study of places or events that, "viewed very close to the ground, may reveal dynamics that are not visible through the more familiar lens of a region or nation." The "close attention to the particular," they argue, will yield a deeper understanding of even the broadest of historical processes.[3]

A microhistory, specifically, the multigenerational story of one family (the approach used by Scott and Hébrard), can serve to vividly illustrate how broad historical processes manifested themselves in the lives of people who lived through Cuba's dramatic transformations from colonialism to republic and, ultimately, to revolution. But more than simply being illustrative, such an approach can craft a more complex picture of how those forces played themselves out "close to the ground," thereby enriching and even challenging the generalizations that many historians have painted in broad strokes. Attention to the "particular" holds the promise of a deeper understanding of how Cubans negotiated and adapted to the tumultuous changes that enveloped them. The historical processes that led to the Cuban Revolution constitute the large canvas within which I am writing a microhistory, based on my family, designed to deepen our understanding of that important event in Latin American history.

This book, therefore, is an attempt, to use the words of the historian Kendra T. Field, "to historicize the privilege of writing openly about one's own ancestors."[4] And it is a great privilege that I do not take lightly. Placing the story of my family within the broader sweep of Cuban history was a challenge, for it required that I dig deep into the historical record to flesh out details and fill in gaps. My research underscored the fallibility of memories and the inevitable tendency to construct a noble family story punctuated by myths and distortions of reality. Where possible, I have corrected any errors in what I was told so as to leave an accurate record. But family lore remains central to the narrative. As the Cuban Republic unraveled during my childhood, this story evolves into a memoir, in which I add my recollections to those I gathered from the memories of others who lived during earlier times, all of it contextualized by the research I conducted.

The rise and legitimization of personal family history as history, a development that Field so ably documents, has been especially evident in recent historiography on African Americans.[5] In *Growing Up with the*

Country: Family, Race, and Nation after the Civil War, Field tells the story of her own ancestors, inviting us to observe "historical change up close . . . revealing how individual lives meet, shape, and upend broader historical patterns."[6] The microhistorical approach is especially valuable in recovering and reconstructing the past of peoples who were enslaved and otherwise marginalized, who struggled and triumphed in the face of adversity, and who have traditionally been absent from mainstream histories and from so many public archival collections. It is through family stories, documents, and artifacts handed down through generations that the histories of marginalized peoples can be written, histories that despite being fundamental to fully understanding the time and place in which they took place are fragile, at risk of being lost unless they are recovered and told.

This story I am telling here is and is not part of the trend in the writing of microhistory. It is clearly not a story about a family that was enslaved or that struggled to survive at the margins of the society in which its members lived out their lives. On the contrary, my family was situated somewhere in the upper levels of prerevolutionary Cuban society. But it is a story that if not recovered and told will be lost, for my ancestors lived in a world that no longer exists, swept away by a tide of revolutionary change.

There is a great deal that is known about the broad historical conditions that inexorably pushed Cuba down the path of revolution, but much less is known about how members of the dominant social class led their lives; how they lived under colonial rule and later adapted to the new social, political, and economic order ushered in by the pervasive influence of the United States; and how they ultimately sowed the seeds of their own destruction. Postrevolutionary historiography has, until recently, treated the elites of the Cuban Republic with contempt, with little interest in writing about anything other than the undeniable abuses of power, corruption, economic inequality, and social injustices. Newer generations of Cubans have therefore barely the sketchiest knowledge of life in that past world. The only clues that it ever existed are its architectural remnants: the decaying yet stately residences and public buildings that surround anyone who lives today in the central areas of Havana, structures that have withstood the onslaught of time and neglect. The lives of those who built those buildings and lived in those homes are a mystery to most Havana residents today, despite the importance of those elites in shaping the course of Cuban history.

I am here chronicling that lost world from the perspective of one family. I therefore acknowledge and give free rein to the elitist lens of the story, without apologies, judgments, or justifications. The stories, characters, events, and my memory all speak for themselves. I have tried not to glorify my ancestors. To write a true microhistory that would leave a historical record and serve as a legacy to my descendants required me to scrutinize family stories that portray those ancestors in an overly positive light, balancing those stories with the realities uncovered by research and presenting those realities without airbrushing any faults, even painful ones. For example, I have no evidence that any of my direct ancestors on my mother's side owned slaves, but it cannot be discounted. The Fonts went to Cuba precisely to get in on the opportunities created by a booming sugar industry that depended on slave labor, and there were members of that extended family that were indeed slave owners. That is not omitted from this story.

Family stories and documents, my memory, and my research are the sources I have woven into a seamless narrative, keeping to a minimum the disruption of attribution in the text, as in "according to," "as I once heard," or "as found in." Of course, archival and secondary sources, especially when quoted, are properly cited. The story does not stray from what can be documented through family oral history and archives, memory, or research. Even when I have allowed myself to imagine the details of some events that I know took place but to which I could not have been a witness, such as the get-acquainted dinner of my grandparents, I cobbled the details together based on the sources. In the case of the dinner, I draw on my mother's recollection of what her father told her about it, embellished, for example, by what my father once told me about where his father kept the H. Upmanns, my aunt's information about Oscar's favorite brand of Scotch, and my own memory of the house and the dinners that were served there. To create fictional events, characters, or stories would run counter to my purpose in writing this book. That clarification is necessary, for my family was not exempt from living what Gabriel García Márquez called "the outsized reality" of Latin America, a reality that, had it not been lived, would be considered a work of fiction.[7] This is not a work of fiction, no matter how fantastic some of the passages may seem.

Despite my claim to write this story for others, I now realize that this project has also been about self-awareness. I always found puzzling many aspects of my childhood in Cuba, especially the strong American influence on my everyday life. All my immediate ancestors were born in Cuba, and the more distant ones were born in Spain. How did such a thoroughly Cuban child grow up in such a binational Cuban and American world? As I assembled and wrote the story of my family, my childhood made sense. When, late in the book, I enter the story with my own memories, I hope that the reader will be able to appreciate, as I did, that my childhood could not have been other than what it was, a product of the historical processes that enveloped my ancestors and determined the course of their own lives, and mine.

In the end, what I have tried to accomplish here is to construct an authentic family chronicle that is rooted in, and reflects, the dramatic history of the place where my forebears lived and where I spent my childhood. Ultimately, this is a story of the antecedents, rise, and fall of the Cuban Republic, as seen through the lives of the members of two families that were united on a February day in 1948.

The stories of those two families were quite different from each other, but they were both emblematic of the course of Cuban history during the time in which they unfolded. As such, I aim in this book to do more than just leave a record for my descendants. I have attempted, I hope successfully, to use the story of my family to write a history, from a micro perspective, of the transformations that characterized Cuban society as it lurched from colony to republic and then to revolution.

1

FONTS

CATALUNYA

The ancient village of Torredembarra, about fifty miles south of Barcelona, is today largely overlooked amid the sprawl of modern seaside villas, condominiums, resorts, hotels, restaurants, and marinas that stretch continuously along most of Catalunya's Balearic Coast. The village's well-preserved medieval center is usually bypassed by the many Spaniards and foreigners on their way to the warm beaches of the Mediterranean.

Torredembarra's history dates to 1195 CE, when the local archbishop had a chapel built in that location. The town that grew around it was named after a nearby tower (*torre*) in what was then the larger municipality, Bará, named after a long-forgotten local notable. Tower-of-Bará, or *Torre-den-Bara* in Catalán, in time became Torredembarra.[1] But despite its origins in the twelfth century, the village is a newcomer compared to its surrounding region. Torredembarra is in the province named after its principal city, Tarragona, a port just twelve miles down the coast that in 218 BCE became a Roman stronghold and the major administrative and trade center for Hispania, the empire's Iberian province. There are Roman ruins strewn all over the region, the most prominent of which is the Tarragona Amphitheater in the city's center, directly on the shoreline.

Just outside Torredembarra, there is a Roman triumphal arch that dates to 13 BCE.[2]

It is not clear why or exactly when Juan José Fonts; his wife, Josefa Fort; and their son, Ramón, left Torredembarra for Cuba. Perhaps the village's economic base of fishing, agriculture (wine, wheat, olive oil, and carobs), and the manufacture of high-quality cloth made since Roman times from the hemp cultivated in the region could not match what the Caribbean island colony was offering newcomers at the beginning of the nineteenth century: a chance to get in on the ground floor of what was fast becoming one of the most profitable industries in the Americas. Stories of the wealth that could be made from the island's booming sugar production no doubt made their way back to Torredembarra, as many prominent Catalonians, several from Torredembarra, had already made their way to Havana.[3]

Juan José and his family may have also felt compelled to leave Torredembarra in the wake of the constant upheavals caused by the Peninsular War, waged by Napoleon to "pacify" Spain and place his brother Joseph on the throne in Madrid. From 1811 to 1813, Tarragona and its countryside became one of the war's principal theaters, as the city's Spanish and English defenders succumbed to a siege by Napoleon's troops in 1811, and in 1813, the English laid their own siege but failed to dislodge the French defenders.[4]

MARRIAGES

Regardless of whether the Fonts family emigrated before, during, or after the Napoleonic takeover of Spain, by 1820 they were in the New World, if perhaps not yet in Havana. That year, at the age of twenty-nine, Ramón, the son of Juan José and Josefa, married nineteen-year-old María Hilaria Palma MacFail in St. Augustine, Florida, which had been, until the year before, the capital of Spanish Florida for more than two hundred years. María Hilaria's father was an Andalusian immigrant who had established a large family and a prominent presence in the city.

Lottery ticket, December 22, 1825. Author's collection.

The transfer of St. Augustine from Spanish to US control eventually prompted the migration of many families to Cuba, and the Palmas were among them. By 1825, Ramón, his young bride, and his parents were already residing in Havana. The marriage to María Hilaria had been a stroke of good fortune for the young immigrant, but perhaps pure chance played a critical role in Ramón's future.

Tucked away in the stamp collection I inherited from my grandfather Oscar, the great-grandson of Ramón, was a small, thick, yellowed envelope that contained a ticket issued by the Royal Lottery of the Always Faithful Island of Cuba for a drawing on December 22, 1825. The ticket was stamped "*pagado*" (paid), which means it was a winning ticket. The prizes typically ranged from the equivalent of about a hundred dollars up to ten thousand dollars, and possibly higher, since prizes during the holiday season were generally more substantial. That the ticket was carefully kept for generations, even as so many of the family's papers have disappeared, is the strongest clue that it was probably not a paltry sum but instead a game changer for the fortunes of the Fonts family. Anything close to ten thousand dollars would have been a considerable sum in those days.

The lottery winnings may have helped Ramón invest in the island's burgeoning sugar industry. By the 1820s, the process by which the island became the world's leading producer was well underway. It has been called the Sugar Revolution because it transformed Cuban society in the span of only a few decades.

The origins of the Sugar Revolution date back to 1762 when, with a swift and bold military maneuver, the British occupied Havana. They stayed for only eleven months before giving it back to Spain, but it was a turning point in Cuban history, as the floodgates of commerce were opened between the island and the rest of the world. For centuries, commerce in and out of Havana's harbor had been dominated by Spanish royal ships carrying treasure and goods from the mainland. During the eleven months of the occupation, however, more than seven hundred merchant ships sailed to Havana, many of them from the British North American colonies.[5] Cubans welcomed the new trade opportunities, but the sinister underside of the commercial opening was that it gave Cuban planters direct access to English slavers without having to go through Spanish middlemen. The cheap and massive importation of slaves was the trigger for the sugar boom.[6]

Three other factors helped propel Cuban sugar production. One was technological: the application of steam engines to power increasingly larger cane grinders, greatly expanding the production of the sugar mill. Another was the discovery, in Louisiana in 1795, of the granulation process, which helped sugar become a marketable world commodity. A third factor was the slave rebellion in the neighboring French colony of Saint-Domingue, which led to the establishment of the independent nation of Haiti but devastated its sugar industry. Saint-Domingue had been the world's leading sugar producer, so the sudden and total loss of its production created a huge void in the world sugar market and a sharp increase in prices. The rush to get in on the profitable sugar market created a self-feeding juggernaut as Cuban planters multiplied their slaves, their land, and the production capacity of their mills.[7]

The results were dramatic. In 1761, the year before the British occupation, the ninety-eight small mills in the Havana region produced a total of 4,300 tons of sugar. At the cusp of the transformation, in 1792, total production had already multiplied to 13,800 tons. But even that increase pales in comparison to what would happen during the first half of the nineteenth century. By 1860, total production exceeded 515 million tons. "The nation," wrote one historian, "became a burnt offering to the god sugar."[8]

Equally dramatic was the impact of the Sugar Revolution on Cuban society. In 1774, nearly three centuries after the Spanish set foot in Cuba, the island only had some 172,000 inhabitants, and slightly over 20 percent of them were slaves. By 1827, however, only fifty-three years later, the total population more than tripled, to some 704,000, with slaves representing 40 percent. Just fourteen years later, in 1841, the population passed the million mark, and the proportion of slaves continued to rise.[9]

The island's rapid population growth was due not only to the slave trade but also to the arrival of Spaniards such as the Fonts, who likely went to Cuba to get in on the expanding economic opportunities. There was a lot of money to be made, not just in sugar production, but in all the ancillary industries and services created by the Sugar Revolution. A new elite arose in Havana and the nearby region and city of Matanzas. This sugarocracy was composed primarily of newly arrived immigrants, many of whom became far wealthier than the old aristocracy that had lived for generations in Cuba under a more limited agricultural and pastoral economy.

By the middle of the nineteenth century, Ramón and María Hilaria had prospered enough to gain a foothold in the upper levels of Havana's society and have their portraits painted by Juan Jorge Peoli, one of Havana's most popular portraitists. Their social status enabled their children to do what Ramón had done: marry well. They had five offspring, three girls and two boys, all baptized in Havana's cathedral. The oldest, Hilaria, named after her mother, was the one who landed the best catch of all. At nineteen,

Ramón Fonts y Fort, painted by Juan Jorge Peoli. Fonts family collection.

María Hilaria Palma MacFail, painted by Juan Jorge Peoli. Fonts family collection.

in 1844, she married Miguel de Aldama y Alfonso, scion of what at the time may have been the richest family in Havana.[10]

Miguel's father was a Spanish immigrant, Domingo de Aldama y Aréchaga, born in a village in Spain's Basque region to a family of modest means. Domingo left for Cuba as a young man, determined to succeed by taking advantage of the island's burgeoning opportunities. He married one of the daughters of his employer, Gonzalo Alfonso, a wealthy Havana merchant and sugar mill owner who had befriended the enterprising young immigrant.[11] Domingo made the most of his new social position and soon amassed his own fortune from the booming business in sugar and slaves. Many of his first investments were in the slave trade, underwriting expeditions to Africa to supply his father-in-law's sugar mills with labor.[12] Eventually, Domingo acquired his own mills as well as controlling interests in the island's major railroads and insurance firms. He built a palatial home in Havana, the first residence to be built outside the city's old colonial walls. The Aldama Palace, as it was called, still stands and is regarded, as one writer notes, as "the most acclaimed building in nineteenth-century Havana."[13]

Domingo and his wife, María Rosa, had four children, two boys and two girls. The oldest son, Gonzalo (named after his maternal grandfather), was rebellious, intent on marrying a beautiful, charming, and educated woman somewhat older than he, but whom Domingo considered an unacceptable match because her family had a lower social status. He sent Gonzalo to New York, where the family sold its sugar, and instructed him not to return to Havana until he had forgotten about marrying the woman. Domingo was inflexible despite his son's pleas, and one morning in 1845 the young man hurled himself from the dormer window of his Barclay Street boardinghouse in downtown Manhattan, landing headfirst on a curbstone some sixty feet below, dying instantly.[14]

That left Miguel as the only son of Domingo and María Rosa. He had been a good student, an obedient son, and trustworthy and effective in managing the family's assets, and he had married Hilaria Fonts, a union that Domingo favored. In time, Miguel became the head of the

Miguel de Aldama and Hilaria Fonts. Carrillo de Albornoz and Aldama Family Papers, Beinecke Rare Book and Manuscript Library, Yale University.

Alfonso-Aldama clan, administering and significantly expanding not only his father's fortune but also that of his mother's family, the Alfonsos. He and Hilaria Fonts had five children, four girls and a boy, but only the girls survived to adulthood.

Hilaria Fonts's marriage to Miguel and into one of Havana's wealthiest families no doubt paved the way for her younger siblings to also enter favorable unions. All four of them married in Havana's cathedral between 1855 and 1857. María de la Concepción married an Alfonso, a member of Miguel's clan, and Adeláida married Justo Mazorra y Cairo, a son of immigrants from Santander. One month before Adeláida's wedding, her brother Ramón Fonts (named after his father) married Adeláida's fiancé's sister, Clara María Mazorra y Cairo.

The youngest of Hilaria's siblings, Juan Carlos, married in 1856. His marriage may not have been as economically advantageous as Hilaria's, but it was certainly a big step for the Fonts in terms of that less tangible, but critical, asset in colonial society: social prestige. Unlike his siblings, who married into Spanish immigrant families that were part of the newly rich sugarocracy, Juan Carlos married into the old Cuban aristocracy. His bride was Leocadia Paula Sterling y Varona, a woman from Puerto Príncipe, in the east-central region of Camagüey. Eastern Cuba was the area first settled by the Spanish, and the families that migrated there from Spain and became landowners could claim to be Cuba's oldest landed aristocracy, most dating back to the sixteenth century. Leocadia's mother was María del Rosario Varona y Zayas-Bazán. The Varona family settled in Puerto Príncipe in the middle of the sixteenth century and became one of the most prominent in the region.[15] Leocadia's father was Nicolás Sterling y Heredia from Santiago de Cuba, in the island's easternmost province. Nicolás's grandfather was born on the island of Hispaniola and moved his family to Santiago shortly after 1795, when the Spanish relinquished control of Santo Domingo to the French in the Treaty of Basel.[16]

Aristocratic families do not necessarily have greater wealth than new money families. The eastern elite families that established themselves early in the colonial period on large pastoral estates saw the island's development bypass them as Havana became the hub of Spanish trade in the New World. Their descendants were also bypassed in the nineteenth century when the western provinces became the center of the Sugar Revolution that created a new elite class in Havana and Matanzas. The easterners remained stuck in a more modest and diversified agricultural economy based on cattle production, so they were less wealthy and depended less on slavery than their western counterparts, selling their cured beef to the English and the French, who had many slaves to feed in their sugar colonies throughout the Caribbean. They lived in relative isolation for generations and intermarried among themselves, as landed gentry tend to do.

Leocadia's family was apparently among the eastern families that decided to take advantage of the sugar boom and move to Havana, where they enjoyed a certain whiff of nobility as one of Cuba's oldest families. It is there where she met Juan Carlos Fonts y Palma. They had five children: Aurora, Carlos, Oscar, Raúl, and my great-grandfather, Ernesto Fonts y Sterling.

WAR, EMIGRATION, AND DEPORTATION

In 1868, less than a year before my great-grandfather Ernesto was born, war broke out in Cuba. Before then, Cuban separatists had been involved in ill-fated and sporadic conspiracies, armed expeditions from abroad, or local insurrections against Spanish rule in Cuba. But what broke out in October 1868 was different. It was the first all-out war for Cuban independence. It originated in Leocadia's home region, where the eastern landowners had endured generations of neglect from colonial authorities and had few sentimental or economic ties to Spain. To them, colonial rule meant only oppression and taxes. Without a great dependence on slavery and sugar and therefore devoid of any stake in the continuation of the colonial or slave regime, the eastern patriarchs, unlike the Havana sugarocracy, had little to lose and were willing to risk all of it, freeing their slaves and organizing an army to fight against the Spanish. Their desire for independence was stoked by a privileged education in Europe, where they were exposed to liberal and democratic ideals. The war they started quickly enveloped eastern Cuba.

The Havana sugarocracy was clueless about the intentions of their eastern compatriots, whom they hardly knew, if at all. On the day the insurrectionists declared war in the east, Hilaria Fonts; her husband, Miguel de Aldama; and their daughters and sons-in-law were on a ship bound for New York on their way back from a European vacation. As was the case with most western sugar planters, the Aldamas had long yearned for greater freedom from the economic and political oppression with which Spain ruled the island, as long as any change did not involve large-scale violence that could threaten their properties and end slavery. Back in 1847, in their new Aldama Palace, Miguel and his father, Domingo, hosted a secret meeting designed to promote the idea of annexing Cuba to the United States. A select group of leading sugar planters attended, as well as Moses Yale Beach, the editor of the *New York Sun*, and John L. O'Sullivan, the prominent New York Democrat credited with coining the term "Manifest Destiny."[17] Annexation as a slave state was an attractive alternative for the planters, who looked to the southern US states as a model of how to fiercely defend slavery while ending the slave trade, something the sugarocrats favored because they feared the consequences of an "Africanization" of Cuba if the slave trade continued. Furthermore, annexation was the best way to peacefully end Spanish rule, since it could be achieved through negotiation, something that at that meeting O'Sullivan committed himself to pursuing. He went to Washington and persuaded President James Polk to make an offer to the Spanish for the purchase of Cuba, an offer that Madrid flatly refused.

The US Civil War, of course, ended all possibility of annexing Cuba as a slave state, and while the western planters such as the Aldamas continued to hold out hope that Spain might reform its colonial rule in less oppressive ways, the easterners saw independence as the only alternative, and they embraced the only way to achieve it: war. In so doing, they forced the Havana sugarocracy to choose sides.

Upon his arrival in New York from his European vacation, Miguel de Aldama had an urgent letter waiting for him from José Manuel Mestre, a cousin who was also his lawyer. Mestre, who feared a "decisive schism," urged him to return to Havana as soon as possible. Miguel rushed home only to find another letter for him, one that spoke volumes about the influential position he had managed to attain through his wealth and contacts. But it was not a letter Miguel welcomed, for it would force him to make the most consequential decision of his life. Dated October 31, 1868, the letter was from Don Carlos de Borbón, the Carlist pretender to the Spanish throne who took advantage of the destitution of Queen Isabel to act as monarch. Don Carlos addressed Miguel in a familiar tone and offered him the position of Civil Governor of Cuba to help the Military Governor "with your influence, your contacts."[18] It was an attempt to recruit him into a figurehead role to help defuse the rebellion in the east.

Miguel was so stunned by the letter that he went to see Francisco Lersundi, the Military Governor, to confirm its authenticity. Lersundi confirmed it. Only a few weeks before, Miguel may have welcomed the opportunity to try to influence Madrid to reform its relationship with the island and avoid violence. But he turned down Don Carlos's offer in a letter that showed just how much the cautious Havana elites had been pushed into accepting the inevitability of the easterners' solution:

> Your offer . . . may have been well received before now by a people that have always aspired to the autonomy of the country as a way to harmonize the union with the metropolis and its own survival and prosperity. *Unfortunately, the circumstances have changed.* Some are fatigued, others are disillusioned, many are exasperated, and all are dissatisfied, and a considerable portion of our inhabitants has thrown itself into a fight, looking to have firearms succeed in the search for liberties and guarantees that could not be attained after thirty years of resigned suffering.[19]

Miguel had taken himself out of the loyalist camp, and the pro-Spanish forces were not pleased. The most zealous of those forces were the *voluntarios*, a paramilitary corps recruited in Spain by Governor Lersundi to ruthlessly assert colonial control. They tended to be young, poor, uneducated, and imbued with a fanatical patriotism and a hatred of rebellious Cubans. One historian described them as an "antisocial and *provocateur* element."[20] By December of 1868, when a new Military Governor arrived in Havana, there were thirty-five thousand *voluntarios* in Cuba, far exceeding the number of regular Spanish troops.[21]

The new Governor was General Domingo Dulce, a longtime friend of Miguel. His initial strategy was to quell the rebellion by granting concessions such as freedom of expression and the press and amnesty to all rebels who disarmed. The reaction from pro-Spanish hardliners was swift. A group of Spanish citizens demanded the Governor take "extreme measures . . . the government cannot make concessions with the larcenists and arsonists that infest so much of eastern Cuba."[22] Defying Dulce's orders, the *voluntarios* ran amok, provoking violent episodes in Havana against perceived sympathizers of the insurrectionists and unleashing a wave of terrorism throughout the city that cost the lives of even women and children. With the *voluntarios* outnumbering regular troops, the beleaguered Dulce was practically under siege in his own palace.

In that climate, Miguel de Aldama's decision not to cooperate with the loyalists proved to be a dangerous one. On January 24, while the entire family was spending a few days at their Santa Rosa sugar mill east of Havana, *voluntarios* from the Third and Fifth Battalions forced their way into the Aldama Palace and ransacked and looted a section of it, slashing paintings with their swords, breaking mirrors, damaging furniture, tearing curtains, and taking valuables. They were eventually dispersed by regular Spanish troops dispatched by General Dulce, who personally showed up to survey the destruction. Three days later, still at the Santa Rosa mill, Miguel penned a letter to "My General and friend" (Dulce) in which he bemoaned the damages "which you know better than I": robbery, arson,

destruction, looting, and even, he added as an afterthought, the "viola-
tion of an unfortunate and defenseless black girl [*negrita*]," presumably
a house slave.[23]

The Governor's accommodating stance toward the rebellion lasted
until early February of 1869, when it was clear his concessions had failed
to appease the insurgents. Under pressure from the *voluntarios* and hardline Spanish loyalists, he had no choice but to do an about-face, reinstating
controls on political expression and expanding the bases for acts considered treasonous, to be judged by a military tribunal: rebellion, conspiracy,
sedition, harboring rebels, subversive expressions, political assembly or association, and alterations of the public order. On the battlefields, the order
was given to carry out executions without trials.

The *voluntarios* zealously went about applying the new repressive measures, initiating a new wave of terror, especially in Havana. The Spanish
were desperate not to lose what remained of their once-vast empire. The
harshness of their repression prompted an exodus of most of the Havana
sugarocracy, especially to New York, where most of the planters sold their
sugar and kept sizable accounts in Manhattan's financial institutions.
One Spanish official noted "the spectacle of an emigration so numerous
and vertiginous that there were days in which ship tickets were violently
disputed and even the cargo holds of ships leaving Havana were filled with
passengers." That official estimated that from February to September 1869,
two to three thousand families left every month.[24]

Most of the Aldamas' relatives and friends left the island during February and March. Miguel resisted leaving, in part because he feared that once
he did so, his properties would be seized, but also because his wife, Hilaria
Fonts, suffered a seizure or stroke that left her somewhat incapacitated
and unable to travel. Miguel may have also suspected that he would not
be allowed to leave given his prominence and influence in Havana society. By April, however, Miguel was willing to risk everything to leave for
New York, as is clear in a carefully worded letter to General Dulce, which
starts by indicating that some conversations he recently held with mutual

friends led him to believe that the Governor would not look favorably on his departure. Acknowledging in the letter that in the event he emigrates, the government may enact measures against his "interests" and even bar him from returning to Cuba, Miguel makes clear that he had decided to leave, not out of concern for his personal well-being, but because of his special family circumstances: an eighty-two-year-old father and a wife and four daughters who, since the attack on their house, "live sequestered, in terror, without guarantees for their safety . . . which has affected my wife to the point that after suffering a serious illness produced solely by the terror, she is prostrated and suffering a paralysis for which she cannot receive treatment." Given those conditions, he wrote to Dulce, and even aware of the consequences and pain of emigrating, he was committed to try to give his family "the health and tranquility they have lost, and therefore," finally getting to the main reason for writing the letter, "I hope to not encounter obstacles in the issuance of our passports." Out of an abundance of caution, he left the letter unsigned.[25]

There is no record of Dulce's reply, if any, but on May 10, 1869, Miguel de Aldama arrived in New York aboard the *Morro Castle* from Havana. It is likely that he left clandestinely, since his name does not appear on the passenger manifest, which does list Hilaria; his daughters; his father, Domingo (who was a widower by this time); and his son-in-law Leonardo del Monte, married to Miguel's daughter Rosa. (Leonardo was also his nephew, for he was the son of one of Miguel's sisters, also named Rosa.)[26]

About a month after the Aldama family emigrated, Domingo Dulce was replaced as Military Governor of Cuba. In poor health, still unpopular with the loyalists, and unable to quell the rebellion, he was recalled to Madrid, where he died not long after. One of his legacies was the decree by which all of those judged to be disloyal to Spain, especially exiles such as the Aldamas, had their properties embargoed. Eventually, more than four thousand Cubans had their properties confiscated, most based on flimsy pretexts. What started as a wartime strategic measure quickly degenerated into abuses, graft, and the massive theft of properties by the Spanish.

For the Aldama family, the embargo on their properties was a serious financial blow, but they were not facing an impoverished exile. For decades, Miguel and his father had been keeping most of their liquid assets in accounts with the New York financial institutions that acted as the commission agents for the sale of their sugar in the United States. A ledger sheet in the archives of one of those financial institutions, Moses Taylor and Company, has an entry of one hundred thousand dollars in the name of Miguel de Aldama.[27] One source, citing someone close to Miguel, estimated that he may have had as much as seven hundred thousand dollars in assets in New York at the time of his migration.[28]

But a more severe penalty than having property embargoed befell one of Miguel's brothers-in-law, the youngest of Hilaria Fonts's siblings: Juan Carlos Fonts y Palma, the father of my great-grandfather Ernesto. Juan Carlos, unlike his more cautious siblings who had a stake in the continuation of the colonial regime, became actively involved in pro-independence activities and was deported to Spain. By August of 1870, the deported Juan Carlos was living in Barcelona, Catalunya's capital, just up the coast from Torredembarra, the town from where his father and grandparents had emigrated half a century before.[29] His wife, Leocadia, and the children migrated to Spain sometime after 1870. Their oldest son, sixteen-year-old Carlos, graduated from a secondary school in Seville in June of 1873 and that same year enrolled in the law school of the Universidad Central in Madrid, where he lived with his maternal grandfather, Nicolás Sterling y Heredia, who had also migrated from Cuba and was listed in the records of the law school as the person responsible for Carlos's tuition. As the war was nearing a close in 1877, Carlos requested that his transcript be transferred to the University of Havana so that he could complete his law degree at the Cuban university, an indication that the family was returning to the island.[30] There is no record, however, of his father, Juan Carlos, ever returning to Cuba or of when and where he died.

Juan Carlos's youngest son, my great-grandfather Ernesto, was an infant when his father was deported. When he was ten years old, in 1879, he was sent to New York and placed under the tutelage of Miguel de Aldama, the husband of his aunt Hilaria. Miguel was still living there and had not returned to Cuba since his arrival in the city ten years before. Those years had been bitter ones for Miguel. His father, Domingo, died in 1870 not long after arriving in New York, and in April of 1871, Hilaria Fonts, who never recovered from her illness, also died. Miguel bought a burial plot in Green-Wood Cemetery in Brooklyn and paid James Bliss, a vault builder and mason, $3,800 to erect a stone mausoleum near the main entrance of that historic cemetery.[31] Miguel interred there both Domingo and Hilaria.

As if the deaths of his father and wife had not been enough, Miguel de Aldama's years in New York were filled with political and financial failures. He had accepted the position of Agent General of the Cuban Republic, with responsibility for coordinating activities in the US to garner political and financial support for the insurgents, raising money, outfitting expeditions to the island, and lobbying Washington for official recognition of the legitimacy of the independence movement.

By 1871, however, about the time of Hilaria's death, those efforts had largely failed. President Grant's Secretary of State, Hamilton Fish, steered the US away from any involvement in the war in Cuba for fear of jeopardizing relations with Spain. Furthermore, Fish had grown weary of the émigrés' violations of US neutrality laws: "misguided individual citizens," read a statement Fish drafted for Grant's signature, "cannot be tolerated in making war according to their own caprice, passions and interests, or foreign sympathies; . . . the agents of foreign governments, recognized or unrecognized, cannot be permitted to abuse our hospitality by usurping the function of enlisting or equipping military or naval forces within our territory."[32]

The US's unequivocal rejection of any support for the Cubans doomed Aldama's efforts to raise money and outfit expeditions. But many of his fellow émigrés attributed his failure to a lack of true dedication on his part to the success of the war. His critics in New York regarded him as a Havana sugarocrat uncommitted to independence whose primary concern was keeping the war from expanding to the west so that his embargoed properties, which he hoped to recover, would not suffer damages. His most acerbic critic, Emilia Casanova, railed in a pamphlet that if "Aldama does not want, can't, nor knows how to be useful to the homeland, he should step aside. . . . His service to the cause of independence is an absurd pretension."[33] Aldama eventually resigned as Agent General, a move that was not unwelcomed by the rebel government he represented.

His critics were not entirely off the mark. Whatever his motives, there is no question that Miguel de Aldama did not set an example of self-sacrifice for the cause of Cuban independence. While others were donating most of their wealth or dying on the battlefields of Cuba, Miguel was busy investing a fortune in the construction of a huge sugar refinery on the Brooklyn waterfront. Named after one of Aldama's embargoed sugar mills, the Santa Rosa refinery was built in 1873 and had a chimney 140 feet in height and a complex of buildings, of which the tallest was a filter house that rose 120 feet. The cost of its construction was estimated at half a million dollars. The *Brooklyn Daily Eagle* hailed it as "one of the largest and finest sugar refineries in Brooklyn and Manhattan."[34] Miguel was making this huge investment at a time when the money to outfit expeditions was increasingly scarce.

The war dragged on until 1878, when the insurrectionists were compelled to give up and Spain retained control of the island. The treaty that ended it granted amnesty and a safe return to the island to all who had opposed the Spanish, but it did not stipulate the return of embargoed properties. By that time, Miguel de Aldama had virtually depleted the funds he had squirreled away in New York prior to the war. The refinery never became fully operational because it required further investments he could not afford. He faced financial ruin but still managed to keep up the appearance of prosperity by hosting a lavish wedding reception for his daughter Leonor, who married a Colombian diplomat at St. Stephen's Church in Manhattan in the spring of 1879.[35] Later that year, Ernesto, Hilaria's nephew, arrived in New York to continue his education in the United States under Miguel's guardianship.

Miguel enrolled my great-grandfather at Mount Pleasant Military Academy near Ossining, New York, about thirty-three miles north of the city, on the banks of the Hudson River. Ernesto was placed under the guardianship of Aldama precisely so he could study in a boarding school in New York, a popular option for families in Havana in the 1880s. Passenger manifests for ships that made regular runs between New York harbor and Havana list several young Cubans during the days immediately before and after the school year, as the youngsters spent their summers with their families in Cuba. Ernesto, for example, appears on the manifest of the *Niagara*, which sailed to Havana from New York on June 25, 1880, and again on that of the *Norfolk*, which sailed the following year on June 24. On both of those trips, he was accompanied by several boys his age with the last names of some of Havana's most prominent families.[36]

Founded in 1813, the Mount Pleasant school was premised on the value of military discipline and adherence to tradition as the best learning environment for boys. The school stood "for that which is permanent and substantial and opposed to the element in the educational world that is crying for change, evidently thinking that all change must be progress," and going even further in extolling conservatism, it favored ". . . holding on to the best of yesterday and not too eager to experiment with the possibilities of tomorrow." Its teaching philosophy centered on "simplicity of life and living . . . honesty, thoroughness, graciousness, real manliness are the watchwords . . . and the keynote of its teaching is service."[37] The school sought to "foster and strengthen those habits of accuracy, perseverance, and self-reliance."[38] Ernesto's education in those traditional values and in strict codes of conduct had a formative impact on him. He also acquired skills that he would use later in his life: military discipline, horsemanship, and the use of firearms. But the most important skill he acquired at Mount Pleasant, one that would serve him well throughout the rest of his life in Cuba, was fluency in English.

By 1885, Miguel de Aldama's last-ditch efforts to make the refinery productive failed, and with dwindling assets in New York, he had no option left except returning to Cuba to try to reclaim his embargoed properties. He would never get them back. Ernesto left with him to Cuba without graduating from Mount Pleasant. Eventually, in Havana at age eighteen, he earned the equivalent of a high school degree in the commercial field, with a specialization in bookkeeping. His older brothers Carlos and Oscar, by that time established attorneys in Havana, hired him to keep the financial accounts of their law offices.

On March 27, 1888, the *New York Times* carried a brief dispatch from Havana with the news of the departure of the steamer *City of Washington*, bound for New York with the remains of Miguel de Aldama, "the wealthy Havana merchant and one-time leader of the revolutionists in Cuba," who had passed away on March 15.[39] His biographer noted that Miguel was unable to rebuild his fortune and died in the most "absolute poverty" (an assertion disputed by some historians) as a guest in a friend's house in Havana. Salomé Malagamba, a former slave whom Miguel had freed years earlier, reported the dying words of his once master: "Do not bury me in this enslaved land, place my bones in a free land."[40] There was, of course, a burial spot available to him in that free land: the mausoleum he had built years before in Green-Wood Cemetery in Brooklyn to bury his father, Domingo, and his wife, Hilaria Fonts.

2

PÉREZ

REMEDIOS

The first Spanish settlements in the New World were in Hispaniola, the island that is today shared by Haiti and the Dominican Republic and that lies only fifty miles from the eastern tip of Cuba. The earliest Spanish incursions into Cuba, therefore, proceeded from east to west. The first Governor of Cuba, Diego Velázquez, was able to finish the first wave of colonization in less than two years and with only some three hundred men that he placed under the command of Vasco Porcallo de Figueroa. By 1519, Porcallo had established the first eight *"villas"* of Cuba. The first and easternmost was Baracoa, and the seventh and westernmost was Havana itself. On his way back east, and almost as an afterthought, he founded the eighth settlement in an unlikely spot: a key off the northern coast of central Cuba, about two hundred miles east of Havana. It would eventually be named San Juan de los Remedios.[1]

The coastal site quickly became unsustainable because of the frequent raids by the pirates that roamed the Caribbean, so it was not long before Remedios was relocated to the main island, not far from the coast.[2] Even in the new location, however, the town remained vulnerable as the raids intensified during the seventeenth century, leading many Remedianos to conclude that the town had not been relocated far enough from the coast to avoid being plundered by the pirates. A safer location farther inland had to be identified, initiating a series of bizarre events that occurred between 1671 and 1696 and altered the course of the region's history. Cuba's leading twentieth-century anthropologist would devote an entire book to chronicling the extraordinary episode, which he entitled *A Cuban Struggle against Demons*.[3]

A local priest, Joseph González de la Cruz, emerged as a strong advocate for relocating the town to an area where his family owned property, which would benefit him financially.[4] Many residents, however, found its soil unsuitable for agriculture. In the meantime, many of the Remedianos had changed their minds about moving and obtained the support of another local priest, Cristóbal Bejarano, for remaining. The rival priests presented their respective cases to the colonial and religious authorities, who delayed for years making any decision on the move. A frustrated Father González, who happened to be the appointed Commissioner of the Holy Inquisition for the region, decided to try a more aggressive approach to force a decision in favor of relocating the town. In a duly notarized affidavit, González alleged that the town had to move immediately, for he had learned from Leonarda, a slave woman who was possessed by Lucifer, that Remedios sat on top of one of the gates of hell. Speaking through Leonarda, on whom the priest performed the requisite exorcism, Satan warned that González was a dog who was not to be believed and that the town should stay in its current location. The priest went on to predict that if the area was not evacuated, demons would possess many of the inhabitants and the town would sink into the depths of hell. That is why, he argued, the devil wants the town to stay, but God wants it to move.

González immediately led a group of terrified families out of the town, but most of the residents decided to stay, even if it meant facing the demons. The Governor of the region, however, had not authorized the relocation and ordered González and the families to return to Remedios or face punishment. Two years later, in 1684, a royal decree authorized the relocation of the town, although not to the place that González had proposed. The population of Remedios split in two, with about half remaining and the other half departing and establishing a new town, which was named La Villa de Santa Clara, also known as Villa Clara or, more popularly, Santa Clara.[5] Situated almost exactly in the geographic center of the island, the new town quickly became a transportation crossroads and its population boomed. It would eventually become the capital of the province and is today Cuba's sixth largest city. Remedios languished, losing inhabitants to Santa Clara and other fledgling towns in the region.

The encounter of the Remedianos with demons was symptomatic of the relative isolation and provincialism of the central region. In the west, Havana quickly became a world-class port, the axis of Spanish commerce in the New World, later transforming itself into the center of the Sugar Revolution that created fortunes for slaveholding families and made it a magnet for wealth-seeking immigrant families such as the Fonts. In the east, the oldest settlements on the island anchored a region characterized by the large pastoral estates of a traditional landed gentry with families such as Leocadia's, the wife of Juan Carlos Fonts.

By contrast, the region that developed around Remedios, in the north-central part of the island, was characterized by a modest agricultural economy sustained primarily by homesteaders who had migrated from humbler classes and regions of Spain: Asturias, Galicia, and the Canary Islands. While some of those homesteaders eventually came to own considerable estates devoted to mixed farming, cattle, or even sugar, many were subsistence-level tenant farmers on *latifundia*, the mostly unused holdings of absentee landowners whose ancestors had been deeded the land by royal grants.

The prevalence of small-scale farming in the Remedios region led to the sprouting of numerous small towns that served as local trade centers where goods were bought and sold and services provided, creating a modest middle class of shopkeepers and service professionals. The towns dotting the region were referred to collectively as "Las Villas" (the villages).

Eventually, that was the name given to the large central province centered on those towns.

Throughout most of its history, Las Villas suffered from poor communications with the rest of the island. Roads in and out of the region were few. Until the nineteenth century, the region's only link with Havana was a road that turned muddy during the rainy season.[6] Even well into that century, if one wanted to travel between Havana and Santiago de Cuba in the east, sea routes were the best option.

The railroads were also slow to arrive in the region. Cuba was one of the first countries in the western hemisphere to build a railroad network, but most of those rail lines were laid in the western region as part of the transportation system that linked the highly capitalized sugar estates with their supply and distribution networks. In fact, the rail line completed in 1838 between Havana and Güines, the town located in the heart of the sugar-producing region east of the capital, was the first rail line built in Latin America.[7] But the rail lines terminated on the edge of the easternmost extension of the western cane fields, some 125 miles from Las Villas. It was not until the second half of the nineteenth century that rail lines started connecting the towns in the region with one another and eventually with Havana. In fact, it was not until the twentieth century, during the US occupation, that the first rail line was built that traversed the length of the island, from Havana to Santiago, linking Las Villas with all points east and west.

It is not surprising that as a relatively isolated agricultural region during most of its history, Las Villas would acquire a reputation as a bastion of provincialism in Cuba, in sharp contrast with the other regions of the Spanish colony that developed around ports. Almost from its founding in 1519, Havana started acquiring a secular character that was both cosmopolitan and tawdry, typical of major port cities. Both the capital and Matanzas, another port city, developed an elite class rooted in sugar and commerce that supported the development of institutions attuned to the latest developments, ideas, and consumer goods from North America and Europe. It was, of course, a worldview fraught with contradictions, given the dependence of that class on slave labor. Even the eastern landed gentry developed a worldly orientation, sending many of its sons to be educated in Europe or Havana and selling the products of its pastoral estates to their French and English neighbors in the Caribbean. Las Villas, however, remained more insular and was largely bypassed by those undercurrents of cosmopolitanism, secularism, and modernity that flowed through Cuban colonial society.

In 1817, the Spanish government lifted its monopoly control over the island's tobacco industry and encouraged the free cultivation and trade of the leaf and the products derived from it.[8] The oppressive royal monopoly was abolished because it had served to depress production. The end of it ushered in, during the first three decades of the nineteenth century, the true birth of Cuba's tobacco industry and proved to be a boon to Las Villas.[9] The leaf requires meticulous attention from the tobacco farmer, or *veguero*, who is involved not just in the sowing, care, and harvesting of the plants but also in the initial maturing process of the leaves.[10] For this reason, *vegas*, or tobacco farms, rarely exceed ten hectares or twenty-five acres in size. Growing quality tobacco leaves, therefore, required precisely the type of small-scale farming that predominated in Las Villas. Additionally, the soil of the region produced a uniquely pungent leaf that was in demand for blends with the milder leaves grown in western Cuba.

By 1859, the Remedios zone, also known as Vuelta Arriba, became one of the largest tobacco regions of the country, producing more than sixteen thousand tons of leaf tobacco.[11] The small towns in the region also benefited from the expansion of tobacco production, as jobs were created for the ancillary activities involved in the processing and warehousing of the leaves, and even in the manufacturing of tobacco products. One estimate is that in the town of Remedios itself there were some two hundred small tobacco manufacturing establishments, or *chinchales*, which in most cases were simply family-based businesses with as few as one self-employed cigar roller.[12]

The Canary Islanders, *isleños*, had the reputation of being the best *vegueros*. Their considerable presence in the region dates to the efforts of several local citizens' groups to attract white free laborers. In Remedios, an organization called "The Society for Spanish Emigration" claimed to have recruited from the Canary Islands more than one thousand families that were transported across the Atlantic directly to the nearby Cuban port of Caibarién. The push for white laborers was prompted by prejudices and fears regarding the "Chinese solution," the strategy of colonial authorities to promote the massive migration of Chinese indentured laborers to replace the dwindling African slave population following the abolishment of the slave trade in 1865. In 1883, *El Criterio Popular*, Remedios's leading newspaper, could not have been more explicit on this point: ". . . it is one of the most important measures taken for the betterment of the country and one we have always supported, the introduction of free laborers of European races . . . every ship that arrives in this town with free laborers distances us more from the threatening and ill-fated solution of the 400,000 Chinese."[13]

Landowners throughout the region offered land, usually under share-renting arrangements, to the new immigrants, encouraging them to go into tobacco farming. In 1872, one prominent citizen of Remedios acquired nearly seven thousand acres for the express purpose of establishing a "great colony of *canarios*" devoted to producing tobacco. The initiative was praised by the municipal authorities.[14]

The *isleños* joined other Spanish immigrants that had settled in the region, especially those from Asturias, who were protagonists in the development of a class of small-town shopkeepers throughout Las Villas. Consequently, by the late nineteenth century, Remedios contained one of the largest concentrations of Spanish-born persons on the island, a phenomenon that, as we shall see, led to divided loyalties among its population during the wars for independence from Spain.

Racially, it also meant that the central region was among the "whitest" in Cuba. It was estimated in 1873 that Remedios and its surrounding towns and countryside had about fifty thousand inhabitants, of which nearly two-thirds were categorized as "white," a high proportion compared to the population of the entire island. The rest of the population of the region was almost evenly divided among "free colored," African slaves, and Asians, the last two groups working primarily in the area's sugar plantations.[15]

LISANDRO

It was in Remedios that my father's father, Lisandro Pérez Moreno, was born on December 9, 1871, only two years after my maternal great-grandfather, Ernesto Fonts y Sterling, was born in Havana. Both of Lisandro's parents were also born in Remedios. His mother, Marina Moreno Montero, belonged to a family that had lived in the town for generations, dating back, on the maternal side, to the time when the Remedianos were fighting demons. Lisandro's father, Manuel Pérez y Perdomo, however, was the son of an immigrant from the Canary Islands, Juan Pérez, who married a local woman, Josefa Perdomo.

Manuel and Marina had ten children. The six oldest ones were all women: Josefa, Quirina, Francisca, Concha, Sixta, and Isabel. The boys were Abelardo, Juan, Lisandro, and Arturo, although "Lisandro" was not my grandfather's first name. It was not until I examined his baptismal certificate a few years ago that I discovered that my namesake was named Leocadio Lisandro. At some point my grandfather must have decided that his middle name was creative enough but that his parents had gone too far with Leocadio, and he never used it. I am grateful to him for that.

Marina died when Lisandro was seven years old. The family scattered, with the younger boys going to live with the three oldest sisters, who were married and living in Yaguajay, another one of the villages of Las Villas, about twenty-five miles southeast of Remedios. Manuel lived out his widowerhood alone in Remedios. He died in 1888, about ten years after Marina.

With about five thousand inhabitants in 1879, Yaguajay had less than half of the population of Remedios. It had only one local public school for boys, and that was probably overcrowded and understaffed and barely served to give Lisandro the rudiments of an education: reading, writing, and little else.[16] It is unlikely he reached the secondary level. Life was not easy in Yaguajay, and he could not continue to depend on the kindness of his sisters. Education was a luxury. He had to get a job.

He found work in a general store in San Antonio de las Vueltas, a town closer to Remedios and larger than Yaguajay that by 1888 was served by a rail line with connections to Havana.[17] The owners of the store were an elderly couple that with time came to depend on Lisandro's hard work and initiative to assume greater responsibilities in the management of the establishment. After several years of saving his earnings, Lisandro made an offer to buy the store, and the owners more than gladly accepted it. By the time he was eighteen, he owned a prosperous store with enough income to make at least one charitable contribution. On May 17, 1890, a fire in the warehouse of a hardware store in the old colonial section of Havana drew the capital's two competing volunteer fire brigades, who eagerly rushed into the building to extinguish the fire, not knowing it housed a large stash of dynamite. When the fire reached the dynamite, the building was destroyed in a fiery explosion heard throughout the city. Thirty-eight people died, including twenty-five firemen, and countless others were injured. It was a catastrophe without precedent in Cuban history, and the entire country was moved by the tragedy and the sacrifice of the firemen. A collection went up for the benefit of the families of the victims, and Lisandro contributed fifty cents in gold to the relief effort.[18]

Almost as soon as he acquired the store, Lisandro started looking for ways to expand his business. Many of his customers were tobacco farmers, who received all their income only once a year when they sold their cash crop. Lisandro would supply them during the year with whatever they needed from his store, with payment due when the crop was sold. In time, he discovered he could make more money by having some *vegueros* pay him in tobacco rather than cash. Eventually, he sold the store to dedicate himself exclusively to buying, processing, and reselling tobacco leaves, the business that was to become his lifelong occupation, one that would enable him to attain an unexpected level of prosperity for an orphan from Las Villas.

3

FOUR BROTHERS

After living as an exile in New York for more than a decade, José Martí, the poet and writer revered by Cubans for his role in the creation of Cuban nationhood, decided the time was right to launch the definitive movement for independence. He founded a newspaper and a political party, and he raised among his fellow émigrés the funds required to start the war that was to lead to the establishment of a sovereign Cuban nation.[1] When all the pieces were in place, he disembarked on the Cuban coast in 1895 with his generals and with the volunteer fighting force he had outfitted, and the island was once again enveloped in a conflict with the Spanish colonial army. The success of the campaign would rest on the willingness of Cubans to join the uprising.

In some families, all the men (and even some of the women) rushed to the battlefields, but in other families, sentiments were divided. Brothers made different choices. The four sons of Juan Carlos Fonts and Leocadia Sterling each responded differently to the call to arms. Carlos and Oscar, the two oldest, continued with their lives and their law practices in Havana, Raúl was living in the Dominican Republic, and Ernesto, my great-grandfather, enlisted in the Cuban independence army.

Of the four, Carlos Fonts y Sterling, the eldest, was the one least likely to have sacrificed for the cause of Cuban independence. He had a well-established practice focusing on property law, and on various occasions he litigated cases on behalf of the Spanish colonial authorities. He even co-authored a legal reference work, which was published in 1880 as an official publication of the island's government.[2] By 1890, Carlos was also serving as Secretary and Legal Counsel to several railroad companies. His professional activities were aligned with his political beliefs. Carlos was an autonomist, which meant he favored a continuation of the colonial regime, but with a greater degree of home rule. By the 1880s, the autonomists represented an important current in Cuban political life, establishing a party that labeled itself as "Liberal," advocating for an end to slavery and warning Spain that without economic reforms and a greater degree of participation by Cubans in governing the island, Cuba was headed for another war for independence, something the autonomists wanted to avoid. It was an attempt to keep Spanish nationality while espousing a Cuban identity and a measure of political control. José Martí and other advocates of Cuban nationhood and sovereignty were severe critics of the autonomists.[3] Carlos's autonomist sentiments may have been influenced by his years of study in Spain, instilling in him an affinity with that country. He would not have abandoned his law practice to risk his life for the cause of Cuban independence.

When the war broke out, Carlos was not married, so family responsibilities would not have kept him from enlisting, even if he was disposed to do so. Some years before the start of the war he had fallen in love with a young Spanish woman of humble origins who had migrated from her Galician village to seek work in Cuba. When he indicated his intention to marry her, his brothers called a meeting with Carlos to convince him that the woman was only interested in advancing her social position. They reminded him that the success of the family in the New World had been largely due to advantageous marriages and that this was certainly not going to be one of them. Carlos relented, and his brothers took care of the rest.

They gave the woman money and a one-way ticket back to Spain. Carlos never married.

By the time war broke out in 1895, Raúl, another of Ernesto's brothers, was living in the Dominican Republic and away from the impending conflict in Cuba. As with Carlos and Oscar, he had also studied in Spain but took a different path: medicine. He married a Dominican woman, had six children, and established a medical practice in Santo Domingo.

Oscar, yet another of Ernesto's brothers and the namesake of my grandfather, was also a successful lawyer and a partner in Carlos's law practice. He continued the Fonts tradition of marrying well. His wife was Dulce María del Junco y de la Cruz Muñoz, descendant of a military man from Sevilla who served in the 1590s as Spanish Governor of Florida. The family moved to Havana in the seventeenth century, making it one of the oldest families in the capital.[4] Oscar was not an autonomist like Carlos and may even have had pro-independence beliefs, but he was very entrenched in Havana's elite financial and social circles and was clearly a man who enjoyed a lifestyle of comfort and leisure. He served on the governing board of the National Bank of Cuba, and in 1887 he appears as a contributor in the masthead of *El Sport*, a weekly publication of "sports, arts, and literature and the official organ of the League of Base-Ball, the Chess Club, the Habana Yacht Club, and the Jockey Club of Colón."[5] Years later, he would serve as the Vice President of the Automóvil Club of Cuba, a large organization of aficionados of the sporty roadsters that became wildly popular in Havana.[6]

A decade before the start of the war, Oscar bought a very spacious home that had been built in the 1830s in the upper-class neighborhood of El Cerro. He expanded and remodeled the house, combining the existing colonial style with Louis XVI accents and furnishings. He replaced the floor throughout the house with tinted marble he rescued from a palatial home that was being demolished in colonial Havana, and he installed windowpanes of stained glass in the classical colonial style. Decades later, the house was featured in Cuba's leading architectural magazine.[7]

Oscar obviously prospered and enjoyed life under Spanish rule and could not have been at all disposed to leaving it all, especially his mansion, for the hardships and dangers of the battlefield. Although he was clearly not going to enlist, in the years leading to the war his house at Four Domínguez Street in El Cerro served as a place where many of his family and friends, including his brother Ernesto, gathered to share their pro-independence sentiments. When the war broke out, many of the men who frequented the house of Oscar and Dulce María enlisted. The first one to do so was the brother of Dulce María, Enrique del Junco y de la Cruz Muñoz, followed by several of their cousins, among them Arturo Acosta y de la Cruz Muñoz. Arturo's sister, María Luisa, was among the young ladies who also joined in the gatherings at the house in El Cerro. Known by her nickname "Malila," María Luisa met Ernesto at the house, and a romance ensued.

Although the war started in February of 1895, Ernesto did not enlist until months later, on October 24.[8] Perhaps it was his relationship with Malila that gave him pause, or perhaps his brothers tried to talk him out of it for his own safety. But Malila's brother and cousin had already marched off to the battlefields, and unlike his two brothers, Ernesto had relatively little to risk except his life. Keeping the books at their law firm was not a proper career. He was twenty-six years old and ready to give greater meaning to his life. He did not share Carlos's autonomist views, identifying, perhaps out of loyalty, with the separatist sentiments of the father who had suffered deportation. Ernesto was prepared to join the war effort because of the skills he had acquired in Mount Pleasant: riding, use of weaponry, and military discipline, and he was eager to put those skills to use, skills his brothers had not learned while studying in Madrid. He enlisted, but not before becoming engaged to Malila.

In Las Villas, another four brothers faced a similar decision as the Fonts y Sterling siblings: the sons of Manuel Pérez and Marina Moreno. My grandfather Lisandro did not enlist. He stood to lose more than just his life, perhaps even more than Ernesto's brothers, who had university degrees and careers they could fall back on. Lisandro had only the business he had worked hard to build for almost a decade, a shrewd business sense, and especially, relations with the tobacco farmers whose *vegas* he purchased. When he started as a teenager, he faced a steep learning curve before he could turn a profit. Through trial and error, he discovered that the quality of a crop, or *vega*, varied greatly from *veguero* to *veguero*, so he had to become an expert at judging the quality of the leaves, a skill that involved closely eyeing, touching, and smelling several samples. This enabled him to buy from the best *vegueros*, eventually establishing a reputation as a dealer with an excellent product and a buyer who the farmers could trust to strike a fair deal. To entice those *vegueros* to sell to him, he had to offer them the best possible price, but one that still enabled him to make a profit, so he became an expert at predicting the trends in the tobacco market. More importantly, he built strong interpersonal relations with the best *vegueros*.

All those skills and relationships took time to develop, and when the war broke out in 1895, he was on the cusp of making real money from tobacco leaves. He was twenty-three, and whatever his feelings on colonialism and independence, the one thing that was certain was that enlisting in the Cuban army would have destroyed the business that had enabled him to escape the poverty to which he seemed destined as an orphan. Las Villas was, as previously noted, a region with a large Spanish immigrant population, many of them the very Canary Islands *vegueros* who supplied him with the leaves for his business and who likely were no friends of Cuban independence.

To be sure, thousands who enlisted to fight for Cuban independence gave up as much or more than what Lisandro was unwilling to risk. But that was the decision he made.

In Yaguajay, however, his youngest brother enlisted on June 12, 1895. Arturo Pérez y Moreno formed part of the "Remedios" Infantry Regiment of the Second Brigade, First Division, Fourth Corps, of the Occidental Department of the Cuban Liberation Army.[9] Both he and Ernesto Fonts survived the war, and by the end of it, Arturo had attained the rank of Lieutenant, while Ernesto rose to the rank of Colonel and became a member of the Liberation Army's cabinet. This was typical. Arturo was an orphan from humble origins who lived in Yaguajay. Ernesto was a member of a well-connected Havana family. Socioeconomic status was an important determinant of the ranks that members of the Cuban army came to occupy, something especially evident in the lowest ranks, where poor and nonwhite soldiers predominated.[10] Those class differences also had implications for the historical record. Not much can be written about Arturo's war experiences, but Ernesto left enough of an imprint on the existing documentation to piece together an account of his activities during the conflict.

4

COLONEL FONTS

Most of my great-grandfather's war stories center on the deprivations that plagued the independence army during the entire conflict. With the Spanish in control of the towns and cities and with no clear battlefronts, the Cuban troops, called *mambises*, operated exclusively in the countryside, shifting from camp to camp and engaging the Spanish troops they encountered. Under such circumstances, the supply lines were unreliable, and therefore the soldiers had to frequently subsist on whatever they could forage or hunt. The inventory of cattle and produce dwindled as the war devastated farmland in many areas, and the island's largest wild mammal, the *jutía*, a rodent native to the West Indies, averages no more than twenty pounds. They became the most plentiful source of protein, and Ernesto recalled roasting many a *jutía*.

The extreme hunger chronically suffered by the Cuban fighters makes Ernesto's most fantastic war story seem almost plausible. Upon entering an abandoned Spanish encampment, his unit discovered a badly decomposed body lying on a leather cot. After dumping the body, they boiled the leather and ate it.

But the Ernesto war story most often repeated in my family is one that occurred on a battlefield and was Ernesto's closest brush with death. At the end of a skirmish, he unexpectedly came upon a fatally wounded Spanish officer laying on the ground, his gun pointed at Ernesto. As his horse reared back, Ernesto did not have time to pull out his weapon, but the Spaniard, realizing his wounds were mortal and that the battle was lost, chose to spare Ernesto's life and instead turned the gun on himself. To honor him, Ernesto took the officer's saber, a European weapon, and "Cubanized" it, removing the hilt and replacing it with a wooden handle, turning it into a machete, the weapon widely used by the independence army. There is physical evidence of the veracity of the story. In the Historical Museum of Havana, there is a glass wall cabinet that displays several of the machetes used by the *mambises*. All have wooden handles, but one is distinctly different from the others in that its blade is curved and slim, like a European saber. That is the one identified in the exhibit as Colonel Fonts's machete. In a nearby display case is Ernesto's .38-caliber Colt revolver.

Upon his enlistment, Ernesto was assigned to the First Division, Fourth Corps, under the command of General Serafín Sánchez.[1] His education and experience in keeping financial records did not go unnoticed by the heads of the government of the independence army, and barely two months after he enlisted he was named Treasurer for the province of Las Villas. He climbed rapidly through the ranks. In July 1896, he was appointed Undersecretary of the Treasury for the entire island, and in February 1897, already holding the rank of Lieutenant Colonel, he was appointed as Chief of the Second Division of the Fourth Corps, Western Department. The rank and file of that division elected him as a delegate to the assembly that in 1897 in La Yaya enacted a new constitution, to which he is one of the signatories. General Bartolomé Masó, as the President of the new government-in-arms, named him to his cabinet as Secretary of the Treasury, making him responsible for the finances of the entire independence army. Effective August 6, 1897, he was promoted to Colonel of the Cavalry, by signed order of Bartolomé Masó, President, and Domingo Méndez Capote, Vice President.[2]

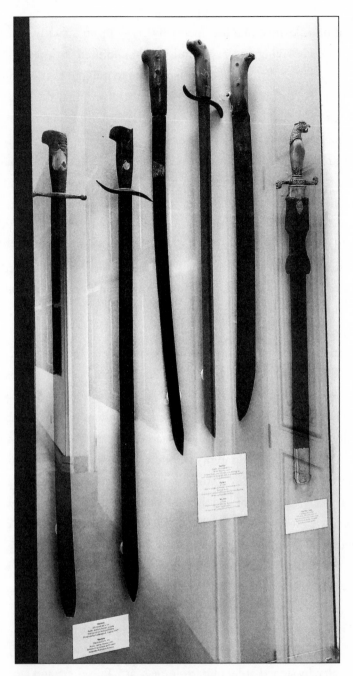

Colonel Fonts's machete (third from left). Historical Museum of Havana.
Photograph by the author.

Colonel Fonts's Colt revolver. Historical Museum of Havana. Photograph by the author.

The cabinet of the Cuban government-in-arms, 1897, Vice President Domingo Méndez Capote seated at center. Standing at left, Treasury Secretary Ernesto Fonts y Sterling. *Cuba y América* 3 (32): 6.

Colonel Ernesto Fonts y Sterling, Treasury Secretary of the Cuban government-in-arms, 1897. *Cuba y América* 3 (41): 9.

In his new position Ernesto allocated funds and oversaw their distribution across military divisions scattered over a large war zone. It was a
difficult role, distributing scarce resources to an army starved for them.
Commanders sent him urgent messages recounting dire circumstances.
One of the first ones to correspond with him was his fiancée Malila's
cousin, Brigadier General Enrique del Junco y de la Cruz Muñoz, who was
also the brother-in-law of Ernesto's brother Oscar. Enrique wrote the letter
from a camp somewhere in Matanzas. After reciting a litany of shortages,
especially of arms and ammunition, he wrote,

> I have a task that exceeds my abilities. I want you to tell me what you think I
> can do under these conditions, and if this allows any margin for one to work, or
> rather to give way to failure or death and be regarded as lazy or cowardly, given
> that it becomes impossible to operate without the necessary resources. I have
> said nothing of this to anyone, but I say this to you because although it is hard,
> friends can be bothered to hear calamities.[3]

Less than two months after sending that letter, Enrique was killed in a
battle along the Hanábana River in southern Las Villas. He was twenty-six
years old. His body fell into the hands of the enemy and was never recovered.[4] The tragedy of war had struck close to Ernesto and to the women in
Domínguez Street in El Cerro. The once lively home of Oscar and Dulce
María was devastated by the news of her brother's death, which had already been preceded, in March of 1897, by the report that Malila's brother
and Dulce María's cousin, Captain Arturo Acosta, was killed in action near
the northern port of Camarioca at age twenty-two.[5]

Letters from his older brothers, Carlos and Oscar, reached Ernesto in the
war zone through informal channels. Ever cautious for fear of reprisals
given their positions in Havana as lawyers and bankers, they signed their
letters with monikers. Carlos was "Mr. Zafiro" (Sapphire), and Oscar was
"the younger brother of Mr. Zafiro." Oscar excused himself for not writing more often by saying that "one incurs grave risks in writing to you."[6]

In one letter, Carlos, whose clients included owners of firms involved in sugar production and commerce, expresses to Ernesto his concern about the rebel army's threat to lay waste to sugar plantations. He writes that businesses could be persuaded to contribute financially to the cause of independence rather than have their properties destroyed.[7] Oscar is more supportive than his older brother of the fight for independence, at one point writing, "The people of Cuba are with all of you in body and soul and until you achieve victory they are willing to suffer the necessary vicissitudes."[8]

Given what he was experiencing on the battlefield, one wonders what Ernesto thought about his brothers' safety precautions and especially about Carlos's concerns regarding the possible losses to commercial properties. Death, injury, pestilence, and harrowing living conditions were a constant part of Ernesto's life during the nearly four years the war lasted. About five thousand Cuban soldiers died in the war. Most were combat fatalities, but many died from yellow fever.[9] He was able to see it all from his perch as the Treasurer of the rebel government. With his staff and escorts, he would travel throughout the war zone, assessing the need for resources and disbursing funds. If the unit he was visiting engaged the enemy, he and his contingent would join in the fray.

Ernesto's role also brought him into contact with the highest officers in the Cuban army, including the head of all the insurrectionist forces, General Máximo Gómez, with whom Ernesto came to enjoy a close relationship, as evidenced by a sustained personal correspondence. General Gómez was a veteran of the previous war for Cuban independence (1868–78). Dominican by birth, he made the Cuban cause his life's mission. When in 1894 José Martí had assembled the organization and the funds to launch a renewed push for independence, he lured the old General away from his home in Central America and persuaded him to again take up arms against Spanish colonialism as commander of the army Martí was assembling. A lifelong military man, Gómez was authoritarian and cantankerous, with very little tolerance for laxity or disobedience in his ranks. He was a severe judge of character, holding few men in high esteem and even fewer in his confidence.

The General exchanged personal letters with only a select few.[10] Ernesto was one of them, addressing my great-grandfather as "my esteemed friend." Gómez may have also had an ulterior motive in communicating with Ernesto. Although he had absolute authority over military operations, the General did have the responsibility of reporting to the rebel government, sending frequent dispatches to the President and the cabinet through a regular mail service established between the respective encampments. Gómez and Ernesto placed their personal letters in the mail pouch carrying the official correspondence. The General used the exchanges with Ernesto as a back channel with the government, obtaining unofficial information and in turn communicating some frank assessments that may have been inappropriate for an official document.

The letters to Ernesto contain criticisms of some of his generals and complaints about the shortages of supplies, especially food. In one letter, he writes that "it pains me a great deal that I have been sacrificed with more than two thousand men, waiting for twelve days, starving to death and cruelly punished by the plague . . . that is not the way to sacrifice men." Many of the letters from Gómez to Ernesto have been published, so at some point my great-grandfather must have donated them to an archive.[11] But he kept two of the letters among his personal papers, perhaps because they reveal a great deal about the General's state of mind and his assessment of the prospects for the war.

Both letters were written in the summer of 1898. By that time, the United States had entered the war against Spain. President William McKinley's hand was forced by the explosion of the USS *Maine* in Havana harbor and the relentless pressure of some of the New York press to wage war on Spain. On April 20, 1898, he signed a resolution passed by Congress declaring war on the Madrid government. It took a while for the US to get ready militarily; it was not until June 22 that invading US troops set foot on the island. The day before, General Gómez penned a letter to

Ernesto from Las Villas with this assessment: "I know nothing of the plan of the Americans . . . in any case, we will now be nothing more than mere auxiliaries in their war against Spain, if for no reason other than they are the strongest and have taken the initiative. . . . I consider the war now concluded by the Americans and not the Cubans."[12] With that, Gómez let Ernesto know, and by extension the Cuban government, that he considered his job done.

In less than a month, the "Splendid Little War," as Secretary of State John Hay called it, was over with an agreement on the terms of Spain's surrender. The General was still in his camp on August 21 when he wrote to Ernesto with an urgent call for the Cuban government to constitute itself into a peacetime governing body, uniting all Cubans into a cohesive political force "to obligate the foreign forces to abandon the conquered land as soon as possible. Any delay in this work poses a danger to the absolute independence of Cuba. That is why," Gómez continued, "there must be haste in this work."[13]

As it turned out, of course, it would take several years for the foreign forces to leave. But the old General was right: the war was over for him, and for Ernesto, who immediately returned to Havana, his family, and his fiancée.

5

AMPARO

The war officially ended on January 1, 1899, when the Spanish handed over control of Cuba to the United States, ending more than four hundred years of Madrid's rule over its largest remaining colony in the New World. It was inconceivable to most Spaniards, especially those living in Cuba, that the "always faithful island of Cuba" would cease being Spanish.

In Camajuaní, a town in Las Villas, the loss of Cuba was devastating news to Manuel Naya y Muiño, a Spanish immigrant who had lived most of his life in the area. In the previous war, from 1868 to 1878, Naya served as a Lieutenant Colonel in the famed Calvary Regiment of Camajuaní, a troop of local volunteers that fiercely fought to keep Cuba in Spanish hands. After that war, Naya retired and continued living in Camajuaní, having formed a family with a Cuban woman from the town. He loved Cuba, which he always regarded as part of Spain. What he had fought so ardently to protect, Spanish rule over the island, was now over, and it was too much for him to bear. On that January 1, the very day the Spanish relinquished Cuba, Naya killed himself.

Two days later, Manuel Naya was laid to rest in Camajuaní's cemetery with full military honors accorded by a regiment of the Cuban independence army commanded by his son, Lieutenant Colonel Casimiro Naya y Serrano. It was an occasion that was perfectly emblematic of that moment in Cuban history. During the war, so many families, especially in Las Villas, had divided loyalties that caused ruptures between Spanish-born parents and their Cuban-born offspring and even between siblings with different political allegiances. But as soon as the war was over, there was an overwhelming desire to repair ties that had always been so intimate, both at the family and national levels. General Máximo Gómez was the first to call for reconciliation and unity when, only five days after Manuel Naya's burial, he left his encampment near Remedios and addressed the citizenry of Las Villas:

> I did not wage war on the Spanish people. I waged war on Spain, its administration. My soldiers have fought for Cuban liberty. We seek to establish the Republic of Cuba for all its inhabitants. . . . We seek the union and harmony of all . . . harmony must reign between Spaniards and Cubans if the country is to be reconstructed.[1]

Besides the Nayas, another prominent family in Camajuaní that experienced sharply divided loyalties during the war was the Vidal Caro family. Salvador Vidal y Tapia was one of the many Spanish immigrants that decided to settle in the central region of Cuba during the middle of the nineteenth century. Unlike many of his compatriots living there, he was not from the Canary Islands, nor was he a tobacco farmer. Salvador was from Catalunya, and he was engaged in commercial activities, first as a traveling salesman and later as the owner of a general store. He married a Cuban woman, Rosario Caro y Reyes, and settled in Corralillo, a small town in Las Villas province, about ninety miles west of Remedios. In 1862, their first child, José, was born. They would have four more children: two boys, Leoncio and Lino, and two girls, Ramona and Rosa.

When war broke out in 1868, Salvador enlisted in the local corps of Spanish volunteers, but by 1870, he became disenchanted and resigned when he witnessed the murder of a ten-year-old boy by his troop, and he, Rosario, and the five children left Cuba and moved to his home region near Barcelona. The family returned to Cuba after the war ended in 1878 and made their home in Camajuaní. The youngest daughter, Rosa, eventually married a local immigrant from Seville, Baldomero Rodríguez López, and had seven children: Alberto, Arminta (known as Chicha), Herminia, Eduardo, Baldomero, Vivina, and Amparo, my paternal grandmother, who was born on October 30, 1884, in Camajuaní.

My grandmother Amparo grew up in a family of both Spaniards and Cubans, with the expected divisions on the question of Cuban independence, divisions that intensified with the imminent outbreak of war in 1895. Her father, Baldomero, the *sevillano*, was among the leaders in Camajuaní, along with Manuel Naya, of the dominant political faction in the town, those who called themselves "conservatives" and pledged their loyalty to Spain.[2] The divisions were most evident among Amparo's uncles and aunt. José, the oldest, quickly established a reputation as an eclectic intellectual: an orator, poet, painter, literary critic, scientist, and inventor. He founded a newspaper in Camajuaní, experimented with the industrial uses of the waste products of the sugar production process, and developed an innovative approach to the process of harvesting the cane stalks.[3] José was also a leader of the autonomists in Camajuaní, professing the same ideals as Carlos Fonts y Sterling: continuation of Spanish rule, but with Cuban autonomy.[4] When the war broke out in 1895, José moved to New York.

The brothers Leoncio and Lino, the other two of Amparo's uncles, were quite different from their brother. They were men of action with separatist sentiments and reputations as political troublemakers in the staunchly loyalist Camajuaní. Five years before the war, Leoncio was expelled from the most important social club in town, the Casino Español, a gathering place for pro-Spanish families, after he was involved in a brawl with one of the members during a billiards game. Leoncio organized a group of friends and a few weeks later founded El Centro Latino, which brought together those families who identified themselves as Cubans, thus establishing a

clear division between Spaniards and *criollos*—that is, Cubans—in Camajuaní's social circles.[5] El Centro Latino featured, among other activities,
a chess club, since both Leoncio and Lino were known as the best chess
players in town.

Ramona, Amparo's aunt, must have looked askance at the activities of
her brothers Leoncio and Lino. In the mid-1880s, Ramona married a Spanish career military officer, Captain Mola, who commanded the Civil Guard
garrison in Placetas.[6] Given the support that Spanish troops enjoyed in the
region, it was commonplace for young Cuban women in Camajuaní and
elsewhere in Las Villas to marry military officers in the service of Spain. In
the 1880s, the newspapers of Remedios and Camajuaní are full of accounts
of weddings between Spanish officers and local young ladies. In several
newspaper stories, Ramona is listed among the *señoritas* in attendance at
balls and other social events to which Spanish officers were invited.[7]

One can only imagine the discussions that my grandmother Amparo
must have witnessed growing up among her extended family in Camajuaní. When the war started in February of 1895 she was ten years old,
and less than a month later her uncle Leoncio was already on the battlefield with the Cuban army, participating in the campaign to take the war
to western Cuba. In June of that year, he was dispatched to the countryside surrounding Camajuaní and was promoted to the rank of Lieutenant
Colonel and given his own command, the Fourth Squadron of the "Las
Villas Regiment," part of the Fourth Corps. He kept a diary of his exploits,
which were numerous and daring.[8] From October 8 to November 25,
Leoncio and his men blew up a bridge, captured a fort near Camajuaní that
was thought to be unassailable because of its location on a steep hill, laid
waste to various commercial establishments in the countryside that were
reputedly supporting Spanish troops, carried out countless skirmishes,
and in the most consequential action of all, derailed an armored military
train and took the occupants as prisoners.[9]

Those feats were even more extraordinary considering Lieutenant Colonel Vidal and his men were operating in a region considered a Spanish

stronghold. The Cavalry Regiment of Camajuaní, the outfit in which Manuel Naya served as a Lieutenant Colonel in the previous war, was still around and even more committed to defending the town and preserving colonial rule in Cuba. Because of its glorious history, the regiment had become a cultural icon that served to cement a proud Spanish identity among the many loyalists in Camajuaní, making them feel safe from the war the Cuban rebels were conducting throughout the countryside.[10] It was impossible to capture the town militarily; the Spanish army had even dug trenches and erected barricades around it.[11] Leoncio challenged the image of invincibility of the famed regiment of volunteers when on the night of November 10, he and a few of his men approached the wall that enclosed the municipal cemetery at the western edge of the town and hung a large sign on it that read "Today we reached the mansion of the dead. Soon we will reach the mansion of the living." According to the local newspapers, the sign caused widespread alarm among the citizens.[12] There were rumors of sightings of Leoncio as he snuck incognito into town at night to visit his family. My grandmother remembered seeing him seated calmly at the dinner table disguised as a priest.

Leoncio recorded in his diary that while his troops were encamped in Manajanabo, about eight miles southeast of Camajuaní, they were joined on January 9, 1896, by the head of the treasury for the region of Las Villas, Lieutenant Colonel Ernesto Fonts y Sterling, who arrived with his staff and escort. Ernesto and his men stayed with Leoncio's troop for five days, accompanying them in several skirmishes with Spanish troops in the region.[13]

In March of that year, a group of citizens of Santa Clara approached General Máximo Gómez with a plan to capture the city. They presented the General with street maps of Santa Clara, pointing out the city's vulnerability to a sudden and swift cavalry attack. Gómez thought it was a risky undertaking but worth a try. The army under his command was scoring victories throughout the Cuban countryside but had yet to capture a town or city of any significance. Santa Clara, the largest city in central Cuba, was an invaluable prize, one that would give a much-needed boost to the Cuban cause.

It was a daring plan, and General Gómez knew exactly who should be entrusted to carry it out: the intrepid Lieutenant Coronel from Camajuaní. Leoncio was promoted to Colonel and placed in command of four columns of cavalry. They would start at different points in the outskirts of the city, advance at full gallop through the streets, following precise routes in which the resistance was thought to be minimal, and meet in the central square to launch a coordinated assault on the garrison that faced the plaza. Leoncio would personally lead one of the columns. One of the other columns would be led by another Camajuaní resident: Casimiro Naya, the son of Manuel, the old loyalist.

The attack took place on the night of March 23, 1896.[14] Contrary to expectations, the cavalry charge met with stiff resistance in the streets. Leoncio's column approached the square ahead of all the others, but he left most of his men behind as he rode his horse in a furious gallop through the streets. He burst into the open square accompanied only by his aide, Corporal Brito, who was immediately shot. Not wanting to leave him behind, Leoncio dismounted from his horse, picked up Brito, placed him astride his own horse, and continued to charge into the square. He did not expect to find the square so brightly lit. During the months he had been fighting in the countryside, Santa Clara had installed electric lights, with much of the wattage concentrated in its large central square, where people tended to congregate at night. Leoncio realized he was now a very visible target for the soldiers defending the garrison. He steered his horse toward the church to seek the cover of the trees that lined its front, but he was met with a fusillade that toppled him from his horse, killing him instantly. Moments later, Naya, who had a reputation as a sharpshooter, arrived at the square and proceeded to shoot out all the lights. In the darkness, no one saw Leoncio's body lying in the square. Naya ordered a retreat to their camp in the countryside, where the troops anxiously awaited the return of their commanding officer. It was only in the afternoon of the next day that they learned the terrible news.

It turned out to be a suicide mission. Santa Clara was evidently not vulnerable militarily. Gómez would not attempt again the capture of a major

Cuban city. Although they were victorious, the Spanish were shaken by the audacity of the attack and carried out retaliatory repressive measures. On March 29, Leoncio's brother Lino was arrested, and a few days later he died in prison.

News of the deaths of Leoncio and Lino reached their brother José in New York. He remained there until after the war, when he returned to Camajuaní and was elected mayor. Years later he served the new Cuban government by occupying diplomatic posts in Bremen, Germany, and in Colombia and Chile.[15]

Ramona Vidal was not in Cuba when her brothers died. A year before the start of the war, Captain Mola's tour of duty in Cuba was over, and he was reassigned to a civil guard post in Spain, where he, Ramona, and their two young sons, Emilio and Ramón (both born in Placetas), settled permanently, first in Gerona and then in Málaga. The boys followed their father, grandfather, and great-grandfather into military careers. Emilio Mola y Vidal, the oldest, graduated from the infantry academy in Toledo and served on the Moroccan front for many years, acquiring a reputation that rapidly earned him the rank of General. In 1936, he was named the military commander in Pamplona, where he coordinated that summer the military coup that attempted to overthrow the government of the Second Spanish Republic. The coup's failure led Mola and Francisco Franco to initiate the war against the republic, with Mola commanding the rebel forces in the northern half of the country. He did not get to see the end of the war. On June 3, 1937, he died when his military plane crashed against a hillside near Burgos in a heavy fog.

My grandmother Amparo's first cousin is widely regarded as the principal instigator of the Spanish Civil War.[16] Despite the General's rise to prominence in the twentieth century, I did not learn of his connection to my father's family until my father also learned of it late in his life. Mola's name never came up in any of the family stories I inherited from my ancestors. I suspect that given the separatist activities of her brothers, Ramona became estranged from her family, especially after her move to Spain,

where she lived out the rest of her life without ever returning to Camajuaní. She apparently had a strict and unforgiving temperament. A Spanish
writer described General Mola, and his mother, with these words: "... he
was smart, harsh, and cold, like the mother who bore him."[17]

General Emilio Mola's uncle, Colonel Leoncio Vidal of the Cuban independence army, became Las Villas' most venerated martyr of the cause
for Cuban independence. After the war, the main park in Camajuaní and
the central square in Santa Clara where he was killed were named after
him, and each feature a bust of Leoncio. My grandmother Amparo and her
entire family, especially Leoncio's widow, who survived well into the twentieth century, were thereafter treated with great deference in Camajuaní.

With the war concluded and lost, the Spanish army left Cuba, but the
many immigrants that had arrived from Spain during the decades before
the war stayed and continued to contribute to the economic and social
life of the country, especially in Las Villas, where they formed the core
of the commercial and tobacco-producing sectors. The reconciliation that
General Gómez championed after the end of the war came naturally to
villaclareños, whose neighbors, employers, and even fathers or brothers
had been loyalists. It was only natural for Casimiro Naya to lead his Cuban
troops in the military funeral for his staunchly loyalist father, a man who
could not stand to live in a Cuba that was no longer Spanish.

Several years after the war ended, my grandmother Amparo became
engaged to a Spanish immigrant, a young salesman who lived in Camajuaní. A wedding date was set, but first the young man wanted to make
a trip back to his village in Spain to personally give the news of his impending marriage to his parents and perhaps persuade them to attend
the wedding and settle in Cuba. Amparo bade him a tearful farewell at the
Camajuaní train station as he left for Havana, where he was to board a ship
for the transatlantic voyage. She never heard from him again, and with
only the sketchiest information about her fiancé's life in Spain, she was unable to locate him. In Camajuaní, where everyone, of course, learned what

Bust of Colonel Leoncio Vidal y Caro in Santa Clara's central park. Photograph by the author.

My grandmother Amparo Rodríguez Vidal, 1907, the year she married my grandfather. The dedication on the back reads, "To the love of my soul, my adored Lisandro, I dedicate this keepsake to whom I love so much and is your faithful, Amparo." Author's collection.

happened, people started referring to her, somewhat cruelly, as *"la viudita"* (the little widow). Her marriage prospects appeared dim.

But a new resident in town took notice of her and told a friend, "I am going to marry that *viudita*." He was thirteen years older than Amparo, having spent his younger years dedicated to building a successful business in the tobacco trade. Lisandro Pérez was finally in the financial position to start a family, and he would do so in Camajuaní with a local girl from a notable family who had diminished marriage possibilities. It was the perfect match for a newcomer who knew no one in town.

Amparo married my grandfather Lisandro in the main church in Camajuaní on November 4, 1907. He was thirty-five, and she was twenty-two. It was a double wedding. Her sister Arminta (Chicha) was also married in the same ceremony. Amparo insisted that the two sisters walk in their wedding dresses from their house to the church so that everyone in gossipy Camajuaní would see that the little widow was getting married.

6

HERE COME THE AMERICANS

The Spanish surrendered Cuba to the United States on the first day of 1899. The US War Department was charged with administering the new acquisition, so a government headed by a high-ranking army officer with the title of Military Governor was installed in the same building where the Spanish Captain Generals had ruled Cuba. The first Military Governor was a Civil War veteran, Major General John R. Brooke, but he was succeeded in December by another army man, Major General Leonard Wood, who would govern Cuba until May 20, 1902, the date he transferred control of the island to an elected Cuban government.

Wood was a dynamic and ambitious man who left his imprint on Cuban history. An army surgeon with a medical degree from Harvard, he volunteered for combat duty in the Spanish-American War as one of the Rough Riders, alongside his friend Theodore Roosevelt. Wood ruled Cuba as befitted a Military Governor: with an authoritarian hand and a paternalistic attitude toward the population, treating Cubans as subjects who needed to be schooled in self-government and American values. He did accomplish two things that greatly benefited Cuba. One was the eradication of yellow fever. He invited Walter Reed and his team to Cuba to conduct experiments designed to test the theory of a Cuban doctor, Carlos J. Finlay, that the disease was transmitted by a mosquito and not by human contact. Once that was confirmed, Wood launched an extensive public sanitation program to eliminate mosquito breeding grounds. The other accomplishment was to facilitate the construction by a Canadian company of a railroad line that ran the length of the island, for the first time connecting the western and eastern halves of the country.

As Military Governor, Wood reported directly to Secretary of War Elihu Root, but his influence in shaping US-Cuba policy was enhanced when his war buddy ascended to the presidency upon the assassination of William McKinley. By 1901, Wood was pushing Roosevelt and Root to devise an exit strategy from the island and subsequently became the point man in implementing a transition from US military rule to an elected Cuban government. Not only did Wood set up a commission of Cubans to draft a constitution, but he also corresponded directly with leading members of the US Congress to enact the legislation that would enable that transition. In fact, his lobbying efforts with Congress were apparently too aggressive, earning him a rebuke from Root. Wood apologized but defended his actions by writing to Root that "in my strict capacity as governor of the Island I am, of course, extremely interested in defending the interests of its people, irrespective of the question of making friends or enemies at home."[1]

For Wood and Secretary Root, the interests of the Cuban people, and certainly the interests of the United States, were best served by ensuring that a government trustworthy and friendly to Washington was installed in Cuba. The culmination of their efforts became known as the Platt Amendment. Introduced in the US Senate by Senator Orville Platt of Connecticut, the amendment was passed by Congress as part of an appropriations bill and set out the conditions for the end of the military occupation and the installation of a Cuban government. Foremost among those conditions was a provision that gave the US the right to intervene to maintain "a government adequate for the protection of life, property, and individual liberty." The amendment was then transmitted to the Cuban commission for inclusion in the constitution they were crafting. Wood made clear to the commission that unless the amendment was included in the constitution, there would be no independence for Cuba. Despite objections from many of its members, the commission succumbed.[2]

The prospect of US intervention should the Cuban government prove unable to maintain order meant that Cuban independence was compromised. Placing Washington as the ultimate authority wreaked havoc on the political system of the new Cuban Republic as rival parties engaged in interventionist politics, creating disorder if they lost an election so that the US would intervene and cancel the results. But another consequence of the Platt Amendment was that Cuba became a magnet for US trade and investments. Not only was the US ostensibly guaranteeing its political stability, but the island was geographically in its backyard, rich in untapped resources and investment opportunities, and practically devoid of competing native capital. The war had left Cuba impoverished such that in 1902 its dependency on the United States was not just political but also financial.

The Platt Amendment swung wide open the doors for a massive inflow of US capital that remained unabated throughout the first three decades of the twentieth century. On the back of that surge in trade and investment rode a growing cultural dependency, with US consumption patterns, lifestyles, and popular culture becoming noticeably embedded in the fabric of Cuban life, especially among Havana's elites. This was a continuation of a pattern that had started early in the nineteenth century, as the United States started replacing Spain as that "other place" in the Cuban consciousness: the place to sell and buy goods, and the desired destination for emigrants or sojourners, as Miguel de Aldama and his contemporaries had done decades before. My great-grandfather Ernesto had been among the thousands of Cuban boys and young men who were sent north to study. The new postcolonial political and economic relationship between the US and the young republic accelerated and cemented that long-standing trend.

The first half of the twentieth century saw the rapid Americanization of Cuba in every aspect of national life, and the Pérez and Fonts families were far from immune to that trend.

FROM COLONEL TO AUDITOR TO MINISTER

In an impoverished postwar Cuba, the economic prospects for most veterans were not encouraging. But Ernesto had a skill set that led to his immediate employment by the US military government that occupied the island. He was fluent in English, had attended school in the US, and had a degree in bookkeeping and experience in the management of public finances. On January 27, 1899, less than a month after the transition from Spanish to US rule, he was named Head of Administration within the Office of the Inspector General of the military government's Treasury Department with an annual salary of three thousand dollars in US gold currency.[3]

At twenty-nine years of age, with a stable financial situation and after serving more than three years in the warring countryside, Ernesto wasted no time in marrying the fiancée he had left behind in Havana in 1895. María Luisa (Malila) Acosta was glad to see Ernesto return unharmed from the war, after having lost her brother and a cousin in the conflict. Ernesto and Malila would have two sons: Ernesto, born in 1901, and my grandfather, Oscar, born in 1903. They moved into a comfortable but modest house that Ernesto purchased on Tulipán Street in the El Cerro neighborhood of Havana, just a few blocks from his brother Oscar's mansion, where he had met Malila.

Although the US military was the final authority during the occupation, a civilian administrative structure was established to handle the tasks associated with governing the island. It was a government staffed almost entirely by Cubans but with no President, since the Military Governor stood alone at the top of the hierarchy. At the national level, Cubans were appointed by the Governor to head, jointly with an American military

counterpart, the various divisions (State, Finance, Justice, Public Instruction, Agriculture, Industries, and Public Works). At the local level,
elections were held for municipal offices. However, partly because of the
sensitive nature of auditing all the financial records and partly because it
required personnel with specialized skills, the Auditor's Office within the
Treasury Department was placed directly under the Headquarters Division of the military government and headed almost exclusively by American officers detailed from the Office of the Quartermaster or brought in
expressly from Washington. There was one exception: Ernesto Fonts y
Sterling, "a capable and experienced Cuban."[4]

Ernesto proved invaluable to his American employer. In his 1901 report
to Washington, Major Eugene F. Ladd, the Treasurer of the military government, noted that he found in Mr. Ernesto Fonts "an apt and progressive student" in learning "the methods of accounting in use in the United
States, the Spanish methods being so elaborate as to be burdensome and
beyond comprehension." Ernesto's department, Ladd continued, "quickly
adopted our methods . . . and I am indebted to Mr. Fonts for valuable assistance and hearty cooperation" in meeting the greater challenge of in-
structing other divisions of the government and the municipal authorities
in the new methods.[5]

As the Auditor's Office continually reorganized to centralize all the financial auditing functions of the military government, Ernesto was promoted to positions with greater authority: Auditor for the Department
of Finance, Deputy Auditor, and Chief of the Internal Revenue Division.
Not only had he learned the American accounting system, but he was the
only Spanish-speaking head of a division, an asset not lost on Major Ladd,
who in his report apparently felt it necessary to justify to the War Department the employment of a Cuban in a position of responsibility within the
Auditor's Office:

Mr. Ernesto Fonts y Sterling is well acquainted with handling collections of
internal revenue and other accounts rendered in Spanish . . . and has perfected

himself in the theories and operation of the present system. His knowledge, too, of the people, and the fact that all such accounts and necessarily the correspondence are in Spanish, make his retention necessary for the best public interests, and demand that his position should have accorded it a proper dignity.[6]

Communicating in Spanish with the municipalities, schools, hospitals, charities, and other institutions that received funds from the government and ensuring that their financial reports were in order, with all expenditures properly entered and documented, was a major task of Ernesto's office, and he hired Cubans as subordinates, training them in the new accounting system the Americans had introduced. It was painstaking work, and Ernesto attended to every detail. The records of the Office of the Auditor of the Military Government in the US National Archives contain hundreds of documents produced by Ernesto's office and personally signed by him. In one letter, for example, dated March 18, 1901, to Sister Isabel de los Desamparados, the Mother Superior of the San José asylum in Santiago de Cuba, Ernesto thanks her for the receipts she submitted in support of her financial report but returns the report to her, asking her to correct and resubmit it because she did not specify the quantity and unit price for the dozens of pairs of footwear ("*pantuflas y alpargatas*") listed on her ledger sheet.[7]

Ernesto's compulsive attention to detail, his penchant for always doing things the right way, was a legacy from his days at the Mount Pleasant Military Academy, where he learned about discipline and service. Those traits helped him become a highly regarded member of the military government that occupied his country. He embraced learning all the fine points of the modern auditing and accounting system the Americans had brought to the island, and that knowledge and skill would serve him well as Cuba, and Ernesto, approached a new future in which the Americans would leave and Cubans would ostensibly govern themselves.

By the end of 1901, Wood had in place all the pieces necessary to proceed with the transition to a Cuban government. A constitution had been finalized (with the Platt Amendment) and a Cuban President had been elected,

Tomás Estrada Palma, whom Wood preferred over the other candidate for the office, General Bartolomé Masó, who had the support of the more nationalist sectors of Cuban society that had pushed for a prompt US withdrawal and opposed the imposition of the Platt Amendment. Estrada Palma displayed all the right characteristics: a man who could be trusted, with a sober presence and a conservative bent who knew the United States well and spoke the language. He went into exile in New York during the first war of independence (1868–78) and for many years was the headmaster of a Quaker preparatory school in the Hudson Valley before he succeeded José Martí as the head of the Cuban Revolutionary Party, which Martí had formed in New York to take the war to Cuba in 1895. Estrada Palma was elected President of the new republic without stepping foot in Cuba and arrived on the island from New York only a month before he took office on May 20, 1902.

Estrada Palma appointed to key positions in his government many of those who had experience in the civilian government during the military occupation. One choice was evident: Ernesto Fonts y Sterling as Auditor of the Cuban Republic. Not only did Ernesto have the experience, but his appointment was designed to ensure a seamless transition in the critical area of financial records. Wood focused on this very point in his February 8, 1902, letter to Secretary Root, in which he summarized the preparations for the transition:

> The Auditor [of the military government] informs me that he will be able to have all American property and money accounts closed by the first of May; such open accounts as remain will be Cuban. Mr. Fonts, the deputy auditor, has occupied his present position since the beginning and will be fully prepared to act as auditor, and will accept the transfer, as he is fully familiar with the exact status of public accounts.[8]

Secretary of War Root, for his part, underscored the need for continuity with respect to the financial accounts when, a month later (March 24), he gave the following instructions to Wood:

The vouchers and accounts in the office of the Auditor and elsewhere relating to the receipt and disbursement of moneys during the government of occupation must necessarily remain within the control, and available for use, of this Department. Access to these papers will, however, undoubtedly be important to the officers of the new government in the conduct of their business subsequent to the 20th of May. You will accordingly appoint an agent to take possession of these papers, and retain them at such a place in the island of Cuba as may be agreed upon with the new government, until they can be removed to the United States without detriment to the current business of the new government.[9]

Those official directives intended to ensure a smooth transition in the control of the public finances were welcomed by Ernesto, who was hoping for a collaborative relationship with his former employer as he assumed his new role for the Cuban Republic. He witnessed the creation of that republic on May 20, when he joined the group of civilian officials and military officers from both governments that crowded into the large marble ceremonial room of what had been the Palace of the Captain Generals. There they heard the formal statements read by Major General Leonard Wood and President Tomás Estrada Palma announcing the passing of the island's government from US to Cuban hands. Wood then proceeded to the roof of the palace, and jointly with General Máximo Gómez, who had commanded the Cuban army during the war, replaced the US flag with the Cuban flag on the palace's mast. The New Englander who had ruled Cuba for more than two years then boarded the USS Brooklyn for his much-anticipated departure to the United States.[10]

With the end of US military rule in Cuba, it was anticipated that the upcoming negotiations between the two governments to resolve several pending issues would be contentious. Estrada Palma, despite being a man the Americans could trust, was nevertheless facing pressure from opposition political groups that had railed against the imposition of the Platt Amendment and considered the new President a puppet of Washington.

For domestic political purposes, he had to try to limit further encroach-
ment by the US into Cuban sovereignty by appearing to act firmly to defend his nation's interests in the upcoming negotiations with the American
government. He signaled this in the statement he read at the ceremony on
May 20. Amid the platitudes and expressions of gratitude directed at the
US, he noted that the ceremony marked the "consecration of the personality of our country as a Sovereign Nation," a characterization that many
Cubans questioned, given the imposition of the Platt Amendment.[11]

One of the issues to be negotiated centered on the provision of the Platt
Amendment that had granted the United States the right to set up naval or
coaling stations on Cuban territory. The number and location of those stations were left unspecified, subject to subsequent bilateral negotiations. Also
left unresolved was jurisdiction over the Isle of Pines, an 850-square-mile
island about thirty miles off the southwestern coast that the Spanish had always governed as a part of Cuba but was still under US control after May 20.
Whether it would remain in US hands or become part of the territory of
the new nation would have to be worked out, since the Platt Amendment
was mute on the question. There was also the issue of the revocation of US
tariffs on Cuban sugar and tobacco, a measure that the Roosevelt administration wanted enacted over the strong objections of members of Congress
who wanted to protect the US sugar beet industry.

These were all weighty issues that could be anticipated to spark the first
intense disagreements in the relations between Washington and Havana.
But contrary to all expectations, especially Ernesto's, the earliest tensions
emerged over the seemingly innocuous question of control of the financial
records, and the new Auditor of the Republic of Cuba unwittingly found
himself in the middle of the controversy.

My great-grandfather Ernesto was eminently prepared and eager to
serve the country for which he had fought so long in the island's countryside. He was confident that there would be a successful transfer of the
financial accounts to the new government (that is, to him), as prescribed
by both Wood and Root. With his usual assiduousness, he had started in

his new role as Auditor of the Cuban Republic long before May 20, working cooperatively, side by side as an equal, with the man that only weeks before had been his supervisor: the Auditor for the military government, Major Jared D. Terrill, who had been detailed to Cuba from the Office of the Controller of the US Treasury. In fact, they both remained in the same office and shared the same staff. Ernesto had learned much from Terrill and enjoyed a good relationship with him, probably because Terrill matched Ernesto in his level of personal discipline and scrupulousness when it came to attention to detail and doing everything by the book.

Unlike what Major Terrill had promised to Wood and what Wood in turn communicated to Root, the accounts of the military government were not closed by May 1, nor even by the twentieth. The delays were not due to any slacking on the part of Terrill and his office, for as he assured the War Department, "My desire to get away from here would lead me to hasten the work as much as possible."[12] The fact is that there were still a sizable number of unspent balances that were in the hands of disbursing officers, and it took weeks to audit all the accounts before they, and the remaining balance, could be turned over to the Cuban Republic. The new Cuban administration was informed on May 20 that a balance of $689,191.02 would be transferred to it from the accounts of the military government, a figure that Estrada Palma made public by quoting it in the statement he read during the ceremony that day.[13] As Ernesto continued to work with Terrill on auditing the accounts for their eventual transfer, he realized that the actual amount would be lower and, of course, felt obliged, as the Auditor of the Cuban Republic, to notify his superiors.[14] No deception or malfeasance was suspected in the shortfall; it was all attributed to the fact that the accounts could not be closed on May 20 and were therefore still in a state of flux, making difficult an accurate quoting of the final balance. Nevertheless, Estrada Palma sent a long letter to Wood with a detailed accounting of the funds signed by Ernesto's superior, the General Treasurer Carlos Roloff, letting the American know that the Cuban government had been shortchanged $54,020.73 from what had been promised.[15]

Wood received the letter in Washington, where he had gone after leaving Cuba, setting up an office at 20 Jackson Place, directly across from the White House, to handle "business pertaining to the late military government of Cuba."[16] It had a skeleton staff directed by Colonel Hugh L. Scott, who had served as Wood's Chief of Staff and second-in-command in Havana.[17] Wood left behind in Cuba the man he came to rely on for help in all administrative matters of the military government, Frank Steinhart, as well as his personal Secretary, a Cuban who had spent most of his life in the United States, Alejandro "Alex" Gonzalez, who was appointed Steinhart's assistant. They both served as Wood's eyes and ears in Cuba as the new government settled in. Terrill, of course, also remained in Cuba as Auditor of the late military government, working with Ernesto to close out the accounts.

Wood had become quite concerned about the financial records, but not because the Cuban President had admonished him about the shortfall, which he dismissed with a perfunctory request to Terrill for an explanation of how the final balance had been overestimated. Wood's concern arose almost immediately after he left Cuba, stoked by accusations from members of Congress about his handling of the finances while he was Military Governor. His aggressiveness in lobbying Congress for the Platt Amendment, his strong support for trade reciprocity with Cuba, and the abrogation of the tariffs that placed Cuban sugar and tobacco at a trade disadvantage had earned him more than a few enemies from the isolationist and protectionist elements in the Capitol. At a session of the House Committee on Military Affairs, questions were raised about the salary "and other compensation" Wood had received as Military Governor.[18] But more serious were the accusations that Wood had made disbursements from the treasury of the military government to pay for the lobbying activities of a Mr. F. B. Thurber of the New York Export Association on behalf of trade reciprocity with Cuba. Mr. Thurber was called to testify before Congress, and Wood was forced to admit that he had indeed authorized the disbursement of about eight thousand dollars from the accounts of the Cuban treasury for the distribution of pro-reciprocity materials to the mailing list of Thurber's association, but Wood defended the action as "suitable to convey to the people of the United States a correct understanding of the needs of the people of Cuba."[19] In an editorial, the *New York Times* indicated its support for Cuban reciprocity but labeled the decision to use public funds to promote it as "foolish, and we cannot see how it was made to seem justifiable."[20]

Although Secretary Root immediately took responsibility for the expenditure and argued that it was totally appropriate, Wood was furious that the reputation he had cultivated as a righteous Governor of Cuba had been tarnished.[21] He had good reason to believe that the incriminating evidence had been leaked from the financial records of the military government. On June 9, he writes a "personal and confidential" letter to the Auditor, Major Terrill:

> You have some men in your office who are giving out information, the contents of vouchers, etc. . . . There is nothing in these vouchers which we object to having known, but we do object seriously to the opportunity being given to every mischief-maker who cares to make trouble. . . . I am aware that you are not in any way informed of the character of some of those men; but they are as a rule known to us from their past history, and while we do not know specifically what men are doing the work, we know a great deal of information is coming out of your office to be used for the purpose of attempting to embarrass either myself or the present Administration. In short we want to close things up now just as quickly as possible.[22]

Wood follows up that personal letter with an official communication to Terrill in which he issues several orders, among them that "in view of existing conditions," the major is to transfer all completed financial records to the office of Frank Steinhart, who as agent for the War Department in Cuba had established his headquarters at Quemados, an area outside of Havana in what later became the suburb of Marianao. The records were to be packed there and readied for shipment to the US. Another instruction affected Ernesto directly:

> You must arrange to sever your connection from the office of the present Auditor, removing such clerks as you may require to Quemados, not later than the 30th day of June ... the original papers must not be permitted to leave your control ... it is desired that your force be reduced as rapidly as can be, and that the entire work of your office be closed as early in July as possible.[23]

Terrill replies in the same manner to Wood, with both a personal letter and an official one. In the former, he writes to Wood that "your official letter came like a thunder-bolt out of a clear sky ... it upsets every calculation that I have made...."[24] He argues that following the order to sever all ties with the Auditor of the Cuban Republic and relocating the office to Quemados

> ... will also result in the removal of Colonel Fonts to the Hacienda [Treasury] building ... up to this time both of us have been using the clerical force with perfect harmony between us ... if the alternative is submitted to the clerks as to whether they will go with me or remain with him, I think you may be assured that most if not all the Cubans will go with him ... that will leave me shorthanded in every respect, and particularly in the assistance of those who understand both Spanish and English, because we have not at this time a single American clerk in the office who thoroughly understands the Spanish language.[25]

Terrill goes on to make a case for protecting Ernesto:

> If Colonel Fonts goes to the Hacienda building under such circumstances the probability is he will go under a cloud, and evil-minded persons would not hesitate to say that he had lost the confidence of the Americans ... the position of Colonel Fonts, and his relations with the Hacienda are anything but satisfactory to him, and if he is separated from the work of auditing for the Military

Government at this time it seems possible that that separation may do him a very serious injury.[26]

In his formal reply to Wood, Terrill pushes back even more forcefully against the order that he sever ties with the Auditor of the Cuban Republic, arguing that it would create inefficiencies and delay the work of closing the accounts.[27] Ernesto took matters into his own hands and went to Quemados to meet with Steinhart and Alex Gonzalez, knowing that both men had Wood's ear, and pleaded the case for keeping the office together. Steinhart was convinced and immediately wrote to Wood:

> Colonel Fonts feels very bad in regard to the removal of the Auditor's office and he begged me to strongly recommend that you allow Mr. Terrill to remain where he is, as the removal is really more a reflection on him than anyone else. . . . I really think Dear General it is best to let the Auditor's office remain where it is.[28]

Gonzalez also weighed in, sending Wood a handwritten note labeled "confidential."

> Colonel Fonts has informed me that Major Terrill has received instructions from you to "sever" all communications with the Auditor for the Cuban Republic. Fonts feels very much hurt about this order, for he feels that after the relations that existed between you and him, and knowing him as you do, he deserves more consideration at your hands, and is at a loss to explain the action taken. . . . I can assure you that the relations between Major Terrill and Col. Fonts are most cordial, a fact I see reflected in the willingness and energy displayed in their work by the whole office staff. . . . Col. Fonts is defending this Institution tooth and nail.[29]

Wood responded to Gonzalez immediately, emphatically clarifying, "There was no intention whatever of reflecting in any way upon Mr. Fonts and no thought of it in mind . . . please tell Fonts that there is not an officer down there for whom I had more respect than himself."[30]

As Ernesto expected, the intercession of Steinhart and Gonzalez with Wood worked, and the General rescinded his order, keeping Terrill working jointly with Ernesto and setting the more realistic deadline of July 31 for the closing of the accounts and the shipment of the financial records to Washington. During Wood's rule in Cuba, Ernesto witnessed on several occasions how Steinhart and Gonzalez managed to talk Wood out of making impulsive and imprudent decisions.[31]

It was not until July 10 that the accounts of the military government were reconciled up to May 19 and closed, with a balance of $635,170.29, an amount that was certified by Ernesto as Auditor of the Cuban Republic.[32] Terrill's work was done, except for his report, and he wrote to Wood that he could do the report in Washington and therefore did not "see any further need of my remaining in Havana any longer than necessary . . . I think that now I shall be able to get away next week" and added the preemption that "I hope no more work will be sent to me from Washington."[33] Terrill departed Cuba on July 26.[34] With his departure, Ernesto was now able to discharge his duties fully and independently as Auditor of the new republic. But the controversies over the financial records would not end there.

Terrill packed the records of his office into 127 cases that he placed under the control of Steinhart, presumably ready to be shipped to Washington, as per Wood's instructions. At the request of the Cuban government, however, Steinhart delayed sending them. Estrada Palma took up the matter directly with Secretary Root in a letter in which he reminded Root that in March the Secretary had recognized that access to the financial records would be important to the officers of the new government in conducting their business subsequent to the twentieth of May and that he (Root) had ordered Wood to "retain them at such a place in the island of Cuba as may be agreed upon with the new government, until they can be removed to the United States without detriment to the current business of the new government." Estrada Palma was asking Root to make good on

that promise and leave the records until May of 1903, since the new government had accepted the assets and liabilities of the US administration
of the island and "many matters of legal contention come up daily" that
necessitated access to the financial records of that administration.[35]

Anticipating that the War Department would deny his request, Estrada
Palma did not wait for a reply from Root before trying the diplomatic
channel, taking his case to the US minister in Havana, Herbert G. Squiers,
who promptly sent a letter to Secretary of State John Hay urging him to
grant the request of the Cuban President. But Squiers went beyond that:
he challenged the authority of the War Department in Cuban matters, arguing that "it is not proper or in accordance with the rules which govern
intercourse with foreign governments to authorize any official relations
between, or correspondence with, this Government and any officer, civil,
military or naval, excepting through the Department of State or its repre-
sentative here."[36] That argument was a valid one, now that Cuba had its
own government. What had been a controversy between the two governments over innocuous financial records had now also become an intra-
Washington jurisdictional issue, with the result that the planned shipment
of the records was further delayed. Both the War Department and Leonard
Wood (from Berlin, where he was on an official visit) strongly pushed for
the immediate shipment of the records. Ultimately, since Steinhart, an employee of the War Department, was in possession of them, the 127 boxes
were finally loaded on October 4 on the *Mexico*, which was bound for New
York from Havana, for ultimate shipment to Washington.[37]

The months-long drama surrounding the Auditor's records was symptomatic of the abnormal birth of the Cuban Republic: titularly independent, but not in reality. Its foundation was predicated on a dependency
that was both political and economic and that would create dilemmas that
reverberated across Cuban society throughout the twentieth century.
How could a country that had fought for more than three decades for self-
determination reconcile itself to a compromised sovereignty? How did
individuals such as Ernesto, who had fought for a free Cuba, navigate

the dualities of nationalism and Americanism, of the ideal of sovereignty and the reality of dependency? No doubt he was a man who, because of his background and education, looked favorably upon the stabilizing influence of the United States in Cuban political life. How did that shape his service to the Cuban Republic? Was he, as Alex Gonzalez believed, someone whom Wood could trust, even while serving as an official of the Cuban government? Was he viewed by his fellow Cubans, especially the war veterans, as equally trustworthy in the pursuit of true nationhood? Given the contradictions inherent in the Cuban Republic, this would not be the last time that my great-grandfather would unwittingly find himself in the middle of conflicting forces.

The closing of the accounts of the military government and the shipment of the records allowed Ernesto to leave behind the turmoil of the transition and settle into the role of Auditor of the Cuban Republic. He was earning a comfortable annual salary of four thousand dollars and had sole responsibility for the operations of the office. His staff was composed largely of the experienced Cubans that had worked with him during the US administration.

Ernesto's exacting nature did not make him an easy boss. Former employees recalled years later that if in reconciling accounts at the end of the day the balances did not match down to the penny, no employee of the Auditor's Office was going home until the error was found. In his personal archive are monthly tabulations of daily employee absences, which he closely monitored to curtail any indiscipline in his staff.[38]

My great-grandfather loved the house on Tulipán Street where he settled into a tranquil home life, something he must have craved after the perils of the war and the challenges he faced during the occupation. Alicia Mendoza, who in 1979 still lived in the same house in El Cerro where she grew up, across the street from Tulipán Park and about a block away from the house of Ernesto and Malila, recalled playing with my grandfather Oscar and his brother Ernesto in the park. As the afternoon light started dimming, the Colonel, as he was still called, would arrive from his office and walk straight

Ernesto Fonts y Sterling, Auditor of the Cuban Republic (seated, center) and his administrative staff, 1904. Fonts family collection.

to the park to pick up his sons and take them home. Invariably dressed in
a white linen suit and wearing a white Panama hat, he would frequently accept the invitation from Alicia's father to come into the Mendoza home
and sit in the mahogany-paneled drawing room to chat about the vagaries
of Cuban national life while enjoying a *cafecito* or perhaps a cordial.[39] Most
Sundays were spent at large family gatherings in El Cerro at the nearby
home of his brother Oscar and Oscar's wife, Dulce María, Malila's cousin.
Routine suited the Colonel's sense of discipline and order.

That tranquility could not last forever given the political instability of
the Cuban Republic. Since the constitution stipulated a four-year presidential term, elections were scheduled for December 1, 1905. Estrada
Palma decided to run for reelection. When he was first elected in 1901,
Estrada Palma did not represent any political party, but for his reelection

campaign he helped organize what became known as the Moderate Party, composed primarily of civilian professionals who had served in the Cuban Revolutionary Party and later in the military government. The opposition party called themselves Liberals and brought together the nationalist elements, many of them war veterans who were formerly led by General Bartolomé Masó and had opposed the Platt Amendment and what they viewed as Estrada Palma's servility toward Washington. The Liberal candidate for 1905 was General José Miguel Gómez, the Governor of Las Villas and a veteran.[40]

To assure himself of reelection, Estrada Palma allowed the creation of what became known as a "War Cabinet," which then proceeded, sometimes without the President's knowledge, to purge local officials as well as appointees of the executive departments of the national government that were not Moderates, placing control of the entire government structure, including local electoral boards, in the hands of the party. Of the 432,000 registered voters, at least 150,000 were fictitious.[41] There was also harassment and even violence against local Liberal leaders. In one incident, a Liberal Party leader in Las Villas, who served as a Colonel during the war and as a member of the 1901 Constitutional Convention, was assassinated by an officer in the Rural Guard loyal to the government.[42] Under such pressure, the Liberal Party withdrew from the election, and Estrada Palma, of course, won by a landslide.

Ernesto was a witness to all these shenanigans from his perch in the Auditor's Office. His office, and the Treasury Department generally, were apparently spared from the Moderate Party's effort to determine the outcome of the election. Estrada Palma had won reelection fraudulently, but even his most fervent detractors agreed that, unlike his successors, he did not leave a legacy of financial malfeasance or wastefulness.[43] One source even characterized his administration as "miserly."[44] After inheriting a paltry sum from the US military government, the accounts of the Cuban Treasury at the termination of Estrada Palma's first term, under the oversight of Ernesto, showed a surplus of more than thirteen million dollars.[45]

In one expenditure, however, the President was certainly not cheap. Once reelected, Estrada Palma no longer concerned himself with trying to counter his image as an acquiescent servant of the Americans, so he was free to act in ways that reinforced that image. Barely a month after the election, he asked the Cuban Congress, where the Moderates held a majority, to appropriate twenty-five thousand dollars from the treasury for the purchase of a pearl necklace as a wedding gift from the Cuban government to Alice Roosevelt, the daughter of President Roosevelt, who was marrying Nicholas Longworth III, a Republican congressman from Ohio.[46] The Cuban minister in Paris was instructed to purchase the necklace and deliver it to Gonzalo de Quesada, his counterpart in Washington, for presentation to Miss Roosevelt, along with a message from the Cuban President that she accept it "as a spontaneous offering of the affection of the Cuban people and . . . as a sincere testimonial of the consideration and gratitude that Cuba feels for your illustrious father, their friend, always their friend, in war as well as in peace."[47] Quesada would later recall that it was not easy convincing President Roosevelt to let his daughter accept a gift from a foreign government and that the bride herself had felt uncomfortable receiving such an expensive present.[48] The gift was finally accepted, but Quesada observed that the gesture did not produce a "good effect" on the American First Family.[49] Estrada Palma, however, did not stop there. When the newlyweds decided to make Havana the first stop on their honeymoon, he invited them to stay at the Presidential Palace and regaled them with a sumptuous formal reception.[50]

If Ernesto had qualms about the "War Cabinet" stealing the election, or with the President's obsequiousness with the Americans, he may well have taken solace in his contribution to Estrada Palma's unblemished fiscal legacy, for he had no reservations about accepting the President's appointment to the second-term cabinet as Treasury Secretary. The formal news arrived in a letter dated March 29, 1906, from Estrada Palma's Secretary, who summoned him to the palace for a swearing-in ceremony.[51]

Ernesto had reached the pinnacle of his career as a public servant. He was now the Cuban Republic's top financial officer. But a storm was brewing that threatened not only his position but also the entire government.

The Liberals had not gone quietly into the night after what they legitimately believed was a corrupt election. Paradoxically for a party that stood for sovereignty and against American control of Cuban affairs, the Liberals took the position that because the election had been fraudulent, Washington should intervene to nullify it and hold a new election.[52] President Roosevelt was not the least inclined to impose a second US intervention, especially since it was not evident at the time that the conditions for intervention stipulated by Article 3 of the Platt Amendment existed, that is, that life and property were threatened. However, if what was required for the US to intervene were threats to life and property, the Liberals could do that; after all, the core of their ranks were veterans of the war who only eight years before had been on the battlefields and no doubt had their weapons and uniforms, maybe even their horses, available to use in a military campaign to overturn the election results.

The first shots were fired in early August of 1906 and after that the rebellion spread quickly in the eastern region. Led by experienced Generals from the previous war, many of them Afro-Cubans who had been excluded from participation in the Estrada Palma government, the Liberals managed to amass a force of about twenty-four thousand that was met with little opposition. The government had no standing army.[53] The Americans had left in place only a Rural Guard scattered across the country for constabulary functions in local communities. By September, it was evident that the government could not defeat the insurgents nor protect life and property as the fighting moved closer to the capital. Estrada Palma, through the US Consul General, transmitted an appeal to Washington for "American intervention and begs that President Roosevelt send to Havana with the greatest secrecy and rapidity two or three thousand men to avoid any catastrophe in the Capital."[54] Both political parties were now seeking US intervention: the Liberals to nullify the election, the Moderates to defeat the insurgents.[55]

Roosevelt did not heed Estrada Palma's appeal for US troops to prop up the government, but he recognized that given the deteriorating situation, US intervention was increasingly becoming inevitable, and he was not happy:

> I am so angry with that infernal little Cuban republic that I would like to wipe
> its people off the face of the earth. All we have wanted from them was that they
> would behave themselves and be prosperous and happy so that we would not
> have to interfere. And now, lo and behold, they have started an utterly unjustifi-
> able and pointless revolution and may get things into such a snarl that we have
> no alternative [but] to intervene.[56]

To "aid the Cubans in reaching a peaceful solution," Roosevelt dispatched to Havana his Secretary of War, William Howard Taft, accompanied by the Undersecretary of State, Robert Bacon.[57] They attempted to forge a compromise that would end the violence and avoid an intervention. A group of veterans who had not joined the rebellion, led by General Mario García-Menocal, had already come forward with their own proposal for conciliation between the Moderates and Liberals but were rebuffed by Estrada Palma, who insisted that before any negotiations take place the rebels had to lay down their arms.[58] Taft became convinced that, although Estrada Palma may not have been personally involved in the abuses perpetrated by the "War Cabinet" on his behalf, the election had indeed been fraudulent, the Liberals had a just cause, and the government was not supported by the population.[59] The proposal that the American representatives presented to the Cuban President had the support of the Liberals and included the annulment of the elections and the resignation of all elected officials, except for Estrada Palma himself, who would govern with a politically neutral cabinet until new elections were held.[60]

In a meeting with Taft and Bacon, Estrada Palma angrily rejected the proposal, insisting that the elections were fair and that to suggest otherwise was to impugn his integrity. He was disappointed that, contrary to his expectations, the Americans were not supporting him in quelling the uprising and instead seemed to be siding with the rebels.[61] In a letter to his wife, Taft described Estrada Palma as "a good deal of an old ass . . . obstinate . . . and difficult . . . and doesn't take in the situation at all."[62] For his part, Roosevelt concluded that "the Palma government has been evidently bent on forcing us to an armed intervention. . . ."[63]

That is exactly what Estrada Palma did. Unable to convince Washington to quell the rebellion and incapable, as one historian put it, of sacrificing his own pride for his country, the President resigned on September 28, as did his Vice President and the entire cabinet, including Ernesto, a collective action that purposely left Cuba without a government.[64] An emergency session of Congress was called to deal with the situation, but most members of the Moderate Party chose not to attend so as to prevent a quorum and forestall any possible action by the legislative branch.[65] Estrada Palma and the Moderates had opted for foreign intervention rather than forging a compromise with the opposition. Roosevelt's reluctant hand was forced, Article 3 of the Platt Amendment was invoked, and immediately William Howard Taft, the Secretary of War and future US President, assumed the office of Provisional Governor of the Republic of Cuba.[66] At Taft's request, Roosevelt ordered the landing of some six thousand US troops that had been stationed in several battleships off the Cuban coast, rapidly dispersing them throughout the island as peacekeepers in local communities.[67]

Estrada Palma departed the Presidential Palace and Cuban history. Eventually, he made his way to his family's estate in eastern Cuba, the home he had left more than thirty years before when he was compelled into exile in New York for his pro-independence activities. Two years after his resignation, in 1908, he died of pneumonia.

My great-grandfather Ernesto's tenure as Treasury Secretary lasted all of six months. On October 2, only a few days after his resignation, he received a note at his house summoning him to a meeting the following day with Taft at the Presidential Palace.[68] A press report of the meeting noted that it was a "lengthy interview" and speculated that it centered on "economic matters."[69] Perhaps it was during that meeting that Taft reached the conclusion that during his entire stay in Cuba, Ernesto was "one of the two honest men he encountered—Palma was the other one."[70] Whatever Taft may have thought about the political actions of the Estrada Palma administration, he could find no fault with the handling of the finances.

Ernesto retreated to his house on Tulipán Street, probably spending more time in the park with his sons, or visiting with his brother Oscar and his family on Domínguez Street, or conversing with Alicia Mendoza's father. He was out of a job. As happened in 1902 during the transition from the US military government to the Cuban Republic, Ernesto found himself in the middle of forces not of his making, faced with dilemmas created by an irregular and unstable political environment. Although he became a casualty of the political turmoil that unfolded after the 1905 election, he was not a mere bystander. He was a cabinet minister, someone in a position of influence and responsibility. He supported Estrada Palma's hardline position of not making concessions to the rebels. Given Ernesto's pro-American sentiments and his character, we can expect him to have favored US intervention over legitimizing the acts of violence and lawlessness that many of his fellow veterans had committed to overturn the election and disrupt the constitutional order. His instinct would have been to remain loyal to Estrada Palma and to go along with the massive resignation of the government. This is clear from the personal letter he received from the former President on New Year's Day in 1907. Addressed to "my dear friend," Estrada Palma expresses his affection for Ernesto, "a consideration formed and cultivated out of an admiration of the noble qualities that characterize you, your rectitude, honesty, and patriotism."[71] Clearly, Ernesto had not broken ties with the President during the lamentable process that led to the second US intervention.

On October 9, just a couple of weeks after Secretary Taft provisionally assumed the administration of the island, his successor arrived in Havana. Charles Edward Magoon was chosen, not only because of his experience as a longtime official of the War Department, Governor of the Panama Canal Zone, and ambassador to Panama, but also because he was a civilian. Roosevelt insisted that this time the US would govern the island with a civilian administration, not a military one, and it would explicitly be a temporary occupation, with Magoon given the title of Provisional Governor. Many of the military officers that had served in the previous US intervention were dispatched to Cuba to serve in key posts. Magoon appointed a cabinet of Cuban civilians, but each of those ministers had a US military "aide" who wielded the real authority in each department. For example, Major Jared D. Terrill, Ernesto's former boss and mentor in the office of the Auditor of the military government, was again asked to leave his position in the Treasury Department in Washington and head to Havana, this time to serve as the aide to the newly appointed Treasury Secretary.[72] Terrill, however, would not be working with his former mentee. Magoon took the position that the ex-rebels deserved to be included in his administration and named a committee of leading Liberals to recommend names for government posts.[73] That committee was not likely to recommend members of Estrada Palma's administration, much less the cabinet ministers who had made the controversial move of resigning and leaving Cuba without a government.

The second US intervention ended with the departure of Magoon from Cuba on January 28, 1909, and the transfer of power to an elected Cuban government. That transition did not signal new employment opportunities for Ernesto in public service. The new President was José Miguel Gómez, the Liberal Party candidate who officially lost the election in 1905 and led the rebellion to overturn it. The Liberals also took both houses of congress and won in most provincial and local elections. Interventionist politics had worked: if the election did not go your way, you could take up arms and threaten life, liberty, and property, creating the conditions for the US to intervene, invoking the Platt Amendment, nullifying the election, and then eventually holding a new one in which you could run again and win. The Platt Amendment was designed to create stability and security, but it had the opposite effect.[74] While the structure of the Cuban Republic was deformed by the imposition of the United States as the ultimate arbiter of the political system, Cubans across the ideological spectrum contributed to that deformity by behaving badly, rigging elections, resorting to violence to settle political disputes, and refusing to compromise. The advice of one prominent Cuban journalist and statesman was not heeded when he called for "domestic virtue" in the face of "foreign meddling."[75]

During his tenure as Provisional Governor, Magoon made some progress in correcting one of the weaknesses of the Cuban Republic that had contributed to the crisis of 1906: the absence of a standing army to protect the government. He reinforced the Rural Guard but also organized an infantry brigade as the nucleus of an expanding regular army.[76] But the Minnesotan left in place a corrosive feature of the Cuban system: the lack of a permanent civil service. This meant, of course, that positions at all levels of public administration could be filled by political appointees. Access to coveted government jobs, an important source of employment for so many, especially displaced war veterans, depended on the results of elections, and as one historian noted, "Public administration became entirely a function of party affiliation."[77]

Once they gained power in 1909, the Liberals embraced the system of political spoils. As soon as he assumed the presidency, Gómez created the first dustup of his administration when protests erupted over a wave of dismissals throughout the vast public bureaucracy, firings intended to make room for the appointments of his Liberal supporters.[78] The protests, of course, went unheeded, and Gómez was able to institutionalize patronage as a fixture of the Cuban political system.

Ernesto clearly had no place in the new government; in fact, he regarded himself, correctly no doubt, as a persona non grata by those in power. In one telling family anecdote, which loses quite a bit in translation, Ernesto and Malila were invited to a reception at the Presidential Palace during the Gómez administration to honor veteran officers of the war for independence. The former Colonel managed to fit into his old uniform, but he was starting to show the stooped shoulders typical of the Fonts men as they age. As he and his wife were about to enter the palace for the reception, Malila whispered to him, "Ernesto, straighten up, you are becoming more and more hunched over." To which Ernesto replied, "Ay, Malila, if these people can't swallow me hunched over, imagine if I straighten out."[79] To say that one cannot "swallow" someone is a Cuban colloquialism that means one cannot abide that person.

The years from 1906 to 1912 were lean ones for Ernesto, Malila, and their two boys. Eventually, Ernesto would have to sell his beloved house on Tulipán Street, but the family stayed in the El Cerro neighborhood in a leased property at 3A La Rosa Street, where Ernesto paid sixty dollars a month in rent.[80] His brother Oscar, who at the time was on the board of the National Bank of Cuba, eventually came through for him with an appointment as Treasurer of the bank. Ernesto was fortunate that family connections allowed him and his family to economically survive those years in which it was not possible to continue in public service. Many other veterans without connections, especially Afro-Cubans and those who served in the lower ranks, were systematically excluded from making a living from the biggest employer in Cuba: the public bureaucracy.

Since the system of political patronage hinged on the outcome of elections, however, there was always the possibility that one's fortune could change. The next elections were scheduled for 1912.

ECHEVARRÍA Y PÉREZ, INC.

In the years after he bought the general store in Vueltas as a teenager, Lisandro was slowly but steadfastly building his tobacco business. At the time the US took over Cuba in 1899 he was twenty-seven years old, his business had survived the war, and he was a well-known and respected member of the small town. When the US military government held elections to fill positions in local civilian governing bodies, Lisandro was elected to serve on the Vueltas town council.[81] It was his first and last experience in politics. He may have developed a distaste for it, or perhaps he concluded that it distracted him from his priority of continuing to build his business.

Not long after the new Cuban Republic was proclaimed in 1902, Lisandro uprooted himself from Vueltas and moved to nearby Camajuaní. He did not do so on a whim. It was a calculated move designed precisely to expand his business. The town was the key to the next step in that expansion.

Camajuaní is one of the newest towns in Las Villas. Centuries after the founding of Remedios and long after towns such as Vueltas, Yaguajay, Caibarién, Placetas, and Cabaiguán were established, the area that was called Camajuaní remained little more than a hamlet that had grown around a large cattle ranch. In fact, it was frequently called the "Camajuaní Corral" or the "Camajuaní Hacienda."[82] In 1858, the area was part of the municipality of Remedios and had slightly less than four thousand inhabitants, most of whom were white and lived in scattered farmsteads and not in the hamlet. The few sugar mills in the zone had about nine hundred slaves. The agricultural population, predominantly white, continued to increase as immigrants from the Canary Islands established tobacco *vegas* on the fertile basin of the Camajuaní River.

On April 4, 1867, the railroad reached Camajuaní with the inauguration of the line that connected the town to Remedios and other towns in Las Villas. The very modest train station built for the occasion was one of the few buildings in the town, which still did not have a school or any other public building. But Camajuaní had now become a stop in the most important local line in the region, one that stretched from Caibarién on the northern coast to Cabaiguán fifty miles to the southeast. The town and its hinterland grew rapidly after that, and in 1879 it was granted its own charter as a municipality separate from Remedios. By that year, the population of the area had doubled to about eight thousand, fueled primarily by the migration of Spanish *vegueros* and small business owners.

The rail line became the central axis of the town's development, which is the reason Camajuaní's human ecological pattern differs from that of almost any other town in the region. Departing from the traditional pattern of the towns that developed early in the colonial period, with a square central plaza or park flanked by a church and public buildings, Camajuaní's central park is essentially a long promenade that runs for several blocks alongside the railroad track, with the municipal building, the railroad station, and other public structures also flanking the line on the opposite side. Unlike other towns in which the train station is somewhat distant from the population center, in Camajuaní the railroad line is the centerpiece of the town, bisecting its central core. It is not surprising that shortly after the inauguration of the line there were two separate incidents of hearing-impaired pedestrians who were struck and killed by locomotives.

But the most transcendental event in Camajuaní's history would come a decade later and was also linked to rail transportation. Up until 1890, the line that ran through the town and served much of Las Villas had no direct connection with the larger network of trains on the island, which meant that there was no easily accessible connection with Havana. That line did not even connect with the provincial capital, Santa Clara. In fact, for centuries the best way to get from Las Villas to Havana was to take a ship from

Camajuaní's park, 1908. Photograph by J. Muros, courtesy of Ramiro A. Fernández.

Caibarién. On March 19 of that year, in an elaborate ceremony, a line from Encrucijada to Camajuaní was inaugurated. Encrucijada, about twenty miles northwest of Camajuaní, had been the terminus of the Sagua line, which had direct connections to Havana and many points west. The towns of Las Villas, from Caibarién to Cabaiguán, were now directly connected to Havana, and that connection was made through Camajuaní. What had been a corral a few decades before was now the rail transportation hub for the entire region. The schedules were timed so that trains leaving Placetas in the south and Caibarién in the north in the early morning would coincide in Camajuaní for the transfer to the Sagua line, with passengers arriving in Havana by sunset. The reverse schedule would be followed for the return trip.

Camajuaní's direct rail connection with Havana had a tremendous impact on the economic development of the town. The ability to travel or ship goods directly to and from Camajuaní and Havana lured businesses to the town. Other localities in the region, especially Remedios, started losing population to the new transportation hub. Not only was the town's population booming, but so was its surrounding countryside, as a rapidly growing number of *veguero* families established their *vegas* along the banks of the Camajuaní River, which snakes through the area. By 1900, the municipality of Camajuaní was far ahead of all the civil divisions of Las Villas in the volume of tobacco produced.[83]

Camajuaní's advantage as a business location did not escape Lisandro's attention, especially after the end of the war when he had settled into a new business model. In the years he was building his business in Vueltas, buying directly from the *vegueros* and processing the leaves, he would sell his inventory to various middlemen who acted as buying agents for domestic or foreign cigar manufacturers. Those buyers were usually based in Havana and would scour the tobacco-producing regions, purchase from processors such as Lisandro, and then sell and ship to the ultimate user of the product, the cigar manufacturer. With the US intervention and the subsequent establishment of the republic under US tutelage, US cigar manufacturers descended upon Havana, buying up more and more of the tobacco produced on the island, especially in Las Villas, which produced a pungent leaf that was blended with leaves from elsewhere to use as the fillers of cigars manufactured in the United States.

With the growth of US demand for his product, Lisandro sought to increase both the volume of production and the efficiency of his operations. He approached one of his main buyers with a business proposition. Rogelio Echevarría was older than Lisandro, with greater experience on the selling end of the tobacco business. He lived in Vedado and owned a warehouse on Belascoaín Street. Rogelio had extensive contacts with US buyers who traveled to the island to place orders for shipments of tobacco leaves. Echevarría would usually meet with the Americans in the Havana hotel where they were lodged to show them samples of the leaves from the lots he had available for purchase. Increasingly, the leaves were those that Lisandro was selling to him, for Echevarría came to rely on the quality of the product that was coming out of the warehouse in Vueltas.

My grandfather proposed to Rogelio a corporate partnership that would integrate all the operations: from the purchase of the *vega* from the *veguero* to the shipping of the processed leaves out of the port of Havana to the US. It was a mutually beneficial proposition. Echevarría, who was based in Havana, could focus on lining up the foreign buyers and handling the inventory that came through the capital from Las Villas for shipment to the ports in the US, leaving all the operations in Las Villas to Lisandro, from the purchase of the leaves to their processing and their shipment to Havana.

Echevarría y Pérez, Inc., was established at about the same time as the Cuban Republic, ready to do business in the new environment that had been created by the Platt Amendment. The logical center for the operations in Las Villas was the new bustling transportation hub, and so Lisandro moved to Camajuaní, where he met *la viudita* Amparo. He was already in his thirties and financially stable, so it was time to start a family. In the November 1907 double wedding in the town's church, Rogelio Echevarría was Lisandro's best man.[84]

The new company built a large tobacco house in Camajuaní, one that would have multiple functions: as a *despalillo* or stemmery, a processing center, offices, and the final warehouse before the leaves were shipped to Havana. It occupied an entire city block in the town, not far from the park and the railroad station. Its most notable feature was a huge high-ceilinged room spacious enough to accommodate about five hundred small desks where the *despalilladoras,* the women who stemmed the leaves, sat to do their work. There were adjoining rooms dedicated to other processing functions and yet other rooms for warehousing the leaves. A loading dock faced the street, and a snack shop took up most of an outdoor patio next to the main room. The offices were located on a mezzanine level with windows that overlooked many of the rooms. Because most of the workers employed there were engaged in stemming, the building was known in Camajuaní simply as *el despalillo.*

The Echevarría y Pérez tobacco house (*despalillo*) in Camajuaní. Photograph by the author (1993).

The warehouse of Echevarría y Pérez in Havana. Photograph by the author (1993).

The company's operations also required a facility in Havana that would warehouse and continue the maturation process of the leaves arriving from Las Villas before they would be shipped through the capital's port to the United States. Rogelio's warehouse on Belascoaín Street was outdated and too small to accommodate the new company's expanded operations. Echevarría y Pérez built a modern warehouse in a neighborhood just south of El Vedado, on the corner of Luaces and Bruzon Streets, less than two blocks from a major artery leading to the port. It had two loading docks that led to several rooms on two floors that were designed to keep the right humidity levels. At the time it was built, it was a state-of-the-art tobacco warehouse.

In the new world ushered in by the establishment of the Cuban Republic, one in which the US played a determining political and economic role, the partnership with Rogelio Echevarría opened for Lisandro that world outside of Cuba, especially New York, that had always been the market and destination for the leaves that had become his livelihood.

Lisandro's earliest personal connection to that world was Isaac Bernheim. Isaac was born in New York in 1863 to Jacob and Rebecca, German
immigrants. Shortly after migrating to New York, Isaac's father, Jacob,
founded the House of Bernheim, which became one of the earliest and
most successful firms involved in importing tobacco leaves and manufacturing cigars, an industry established in New York primarily by immigrant
German Jews.[85] By the time Isaac was born, it would have been difficult to
throw a stone in Lower Manhattan without hitting a tobacco-related establishment. An 1867 directory of manufacturers, importers, and dealers in
tobacco listed 1,309 entries for Manhattan.[86] The city became "the capital
of the North American cigar industry."[87] The House of Bernheim, with
offices at 187 Pearl Street, was a leader in manufacturing cigars using what
were known as "Clear Havana" leaves, which as early as the 1850s started
to enjoy popularity in the US as the best and most expensive smokes. The
1880 US Census found Jacob and Rebecca and their seven children living at 111 E. Seventy-Eighth Street. Isaac was seventeen years old by that
year and already involved in the family business, possibly on the sales side,
since he listed his occupation in the census as "tobacconist."[88]

Isaac and his younger brother Henry assumed progressively greater
responsibility for the operations of the firm, especially after their father
died in 1905. Taking advantage of the end of the war in Cuba and the new
business climate created by the Platt Amendment, the Bernheim brothers
sought to expand their manufacturing capacity by increasing their imports
from the island. Isaac, who knew some Spanish, was the one making the
trips to Havana to place orders from sellers such as Rogelio Echevarría. But
Isaac was not content with just examining the samples that Rogelio showed
him in a hotel room. He wanted to learn the business from the ground
up—how the leaves were grown, harvested, and processed—so he spent
days and weeks with Lisandro, observing every aspect of the operations
of Echevarría y Pérez in and around Camajuaní. The two men developed a
lasting friendship. When Isaac turned fifty in 1913, Lisandro hosted a huge
birthday party for him at a picturesque farm outside Camajuaní, inviting

prominent members of the community and owners of tobacco businesses in the area. The chef of the Cosmopolita Hotel was hired to prepare a lunch of arroz con pollo, roast pork, fried plantains, and a variety of desserts, accompanied by Rioja wines, champagne, *café*, and of course, cigars.[89]

After Isaac's only son, Leonard, graduated from Dartmouth College and Harvard Graduate School of Business, he was sent to Cuba for several months to learn the tobacco business under the tutelage and hospitality of Lisandro. Leonard eventually decided to go into another line of business, so early in 1927 Isaac and Henry dissolved their company upon their retirement. That same year, on April 28, Isaac collapsed and died of a heart attack while standing at the corner of Park Avenue and Forty-First Street.[90] He was sixty-five years old. A few days after his death, his widow, Rena, was surprised by a message from the Cartier store on Fifth Avenue informing her that the item that her husband had ordered was ready to be picked up or delivered. It turned out to be a gold cigarette case, engraved on the front with the initials "LP." On the inside of the lid was another engraving that read, in Spanish, "An affectionate remembrance from Isaac Bernheim to Lisandro Perez, April 28, 1927." That was the date Isaac passed away. Isaac had ordered the cigarette case, probably on the day he died, as a gift to my grandfather. Rena sent it to Havana, where Lisandro always kept it in his desk without ever using it (he did not smoke cigarettes). The case eventually made its way to my father and then to me.

The debt of gratitude that the Bernheims felt they owed my grandfather was not expressed solely with that cigarette case. In 1961, a few months after my family left Cuba for Miami, my father went to New Jersey for a job that his brother Rubén had secured for him as a retail distributor in the Newark area for the General Cigar Company. Before he could establish himself there and have my mother, my brother, and I join him in New Jersey, he suffered a retinal detachment and needed immediate surgery if he was to see again from that eye. Newly arrived in the US, he had no medical insurance and little money. Leonard Bernheim, Isaac's son, learned of the situation, immediately had my father admitted to the Manhattan Eye, Ear, and Throat Hospital, and paid all the expenses of the operation.

After enduring the medical emergency and a winter up north, my father decided to return to Miami, so our family's relocation to New Jersey never happened. But he was appreciative of the solid business and personal relationship his father had built decades before with the Bernheims. That was a constant in my grandfather's life and the very basis of his financial success: strong personal relations based on trust and loyalty with a broad network of friends, partners, business associates from Havana to New York, the townspeople of Villa Clara, and especially, the people he depended on most: his employees and the *vegueros*.

* * *

Cuba's transition from colony to republic was tumultuous. The Platt Amendment, two US occupations, and the failure of the governing elites to act with integrity to overcome the challenges posed by foreign tutelage had created a fragile political environment. For my great-grandfather Ernesto, a veteran that had emerged from the war without any wealth and dependent on public service to support his family, the fragility of the political system placed him in a precarious situation. For my grandfather Lisandro, however, who had decided to concentrate on building his business instead of going to war, the economic order ushered in by the Cuban Republic meant gaining expanded access to the US market for his product, creating new financial opportunities.

The contrasting experiences of the two men, born only two years apart, was emblematic of the way the country had emerged from the long struggle for independence. Veterans, who had sacrificed so much during that struggle, did not fare well in the new republic in comparison with their contemporaries. Ernesto was fortunate that his family connections yielded a lifesaving opportunity during the years he was ostracized by the ruling party. But others were not so privileged, and the marginalization of many veterans from participation in the life of the nation remained a festering sore throughout the early decades of the twentieth century.

✳ 7 ✳

CHAPARRA

One war veteran who made a very successful transition to the new republican order was General Mario García-Menocal y Deop. A descendant of a large aristocratic family from northern Spain that dated its presence in Cuba to the late seventeenth century, Menocal (as he was commonly referred to) had formed part of the large flow of young men sent to the United States to receive an education while Cuba was still a Spanish colony.[1] He graduated with an engineering degree from Cornell University, following in the footsteps of his uncle Aniceto García-Menocal y Martín, who was also an engineer and an 1862 graduate of Rensselaer Polytechnic Institute in Troy, New York. Aniceto had a long career as an engineer for the US Navy, and the young Menocal (Mario) spent most of his youth living in the United States under the guardianship of his uncle.[2]

During the war for independence, Menocal rose rapidly through the ranks, eventually becoming one of the youngest Generals of the rebel army. His most famous battlefield exploit was leading a charge that stormed a Spanish military blockhouse near Las Tunas in northeastern Cuba. After the war, he served briefly in the US military government before resigning to act as the agent and contact person in Cuba for Texas

congressman Robert Hawley, a sugar broker from Galveston who had assembled a group of New York investors eager to take advantage of the new
opportunities on the island the US had just acquired from Spain. Hawley
was impressed by Menocal's binational and bilingual credentials, and
the General became the middleman for the Texan's operations in Cuba.[3]

Menocal advised the Hawley group to purchase an old sugar mill, the
Chaparra, and sixty-six thousand acres of surrounding land in northeastern Cuba, near the bay at Puerto Padre.[4] Menocal was very familiar with
the untapped potential of the area, since it was primarily in that region that
he served during the war. The newly formed Chaparra Sugar Company
transformed the old mill into a huge modern sugar factory, a *central*, then
acquired a nearby mill, the Delicias, and additional land, making the combined property the largest sugar estate in the world.[5] In 1906, the company
changed its name to the Cuban American Sugar Company, with Hawley
as President and Menocal on the board of directors.[6]

Hawley and his group were not the only American investors in the sugar
industry in eastern Cuba. At the time of the US occupation, the region was
among the least developed on the island, sparsely inhabited by subsistence
farmers, with many areas covered with virgin forests.[7] The sugar estates
had been concentrated since the eighteenth century in the west, around
Havana and Matanzas. But US investors such as Hawley, in collaboration
with Cuban middlemen such as Menocal, saw unparalleled opportunities
to invest in the east, where land was incredibly cheap. About seventy miles
east of Chaparra, near the Bay of Nipe, the United Fruit Company's twin
giant *centrales*, the Boston and the Preston, were grinding cane grown on two
hundred thousand acres of land the company purchased in 1902 for
two dollars an acre.[8]

The Cuban American Sugar Company entrusted Menocal with all the
operations of the Chaparra and the Delicias. Despite the remoteness of
the area, he embraced the opportunity to be an on-site administrator; after
all, he was born in a sugar mill that his father managed in Matanzas. In
Chaparra, he built for himself and his family an elegant chalet-style house

in the residential area of the *central*. The company's 1909–10 annual report boasted that the Chaparra and Delicias harvested 9 percent of Cuba's total sugar crop during that fiscal year. The report also included an announcement that the company was buying yet another sugar estate, the San Manuel, with its ninety-two-thousand acres.[9]

Despite his fondness for life in Chaparra, Menocal was politically ambitious, and he started involving himself in national politics. In 1906, he tried to broker a deal between the Liberals and the Estrada Palma government, representing Moderate veterans who were not aligned with the Liberal uprising. He stepped into the void created by Estrada Palma's exit from political life and established the Conservative Party, which brought together many of the members of the old Moderate Party. Menocal ran for President against José Miguel Gómez in 1908 and lost. He returned to Chaparra and to the task of increasing the profitability of the growing sugar enterprise.

Although Menocal met my great-grandfather Ernesto when they served as officers in the war for independence, it was during the early years of the republic that they became friends. Ernesto and Menocal had much in common: educated in the US, bilingual and in many ways binational, an admiration for the American political system, a favorable view of US influence in Cuba, and perhaps more importantly, somewhat similar personality traits. Both men had reserved demeanors, a seriousness of purpose, and a strictness as administrators. Menocal was familiar with Ernesto's reputation for honesty and punctiliousness while running the Auditor's Office.

As he prepared to run for the presidency again in 1912, Menocal hired Ernesto as one of three subadministrators of the Chaparra complex, with the specific responsibility of supervising the expansion of the *central* Delicias, the adjacent property that had been acquired by the Cuban American Sugar Company.[10] The position carried a much higher salary, and a greater challenge, than Ernesto's position at the National Bank, so he, Malila, Ernesto Jr., and my grandfather Oscar moved from the capital to a sugar *central* nearly five hundred miles away in the middle of nowhere.

In the 1912 elections, the Liberal Party was divided, and the Cornell engineer was elected President of Cuba. With the Liberals out and his friend in, everything pointed to Ernesto's return to public service. Before assuming office in January 1913, Menocal placed on his cabinet some men with experience in the Estrada Palma administration, but Ernesto was not among the appointees.[11] Menocal had other plans for him.

Chaparra was Menocal's baby, his investment, his source of income, and his home, and he was held responsible for its successful operation by the company's board and shareholders in New York. If he was to leave the day-to-day administration of the complex of *centrales* to move to Havana and run the government, Menocal needed someone with whom he had absolute confidence to take over at Chaparra. The new President could appoint any number of men as Treasury Secretary, but for Chaparra he needed a man with a unique set of skills and attributes, one who was trustworthy, loyal, judicious, a highly competent and strict no-nonsense administrator who went by the book, and very importantly, someone who could easily communicate, linguistically and culturally, with the company executives in New York. He offered the position to Ernesto not long after the election results were announced on November 1, 1912.

Although isolated, the Chaparra and Delicias complex was a self-sufficient privately owned enclave larger than many towns in Cuba.[12] By the time Ernesto took over as General Manager, it was home to more than five thousand people, contained upwards of six hundred housing units (from barracks and very modest dwellings to elegant houses for the administrators), and had broad avenues with electric streetlights and cleaning crews, its own power plant, schools, a hospital and a pharmacy, a hotel, a post office, recreational and sports facilities, a security force, and a huge commissary stocked with American and Spanish goods. A network of roads and rail lines linked the *centrales* to one another, stretching out to the cane fields and to the company's private port facilities thirteen miles away in Puerto Padre.[13]

President Mario García-Menocal y Deop and my grandfather Oscar on a train in Chaparra. Fonts family collection.

The production facilities alone employed about three thousand work-ers.[14] The industrial equipment in the sugar factory was the most modern and largest of any *central* in Cuba, with the first twelve-roller mill in use on the island.[15] A Spanish journalist who visited Chaparra in 1916, Eva Canel, wrote of the incessant activity of the machinery during harvest season, "the infernal heat and deafening noise, and that complex of cyclopes, rude and intense, the dynamos, grinders, and pressure valves."[16]

Ernesto was suddenly responsible for managing a behemoth, as evi-dent in one press description written the year he arrived in Chaparra: "The work is so colossal . . . one cannot conceive the immensity of the machinery . . . the extent of its cane fields, the multitude of accessories and hands necessary for its proper direction and operation, the complexity of the management of its laborers and purveyors, and the thousand other details involved in the manufacture, storing, and shipment of the precious product."[17]

In addition to the complexities of managing the harvesting and production process, there was also the administration of the entire enclave, a
function akin to that of a municipal mayor, except that Ernesto was managing a privately owned community, with absolute authority and responsibility over every aspect of life within it: policing, quasi-judicial functions,
health, sanitation, and education services; maintaining all buildings, infrastructure, utilities; ensuring an adequate inventory of housing and supplies;
and managing a diverse and stratified workforce. Spaniards and Cubans
worked in administrative and clerical roles and in construction and the
railroads. Chinese immigrants were recruited to work in the factory and
provide a myriad of services. Starting in 1910, the company received permission from the government to start importing labor from the British,
French, and Dutch Caribbean islands to work in the fields, occupying
the bottom rung of Chaparra's hierarchy.[18] Canel, the Spanish journalist, noted the heterogeneity she saw everywhere in the community: "it is
town, village, and factory . . . one sees a lot of people bustling about, men
of all semblances, races, and types; well-dressed women, coquettish and
corseted, like in Havana."[19]

A multitude of issues arose daily in the management of such a complex
and diverse enterprise. In May of 1916, for example, Ernesto received a petition signed by more than forty workers asking that he consider bringing
into Chaparra the laundry businesses operated by the Chinese ("*trenes
de lavado*"), which, the petitioners alleged, were far more efficient and
prompter than the services they were receiving from the laundries that had
been authorized to operate in the community. Those authorized laundries
conducted business with a great deal of "informality and against our best
interests . . . retaining our laundry until it suits their business to return it to
us."[20] There is no record of Ernesto's response.

Ernesto was so successful as the General Manager of Chaparra that he
earned the same level of confidence the company gave to Menocal. One
company executive wrote to Ernesto that Mr. Hawley and the board of
directors had come to regard "the persons of Menocal and Fonts, Fonts

and Menocal, as the incarnation of Chaparra."[21] The two Cubans were given complete control of the administration of one of the largest US investments in Cuba, an example of how, despite the takeover of the Cuban economy by US corporations during the first decades of the twentieth century, Cubans exerted considerable agency as the middlemen and administrators.

The company rewarded Ernesto handsomely. In the summer of 1916, for example, as the fiscal year was ending, the board of directors in New York voted to send him a check for ten thousand dollars as "additional compensation," not a paltry sum for the time, but then Ernesto was responsible for the successful management of the company's operations and huge investments.[22] That same fiscal year, Cuban American had invested $768,409 buying even more land, bringing the total acreage under its ownership to 465,353 acres.[23]

My grandfather Oscar fondly remembered his life in Chaparra, which spanned from the time he was nine years old to just before his fourteenth birthday. The family's financial situation had improved substantially, and they lived in a large comfortable house in the exclusive residential section of the *central* (not Menocal's house, which was the largest house and the one the Cuban President kept for himself for occasional holidays in Chaparra). Oscar attended an excellent private school, and his father spent more time with him and his brother Ernesto Jr. than when they lived in Havana. The Colonel, of course, had a busy schedule running the entire operation, but the isolation of Chaparra meant that there was a domesticity to the evenings, free of the distractions and the social commitments that Ernesto and Malila had to fulfill when he was in public service in the capital. There was also more time for family life during the offseason, when the cane was not being harvested and the mill was not grinding. Ernesto spent much of that time with his sons, passing on to them one of his most important skills: fluency in English. He spent $120 on an English-language encyclopedia that was shipped to Chaparra from the New York offices of the publisher Thomas Nelson and Sons.[24] There were also more opportunities to travel. Not only did they take frequent trips to Havana, but Ernesto occasionally had to go to New York to meet with the company's executives. The ship manifests show that he always took the family with him.

It was in Chaparra that Oscar started to collect stamps. The employees in the administrative offices of the *central* would cut out and save for him the stamps affixed to the letters and packages they received. The bulk of the mail was received from Havana and New York, and so the collection was limited largely to US and Cuban stamps issued during the years the Colonel was the manager at Chaparra.

Among my grandfather's fondest memories of Chaparra were the occasions when his uncles, aunts, and cousins would visit from Havana and their house in the *central* became the site of noisy family reunions. Ernesto would start the festivities by offering his guests a cocktail created by him, or perhaps by Menocal, dubbed a "Chaparra" or "Chaparrita," essentially a Manhattan with rum.[25] For lunch, the Colonel would have a pig roasted over an open pit and he would take over the kitchen to cook his version of that quintessential Cuban dish: black beans. (The recipe, which has been handed down to me, is in the appendix to this book.) The beans were then served over a bed of white rice, accompanied by pork, yuca, and fried ripe plantains. A table long enough for all the guests was set, and Ernesto would sit at the head of it with his sons seated on either side of him so he could keep a close eye on their table etiquette. Typical of the time, the men and boys would wear white linen guayaberas and pants on such special occasions. At the sight of any food stains on his sons' clothes, especially black beans, which show up well on white, the Colonel would calmly reach out, pinch the guayabera of the offender at the shoulder, lift him from the chair, and order him to go to his room and change into a clean shirt before returning to the table.

Life was good at Chaparra for Ernesto and his family. It was also good, at least in relative terms, for most of the residents and workers in the *centrales*. They enjoyed benefits that most of Cuba's rural population did not:

Family and friends at Chaparra, circa 1914. Colonel Fonts and my grandfather Oscar stand-ing at right. Fonts family collection.

housing with electricity and running water, access to a fully equipped hos-pital, schools for their children, an amply stocked commissary, and recre-ational, social, and religious activities. The journalist Canel observed that many residents expressed their gratitude to the company and to Menocal. But the darker side of that beneficence was social control.[26] It was not lost on Canel: ". . . in Chaparra no one thinks . . . individual volition does not exist in any person sheltered under the shadow of the sugar company . . . all speak in unison as if guided by a baton . . . no one complains, all is good . . . one must be prudent."[27]

From the very inception of the Chaparra project, Menocal established a culture of order and security in the *centrales*. Not only did Chaparra have its own security force, but a building within the complex served as barracks and an outpost for the Rural Guard, which was expected to protect the interests of the company. Menocal had good reason to pro-vide for Chaparra's security. Eastern Cuba had always been the region of the island most prone to armed uprisings and lawlessness, dating back to the struggles for independence. The Liberal uprising of 1906 was based in the region, and in 1912 yet another bloody uprising took place in the east. It was a racial conflict. Many Afro-Cuban veterans took up arms against the Gómez government as a last resort for combating the racism that had kept them from participating in the republic they had fought to create. The revolt was crushed by the Cuban army and its leaders were summarily executed. The conflict had left may conservative elites such as Menocal uneasy, and it reinforced his conviction that Chaparra needed to be militarized to defend the huge investments being made in its development.

Those security forces were also employed, however, to enforce control of the residents and employees of Chaparra. Menocal managed the *centrales* with little tolerance for any disruptions of the public order, especially any manifestations of worker discontent or labor organizing, punishing or banishing any offenders from the property. Chaparra was a world unto itself, owned by the company, so Menocal could assert those mechanisms of control with impunity. Furthermore, since the Cuban American company owned the rail lines leading in and out of the complex, it also controlled access to and from the property.

Given Menocal's rightfully earned authoritarian reputation managing Chaparra, some critics in the national press predicted when he was elected President that Cuba was about to be governed by a leader with autocratic tendencies, dubbing him "El Mayoral," The Overseer. Many Cubans greeted the arrival of the new President in Havana with a little ominous ditty that was surreptitiously sung in Chaparra and went like this:

> Cut the cane,
> Step lightly;
> Hurry, here comes Menocal
> Cracking the whip.[28]

That is the managerial culture that Ernesto stepped into in 1912 when he took the helm of the Chaparra. Not only did Menocal expect the Colonel to uphold the level of control that he had instituted for the *centrales*, but he picked him precisely because his record and personality reflected a disposition to continue the tradition of authoritarian management at Chaparra. The flip side of Ernesto's laudable attributes of rectitude, honesty, and trustworthiness was his tendency to be a stern taskmaster who embraced order and obedience, a product of his military education and service. He had been an exacting supervisor at the Auditor's Office, and he had refused to compromise with the rebellious Liberals in 1906. Ernesto was a man of conservative beliefs, intolerant of laxness and rule-breaking in any form, even when it came to table etiquette and black bean stains on the guayaberas of adolescents. Menocal knew the man he was picking for the job, and Ernesto met his expectations as the General Manager of Chaparra.

The historian Gillian McGillivray recounts an incident that allegedly took place under Ernesto's administration:

> One case, under Fonts Sterling's rule in 1914, made it to the pages of the national *Heraldo de Cuba* newspaper. After demanding a salary increase, a Spanish worker named Eloy Vázquez was forced to walk sixty-nine kilometers along the railroad until he left company territory, leaving all of his possessions behind. A Rural Guardsman escorted him off company land and then gave him the *Plan de Machete*—a beating with the side of his knife.[29]

Another Spanish worker at Chaparra complained to Madrid's ambassador in Havana that he had been mistreated and that Ernesto had ordered the removal of the makeshift house that the worker had built for himself on company property. In his response to the ambassador, which is among the Colonel's papers, Ernesto was unapologetic, strongly asserting the right of the company to disallow any "unauthorized construction contrary to all rules, especially of a shack built with scraps of discarded wood, without any value, prejudicial in every way . . . with a bad appearance." Ernesto went on to inform the ambassador that the individual in question was already in his crosshairs because of his "irascible character and barbarous treatment to which he submitted his poor wife." Just in case there were any concerns about the treatment of Spanish nationals at Chaparra, Ernesto assured the diplomat that "the Spanish element that resides here, as with all workers, are treated with the utmost consideration, except in a case such as this one, in which an individual presumes to impose himself upon the Company, which has the perfect right to dictate its own regulations."[30]

The order and security that Menocal so valued for Chaparra, and that Ernesto upheld, was threatened in the aftermath of the 1916 elections. Menocal was running for reelection, and his opponent was Alfredo Zayas, who had served as Vice President during the Gómez presidency. It was the second time the Liberals were up against an incumbent, so they anticipated that the sitting President would use the power of the office to remain in power, as happened in 1906, and they were prepared to challenge the outcome of the November 1 election with an armed rebellion if necessary.

On election day there were scattered incidents of violence, but by all accounts, the voting process was honestly conducted.[31] The next day, as the results started coming in, it became evident that the Liberals were building a winning edge.[32] In its editorial, the New York Times concluded that there was "no doubt of the triumph of the Liberal Party and the election of Dr. Alfredo Zayas to the Presidency."[33] Menocal stepped in and brazenly interfered with the tabulation process, cutting off all communications between local precincts and the General Election Board, altering election totals, and halting altogether the reporting of any further results. Tensions mounted, and even after the Central Electoral Board's ruling in favor of the Liberal Party was upheld by the Supreme Court, Menocal refused to give up. The government declared that Menocal had won the election and mobilized the Rural Guard to intimidate election officials and others to make sure the Conservatives stayed in power.[34]

The Liberals were once again on the losing end of a fraudulent election conducted by the incumbent administration, and as in 1906, they organized an armed rebellion. The country was on the verge of a civil war, this time made more ominous by the fact that many army officers supported the Liberals, since it was during the Gómez administration that the regular army was fully constituted, with the Liberals responsible for most of the appointments of the top military commanders. As before, the uprising centered in the east, with the Liberals eventually controlling most of the region where US companies had made huge investments in the sugar industry.

Although a great deal of the violence took place in the southeast, around the cities of Manzanillo and Bayamo, the *centrales* in the north were threatened by acts of sabotage and sporadic combats, especially United Fruit's Preston and Boston *centrales*. Located farther west, the Chaparra complex was not as affected, but Ernesto was nevertheless ordered to place the security forces of the complex on high alert, and Menocal, wielding his authority as President to protect his interests, deployed military supplies and troops to Chaparra.

The bucolic peace that Ernesto and his family had been enjoying at Chaparra was shattered, and Ernesto once again found himself unwittingly involved in a conflict not of his making, one created by the political fragility of the Cuban Republic. If he thought that leaving Havana would afford him the opportunity to remain distant from the intrigues of national politics, he was wrong. As early as January of 1917, when it became clear that a war was about to start, he received a message from Menocal's Secretary to expect the arrival, through the company's port at Puerto Padre, of 150 weapons and 150,000 rounds.[35] A couple of weeks later, Lieutenant Rodríguez from the garrison at Victoria de las Tunas sent him a terse and ominous telegram: "Colonel Fonts, Chaparra: arm the largest possible number of men situation difficult."[36] It was as if he was again a Colonel on the battlefield. Under different circumstances, Ernesto may have relished returning to that role, but at about the same time the uprising started he suffered a serious spinal injury when he was in the field supervising the harvest. His horse became startled and reared back, and Ernesto was thrown off the saddle and onto a rail line. My great-grandfather was never the same after the injury, suffering bouts of severe pain and impaired mobility.

Injury notwithstanding, Chaparra had to be defended. Troops had to be garrisoned and fed and their horses stabled, defenses built around the perimeter, recreational facilities converted to military use, railroad cars armored to make them less vulnerable to sabotage, and facilities constructed to store ordnance, and all this in the middle of harvesting and grinding season.[37] In the end, the precautions proved to be excessive, since the war never reached the Chaparra complex.[38] The only losses were isolated sporadic fires set in the cane fields by saboteurs. By April, the Liberals had been defeated. Although controlling much of the eastern region, they were unable to inflict damages on the sugar estates after the US landed groups of marines to protect American properties, primarily in the south and around United Fruit's *centrales*.[39] The Liberals were also unable to take any cities in the west, but they had stirred up much more trouble than they had in 1906 and were counting on the US invoking the Platt Amendment and intervening, as happened before. They were disappointed. Facing a war in Europe, Woodrow Wilson was not about to commit troops and resources to a third intervention in Cuba, especially since the State Department favored the continuation of the Menocal presidency, which had supported massive American investments during his first term. Mario García-Menocal and his Vice President, Emilio Núñez, were inaugurated for a second term on May 20.[40]

Although the properties of the Cuban American Sugar Company had emerged relatively unscathed from the conflict with the Liberals, Menocal was not happy that his precious Chaparra had suffered even minor losses. On April 17, he wrote a terse personal letter to Ernesto, on presidential stationery, expressing his dissatisfaction:

The burning of cane there has been an unpleasant incident for me which I consider unjustifiable given that, according to reports, the fires were set by only eight men, and that while they were burning not the slightest effort was made by the armed forces to prevent them or extinguish them. I may or may not be mistaken, but I can assure you that no one can convince me that with the troops that Chaparra had since the earliest moments there could have been any danger.[41]

Ernesto was incensed by Menocal's recriminations. Even with his diminished health, he had protected Chaparra from major losses and, with great effort, managed to avoid any interruptions to the harvest and grinding process. The company's annual report issued a few months later, in fact, would show that the total cane harvested that season increased from the previous year, as did the total raw sugar produced.[42]

There is no record that Ernesto responded at all to Menocal's complaints, and in his anger, he apparently cut off all communication with the President. Ernesto's older brother, Carlos, a senator and prominent member of the Conservative Party, wrote to him on May 22 with some brotherly advice:

> I learned yesterday that M. is very upset with you because you have not been reporting to him, as was customary, the figures relative to the mill. If this is so, I will tell you frankly that you have committed a grave error . . . you should proceed immediately to send him the data, giving some explanation for the delay. . . . Listen to this advice from a father more than a brother. . . .[43]

On June 10, Chaparra's legal counsel, who was also a close friend of Ernesto's, had a long meeting with Menocal in Havana. The attorney subsequently wrote a lengthy letter to Ernesto detailing what Menocal told him in that meeting, noting that when the topic of the events in Chaparra came up, "his eyes changed color and he told me that it was a real shame, and a bunch of other stuff, and then he expressed his surprise and indignation for having his house turned into a garrison."[44] Apparently the foremost reason for Menocal's indignation was even more petty than the marginal losses sustained in the cane fields: his cherished chalet had been used as part of the defense of Chaparra, housing offices and troops, troops that he sent in large numbers precisely to defend the property. Ernesto must have bristled even more upon reading that, and he could not have been assuaged by Menocal's subsequent words as quoted in the letter from the lawyer: "Ernesto has done everything he could and of his loyalty and true friendship I do not doubt, but I should have summoned him at the outset so that we could have understood each other well and he could have grasped the situation. . . . I failed in that detail."[45] The attorney gave Ernesto the same advice as his brother Carlos: "write to him, write to him directly and frequently." The only part of the letter that could have brought some gratification to Ernesto was the news that "Mr. Hawley [the company President in New York] is very satisfied with your actions during the uprising and he blindly supports you."[46]

Frustrated, disappointed, and in poor health, Ernesto resigned as the General Manager of Chaparra, and he and the family moved back to Havana to a house he rented in Vedado, on Sixth Street, between Twenty-First and Twenty-Third Avenues. He secured a position in the capital as General Manager of the Cuba Cane Sugar Corporation. It is likely that he met with Menocal upon his return to Havana and the two friends may have reconciled, but there is no evidence of that meeting among Ernesto's papers or in the press.

On Sunday, February 24, 1918, at his home in Vedado, Ernesto sat in front of his typewriter to write a personal letter to Mr. J. H. Land, the Assistant Treasurer of the Cuban American Sugar Company in New York. Carefully worded in Ernesto's impeccable English, the letter poignantly reflects his health and financial situation, as well as his desire to reclaim his reputation as an effective administrator and loyal employee, a reputation very important to him.[47] "Your unquestionable good will towards me," the letter starts, "prompts me to trouble you once more about a personal matter." Ernesto goes on to point out that since Menocal accepted his resignation as manager of Chaparra, effective on December 31, 1917, "I am entitled to the extra compensation paid from the New York office corresponding to the months of October, November, and December amounting to $600.00." After laying claim to the money he feels is owed to him, and that he undoubtedly needs, the letter refers to the company's latest annual report: "I was glad to look over the balance of the Cuban American Sugar Co. for this last year and see that the earnings of the Chaparra and Delicias were the highest ever obtained notwithstanding the revolt which played such a havoc with our neighbors. It has been a source of great satisfaction to me to see that my efforts on behalf of the company were quite successful." He closes the letter by informing the American that "I am still struggling to recover from the serious illness which resulted from my strenuous life during the last period of my management of Chaparra." The carbon copy of the letter is the last piece of correspondence in the Colonel's surviving archive.

In its April 18, 1918, edition, the leading Havana daily, *Diario de la Marina*, included a note in its social news column announcing the return of Ernesto Fonts y Sterling to Havana from the sanatorium in San Diego de los Baños, Pinar del Río province, where the medicinal sulfur baths "failed to alleviate his aliments . . . Señor Fonts y Sterling has been suffering from an intense rheumatic aliment, finding himself totally prostrated."[48] What was labeled "rheumatism" may have been the long-term complications from his spinal injury.

A month later, on May 20, 1918, the sixteenth anniversary of the day that Leonard Wood left the island and the Cuban Republic was inaugurated, Ernesto passed away in his home in Vedado. At his side were his wife and sons, and President Menocal, who had rushed over from the Presidential Palace. He was forty-eight years old.

Ernesto's funeral and burial attracted huge crowds and, without exception, the most prominent figures of Cuba's political, social, and economic life, irrespective of political party. All of Havana's news media provided extensive coverage of his death, funeral, and burial. Numerous editorials and essays eulogizing him were published in the newspapers and magazines.[49] In honor of Ernesto, the Cuban Senate canceled its session scheduled for the day of the funeral, and members of the House of Representatives stood in a moment of silence during its first meeting after the burial.[50]

From the funeral home in Vedado, the body was taken in a hearse pulled by three pairs of black horses to city hall, the historic Palace of the Captain Generals, which until four years before had been the Presidential Palace and since the eighteenth century had housed the Spanish Military Governors that had ruled over Cuba. The casket was placed, surrounded by candelabra, in the same ceremonial room where Wood and Estrada Palma had made speeches marking the end of US military occupation and the inauguration of a Cuban government, a ceremony Ernesto had no doubt attended. After the overnight vigil and the procession of mourners, the funeral cortege, led by President Menocal, wound its way through Havana's principal streets: O'Reilly, Zulueta, Neptuno, Prado, San Rafael, Galiano, Carlos III, and finally Zapata to the Fonts family gravesite at the Colón necropolis, where he would be joined in the subsequent decades by the bodies of Malila, his sons, and his brothers Carlos and Oscar.[51]

Of all my ancestors, Colonel Ernesto Fonts y Sterling has the most footprints in historical records. He even left a collection of papers, which I was privileged to inherit. Tracing his footprints in archives and databases commanded most of my research time for this book. Despite his historical importance, however, the body of family memory about him was sketchy and, as I discovered, sometimes flawed in the details. The original source of that inherited memory was my grandfather Oscar, who was only fourteen when his father died. Ever since I can remember, Oscar and Oscar's children spoke to me about the Colonel with pride and admiration, extolling the sacrifices he made during the war and his reputation for honesty as a public servant during the days of the republic.

After thoroughly researching his life, I have no reason to contradict the reverential image of Ernesto that was passed on to me. But my research did allow me to arrive at a more nuanced picture of him. His life was charted by certain innate personality characteristics that were molded by a military school education in the United States during his most impressionable years and by the harshness of the Cuban battlefield. He had a profound respect for authority and an admiration for American society and culture

The Fonts family gravesite at the Colón necropolis. Photo by the author (2020).

that led him to view favorably the influence of the United States in shaping the destiny of Cuba. More than once his loyalties were tested as he found himself in the middle of forces unleashed by the political volatility of the Cuban Republic. Although he undertook actions that could be judged as questionable or misguided, they were actions wholly consistent with his character and beliefs. His decisions were guided by his sense of duty and personal integrity, decisions that cost him the level of prosperity and influence enjoyed by others around him, and ultimately cost him his health and his life. Ernesto's loyalty and sacrifices went largely unrewarded in that republic in which many of his fellow war veterans lost their way,

CHAPARRA   ◈   125

cashing in on the ample opportunities for corruption. It is difficult, given the trajectory of his life, not to feel a sense of pathos at his untimely death.

His distant cousin, the statesman and journalist Manuel Márquez Sterling, eulogized Ernesto with these words in a newspaper column:

> Unsurpassed in his integrity, a man without guile or malice, clear and transparent, he traced his life in a straight line that no one ever managed to twist. Despite deserving it, he never sought higher public office. He did not have the temperament for the intrigues and the maneuverings of party politics, and he distanced himself from them, in these times, when those who rule us do not seek the best path for us to follow.[52]

8

GENERAL CIGAR

The 1920s roared into Cuba. With the price of sugar reaching new heights, the country was flush with money, enjoying what became known as "The Dance of the Millions." US investments multiplied, creating opportunities for many Cubans to profit handsomely.

The business partnership of Rogelio Echevarría and Lisandro Pérez flourished during the 1920s, but it faced a welcomed challenge. The demand for their product continued to grow as more US cigar manufacturers sought to acquire the leaf from the central region of Cuba. More land was converted to *vegas*, especially in the regions of Placetas, Cabaiguán, and Zaza del Medio, areas farther away from the hub of Echevarría y Pérez in Camajuaní. To keep up with demand, the partners had to territorially expand their operations across a wide swath of Las Villas, and that was the challenge. In their business, broadening the area of operations required significant investments in infrastructure. While Camajuaní was the nerve center of the operations, with the largest warehouse and direct shipping connections to Havana, all of the company's functions could not be centralized there. The initial warehousing and processing of the leaves had to be a local operation not far from the *vegas* where the leaves were collected. At that time, the transportation of the product from the *vega* to the company's facilities was done using large oxcarts that had to lumber their way through roads that were often narrow and unpaved. The distance from Camajuaní to the area around Zaza del Medio, where some of the most distant *vegas* were located, is fifty miles. The leaves collected from the *veguero* were not packaged in a way that could withstand such a long trek without some damage, given the hot and possibly rainy conditions. It was therefore necessary to have a facility in each of the towns near the *vegas*, towns with rail connections, where the leaves would be processed and packed for the trip to Camajuaní, and eventually to Havana.

There were also labor considerations. The most labor-intensive phase of the operation was the stemming of the leaves (the process of removing the middle rib of the leaf), for which a large female labor force was seasonally employed. This required a decentralization of the processing functions, since Camajuaní, or any other single locality, could not provide the necessary number of women to work as *despalilladoras* (stemmers) if the company's operations were concentrated in one facility. It was necessary to tap into different local labor markets, especially since the women, who were employed seasonally and compensated on a piecework basis, and most no doubt had traditional domestic obligations as well, could not be expected to relocate or commute a long distance to a central facility.

Before the 1920s, Echevarría y Pérez had already acquired or built, and staffed, *casas de tabaco* in several localities. But the increasing demand and the extension of *vegas* throughout the region required that many more be established if they were to keep ahead of the competition in purchasing the best *vegas*. A substantial investment had to be made.

It was at that critical moment that an important American cigar manufacturer made the decision to enter the Cuban market as a buyer. The General Cigar Company, with corporate offices at 119 West Fortieth Street in New York, was the producer of the popular brands Robert Burns, Van Dyck, White Owl, and William Penn, all manufactured at the time with tobacco leaves from Pennsylvania and Connecticut. It had its primary processing and manufacturing facility in Lancaster, Pennsylvania, near some of its tobacco fields in that county.[1] Its corporate precursor, United Cigar Manufacturers Company, dates to at least 1909. It changed to General Cigar in 1917, the year that name first appears in the corporate annual reports.

The company's incursion into Cuba was its first attempt to internationalize the sources of its raw material. Its 1921 annual report lists all the company-owned manufacturing, warehouse, distribution, and retail outlets, and none were located outside the US.[2] They discovered, however, that the pungent leaves from Las Villas, when blended with their own Pennsylvania leaves, produced a better smoke.

The customers of the processed leaves sold by Echevarría and Pérez, such as the House of Bernheim, were typically family-owned businesses that were involved only in manufacturing, purchasing leaves ready to be rolled into a cigar. General Cigar was a bigger company, with experience not just in manufacturing but in all aspects of cigar production, including growing and processing the leaves. Their business model led them to decide on a more far-ranging presence in Cuba than as simple buyers of the processed leaves. The company set out to do what Echevarría y Pérez was doing: purchase from the *vegueros*, process the leaves, and ship them to the United States. In their case, the leaves would be shipped to New York and then on to Lancaster, where they would be blended with their Pennsylvania leaves to form the filler that was then encased in Connecticut wrappers, also from their farms. Although General Cigar was also a grower in the United States, they knew that in Cuba that function was best left up to the *vegueros*, but their corporate profile predisposed them to engage in the processing of the leaves.

The company had two alternatives in Cuba. One was to invest in building the infrastructure and in recruiting the personnel needed to compete with the Cuban companies, such as Echevarría y Pérez, that had years of experience and contacts in Las Villas. The other, the smarter move, was to just buy one of those companies and acquire their facilities and their

experienced personnel. Isaac Bernheim, who was starting to wind down
his business as he contemplated retirement, placed the executives of General Cigar in touch with my grandfather. The company made an offer to
acquire all the facilities of Echevarría y Pérez, including the warehouse in
Havana, and to retain its full-time employees, that is, Lisandro and the
administrative, clerical, and skilled employees.

My grandfather had misgivings about selling what he had worked so
hard to build. Still in his mid-fifties, he was in his prime as a businessman and was looking forward to more years of running an operation to
which he had devoted his life and developed so many personal and working relationships, most of whom depended on Echevarría y Pérez for their
livelihood, from the *vegueros* who loyally sold their *vegas* to him to the
employees in each of the *casas de tabaco*. It seemed as if he was abandoning
them for an uncertain future in the hands of foreigners.

But there were compelling reasons favoring the deal. To stay competi-
tive, Echevarría y Pérez had to make significant investments to expand
its operations. If the offer from the Americans was refused and General
Cigar, with its capital, became a competitor, then it could have spelled the
end of Lisandro's business. And then there was the situation of Rogelio
Echevarría. Echevarría y Pérez had built a roster of loyal recurring buyers
such as the House of Bernheim, so Rogelio's job as the salesman of the
product had become practically obsolete. More than a decade older than
my grandfather, he was already in effect a silent partner. By 1919, Lisandro
was managing the entire operations of the company from Havana, where
he had moved with his family. Rogelio was ready to cash out and retire, so he
strongly favored selling out.

At some point in the negotiation process, Isaac Bernheim passed on to
the President of General Cigar, Fred Hirschhorn, the critical piece of advice
that persuaded Lisandro to embrace the deal. Bernheim and Hirschhorn were
probably well acquainted: both were sons of German Jewish immigrants,
contemporaries who started in the tobacco business as teenagers, and active in New York cigar manufacturing and philanthropy circles. Bernheim

My grandfather Lisandro, circa 1930. Author's collection.

made his colleague realize that the most important asset General Cigar would be acquiring in the deal were not the facilities but rather Lisandro's expertise and deep contacts in the region. No manager sent from Pennsylvania to Camajuaní was going to be able to match the deep knowledge and extensive network my grandfather had built over decades. "Give him full authority in managing the entire operation," Isaac advised.

That is precisely what General Cigar included in the deal, offering to hire Lisandro to be completely in charge of the company's operations in Cuba, naming him as President of the newly incorporated General Cigar Company of Cuba, Ltd., a wholly owned subsidiary of the General Cigar Company. Lisandro accepted on one condition: while all the other employees would receive a salary or wage, he wanted to be compensated by commission based on the amount of tobacco shipped to New York. Ever since he bought the general store in Vueltas when he was a teenager, Lisandro made a living based on what he produced, not on a wage, so the arrangement with General Cigar suited him best and was consistent with the autonomy he was given to manage the entire business.

Working on a commission basis was also meant as an assurance to the Americans that he would continue to devote himself to running a profitable business that produced a quality leaf. The agreement read, "L. Pérez commits himself to dedicate all his time to the business of the General Cigar Co. of Cuba Ltd. in the warehouse, the *despalillos*, and everything related to the business in Cuba."[3] He was now working for the Americans, but the job remained the same: managing the operations involved in taking the tobacco leaf from the *vega* in Las Villas to the docks in Havana for shipment to New York.

Lisandro received $2.50 for every *tercio* of tobacco leaves that he shipped to New York. *Tercios* were the packages used to transport the leaves at various stages of their processing, including the final shipment to General Cigar. It was a unit of volume rather than weight: a cube with sides measuring about three feet, packed with carefully laid layers of tobacco leaves and wrapped in *yagua*, the thick woody sheathing leaf base of the royal palm, and then sewn tight with burlap. A *tercio* could weigh as much as one hundred and thirty pounds if it contained leaves that had not been stemmed, or as little as eighty-eight pounds with stemmed leaves.

In 1933, Lisandro's commission came to $27,303.[4] He still managed to make that sum in the depths of the Great Depression because the tobacco he shipped that year had already been maturing in the Havana warehouse for several years. The year before, however, General Cigar ordered Lisandro not to buy any tobacco because the company faced a loss of profits and had enough inventory given the depressed market. Essentially all field operations were to cease, with personnel placed on unpaid leave. Lisandro could not do the latter. A great part of his success was due to the cadre of administrators he had trained and who worked for him all their lives managing the operations in the major tobacco houses, men such as Abelardo Cangas in the Havana warehouse, Higinio González in Camajuaní, and Antonio Barquín in Cabaiguán. With the acquisition of Echevarría y Pérez, they had become General Cigar employees with salaries ranging from $2,500 to $3,500, and the company ordered them furloughed. Lisandro met with the employees and proposed paying them half of their annual salary for working on a drastically reduced schedule managing the minimal processing operations of the tobacco that had already been purchased years before. He paid those reduced salaries out of his pocket. Apart from his loyalty to those lifelong employees, he could simply not afford to lose them if they went elsewhere for employment.

General Cigar invested in the necessary expansion of facilities across the tobacco-producing regions of Las Villas. Even before that expansion, managing all the operations was a complicated task. It had now become even more complex, with more facilities, more employees, and more inventory. By the late 1930s, the General Cigar Company of Cuba, under Lisandro's management, was operating out of fifteen tobacco houses spread throughout central Cuba, in addition to the warehouse in Havana.[5] Some of those facilities were only large enough to serve as the places where the newly purchased tobacco was brought in from the nearby *vegas*, sorted, initially

HAVANA—
bought to the
best advantage

MORE fine Havana goes into Robt. Burns than is required for any other cigar made in America.

Immense purchases naturally give the makers of Robt. Burns unusual buying advantages—both as to price and selection of leaf. The General Cigar Co., Inc., has always shared these advantages with the smokers of Robt. Burns.

ROBT. BURNS
Perfecto
Actual Size
2 for 25c
Box of 50—$6.00

PERFECTOS: 2 for 25c
INVINCIBLES: 15c straight
(Foil Wrapped)
EPICURES: 2 for 25c

General Cigar Co., inc.
NATIONAL BRANDS
NEW YORK CITY

*Robt. Burns Cigar
is Full Havana Filled*

General Cigar ad, circa 1940. The inclusion of Cuban leaves in their cigars became a major selling point for the company.

processed, packed, and provisionally stored, that is, the process known as the *escogida*. Those smaller houses were given the name of that process, *la escogida*. The larger facilities, seven of them, functioned as both *escogidas* and stemmeries (*despalillos*). They were larger because they carried out both functions, and eventually all the inventory was funneled through them for final processing, including stemming, which required space for all the desks where the *despalilladoras* performed the delicate task of removing the stem from each leaf. Camajuaní was the largest of the *despalillos* and the nerve center of all field operations.

The process of taking a leaf from the *vega* to the dock in Havana involved a multitude of steps in which the leaf was sorted, packed, shipped to Havana, aged, shipped back to Las Villas, unpacked, fermented, stemmed, repacked, shipped again to Havana, and stored before it was finally loaded on a ship to New York. A leaf's journey through that process normally took seven years. Adding to the complexity of the operation was the management of both a permanent and temporary workforce that during peak periods could exceed a thousand workers in the tobacco-processing facilities scattered throughout the region. All this required an efficient cargo transportation network linking those facilities with one another, with the *vegas*, and with Havana. And then there was the maintenance of the facilities and the purchase of all the ancillary supplies needed to process and pack the leaves, such as the *yaguas* for *tercios*, which were purchased directly from individual farmers. It was a business that was no less complex, perhaps even more so, than any of the industries involved in processing an agricultural commodity into a fine product with a worldwide reputation, such as wine or distilled spirits. The operation Lisandro managed was perhaps more intricate than those of his competitors, for he took no shortcuts, managing a system he had developed that produced a processed leaf with the quality that established his reputation and attracted General Cigar as a buyer.[6]

The process started while the leaf was still on the plant, in the *vega*. Lisandro had buyers in the field whose job was to keep a running account on each of the tobacco farms in their assigned territories. They were to record the date the *veguero* planted the seedlings, the provenance of the seedlings, and the changes in temperature and levels of precipitation in the area. Since the tobacco plant is harvested in stages, depending on the maturity of the leaves in each plant, the buyers would also record the dates of the first cut, second cut, third cut, and so on. Once the entire *vega* had been harvested and the *veguero* had hung the leaves in stitched bundles in his curing house, the buyer would estimate the size of the *vega*, the adequacy of the curing conditions, and the quality of the leaf. All this information, plus the farmer's reputation, was factored into the decision on whether or not to make an offer on the crop.

To meet the volume of tobacco that General Cigar expected from its investment, Lisandro had to rely on the reports of those carefully chosen buyers to make decisions on those *vegas* with which he was personally unfamiliar. He was now operating in an expanded region, and he did not have firsthand experience with all the new *vegueros* that could potentially supply him with inventory. However, those *vegueros* who were his long-standing suppliers were not scouted by a buyer. Lisandro knew their reputations for producing quality leaves and would every year buy their crop without inspection.

The trickiest part was setting the price and deciding when to offer it. Prices generally ranged from eighteen to twenty-five *pesos* per *quintal* (100 kilograms or about 220 pounds). Lisandro considered not only the buyers' reports but also the trends in the world tobacco market and the size of his inventory from previous years. In terms of price, some years the constellation of factors favored him, and other years they favored the *veguero*, but he knew that since this was an annual process and he wanted to keep buying from the best *vegueros*, he had to settle on a fair price, one that would not be exploitative when it was a buyer's market. This is why some *vegueros* were his loyal suppliers, trusting that the price he set was a fair one, and why his competitors looked to him as the standard when setting their own purchase prices in the region.

There were years in which some of his competitors would start making offers to a few *vegueros* at a price that Lisandro considered unreasonably high. They wanted to drive up the price because they had a glut in inventory and had no intention of buying much of the new crop but did not want that inventory devalued with a lower price that year. This would usually set off panic buying from others who were concerned that the best *vegas* would be bought up. One year, that panic reached the boardroom in New York, and General Cigar sent Lisandro a telegram ordering him to start buying at the higher price. But Lisandro knew the game and held fast, telegramming the Americans, in Spanish, that if they wanted to buy at those prices, they were welcome to go down to Cuba and do it themselves, because he was not going to do it. He was in charge of operations, he reminded them, and he would decide when to buy and at what price. New York backed down, the panic subsided, and he made offers that year that were in line with the actual market. The suits in the offices on Fortieth Street never meddled again.

Once the *veguero* accepted the price Lisandro and his buyers offered, the deal was sealed with a handshake. It was an irrevocable oral contract. Neither party could afford to damage its reputation by trying to go back on it. A date would be set, sometime between May and September, the season for the *escogidas*, to pick up the crop and pay the farmer. The calendar was set calculating it would take an entire day to load the *vega* and then unload it at the tobacco house. Some ambitious *vegueros* produced crops that could take two or three days to load and unload, but such large *vegas* were the exception.

On the appointed day, the oxcarts (eventually replaced by trucks) would arrive at the farmer's property, along with the personnel from General Cigar, to start the *escogida* process. The oxcarts were owned and operated by independent contractors, and the number hired for that day would depend on the estimated volume of the crop. At the farmer's curing house, as the *matules* (bundles) of leaves were unhung from their perches, batches of them would be stacked on a large scale to weigh them. The buyer's workers would then form a line from the curing house to the oxcarts, passing from person to person the *matules*. When the loading was over, the amount owed was calculated, and the *veguero* was handed a voucher that showed both the volume he produced and the amount he was due. It was then customary for the farmer and his family to invite all who had worked that day to a lunch of either arroz con pollo or a roasted pig that had been slaughtered for the occasion. The *vega* was then transported to the *escogida* plant and carefully unloaded.

The next day the *veguero* would go to the company's tobacco house in town and redeem his voucher for a check payable at the City Bank branch in that same locality. Starting in 1907, when it entered the Cuban market, City Bank expanded rapidly throughout the island, so that by the 1930s it had established a ubiquitous presence, making possible the transfer of funds from the United States to almost any locality in Cuba.[7] In anticipation of the *escogida* season, Lisandro's office would send a detailed breakdown to General Cigar of funds that needed to be deposited in each branch in the region, based on estimates of the monies they anticipated would be disbursed to *vegueros* in each locality. The office in New York would then wire the money to City Bank in Havana, with instructions on the distribution of those funds among its branches in Las Villas. The pervasive presence of US companies in Cuba, including banks, made it possible for a *veguero* somewhere in central Cuba to form part of an international financial system.

In the *escogida* house the *matules* were disassembled and the leaves were laid on the floor, sprinkled with water to prevent brittleness, and then sorted by color, size, and quality into one of seven descriptive categories. The leaves in each category were retied together in circular bundles of about 160 leaves each and carefully packed in *tercios* made of *yagua* for shipment to the warehouse in Havana, where they would be cured for two or three years. The logic of shipping them to Havana was that the warehouse there had ample space and the optimal environmental conditions for curing the leaf. The *escogida* houses did not have the humidity requirements nor the space to store two or three years of inventory.

Each *vega* was processed separately so it could be tracked. Every *tercio* was stamped with the name of the *veguero* and the date the *vega* was picked up. Those identifiers would remain in place in subsequent packaging throughout the entire process so that the *tercios* that eventually arrived in Pennsylvania could be identified by their exact provenance in Cuba.

Once the *tercios* had spent enough time in Havana, they were shipped back to Las Villas, but not to the original *escogida* house. They were redirected to one of the seven *despalillos*, mostly to Camajuaní, where they would be unpacked, the leaves moistened again, and then the bundles hung on a structure made of hollow poles, with thermometers protruding from the end of each pole. Those structures were then completely covered with several heavy blankets so the leaves would "sweat" and run a "fever" for several days, and the thermometers would be checked periodically. It was akin to a fermentation process designed to enrich the flavor of the tobacco. On the day the blankets were removed, only the employees handling the operation could be inside the *despalillo*. The fumes that were dispelled had a potent smell similar to ammonia that could be detected as far as Camajuaní's park. Evacuating the personnel on those days was a practice adopted after several *despalilladoras* working in the big room on the farthest end of the facility fainted from the fumes.

The next step was the stemming of the leaves. Stemming was seasonal piecework done by women, using only their fingernails to remove the central rib or vein, leaving the leaf with a sort of double kidney shape. Each woman would disassemble her assigned bundle, stem each leaf, and then retie the bundle again and attach her distinctive tag. The days, weeks, and months when stemming was taking place was when the *despalillo* in Camajuaní turned into a lively, bustling place, with as many as five hundred *despalilladoras* on the main floor. On those days, Regina Depestre, the tall black woman who ran the cafeteria in the central patio of the *despalillo*, made a hefty profit turning out batches of the incomparable cod fritters that everyone just had to have for lunch.

The final step was to pack the leaves into *tercios* again, in carefully laid out layers separated by kraft paper. For this last packaging, the *yagua* tercios were wrapped tightly with a layer of burlap that was handstitched in place. They would go back to Havana to be stored and cured for another two or three years before they were transported to the port and shipped to New York.

This complex processing regime that Lisandro had instituted for his business was followed every year in every one of the facilities in Las Villas by a loyal and experienced administrative cadre that had worked for him their entire lives. The process was so routine that it was almost a ritual. Once he moved to Havana, Lisandro could have delegated the field operations to those administrators. But he could not conceive of the idea of running his business exclusively from his office in the warehouse in Havana. The quality of his product was determined by what happened on the ground in Las Villas, in the *vegas* and the tobacco houses, and if he had personally guaranteed to General Cigar that he would uphold those quality standards, then he had to remain active in the field.

For more than three decades after moving to Havana he followed a weekly routine from which he very rarely deviated. Every Wednesday around five in the morning, he would descend the stairway from the terrace of the house on G street to the driveway carrying a small briefcase with papers and his inseparable notebook. The black Buick was waiting for him at the bottom of the stairs with César holding open the door to the back seat. César was his chauffer for all business-related automobile travel, and his services, as well as the Buick itself, had been negotiated in the deal with General Cigar. Lisandro never learned how to drive, and so it was critical to have a chauffeur, especially for the weekly two-hundred-mile jaunt to Camajuaní. César was an employee of the company, and the Buick was owned by General Cigar.

After a stop in Colón, Matanzas, for breakfast, Lisandro arrived in Camajuaní at eleven in the morning, but not directly to the *despalillo*. Lisandro arranged to rent an enclosed parking space adjoining a private residence in a quiet area of town near the *despalillo*. César would park the car there, and Lisandro would walk to his office in the tobacco house. During his entire stay in Camajuaní, he would walk everywhere, and the Buick would stay sequestered. Lisandro did not want to give an image of ostentatiousness by being driven around the town in a luxury car.

Lisandro would conduct business from his office in the *despalillo* in Camajuaní, although occasionally he would go out to Placetas or Cabaiguán to check on the situation in those tobacco houses. Some of his administrators in other facilities would go to Camajuaní to see him regarding any issues they were encountering. He would stay in Camajuaní until midday on Friday, when César would drive him back to Havana. Lisandro slept the two nights in a dormitory he had set up on the second floor of the *despalillo*. It was so austere it looked like a hospital ward, with six single white metal beds arranged along the walls and a small adjoining bathroom. César also slept there, as well as any guests. When they were older, my father and his brother Rubén accompanied him on these weekly trips, and they would sleep there as well. Lisandro did not afford himself the luxury of a private room. He indulged in some luxuries in Havana, as evidenced by the house on G street, but in Las Villas, where he had lived most of his life in fairly humble conditions, he never allowed himself any ostentatious display that could be interpreted as showing off the wealth he had acquired. My grandfather may have moved to the glittering capital, but his essence was still that of an orphaned boy from Remedios, and he never wanted to do anything that would alienate him from that environment that had been the key to his success.

Nevertheless, everyone knew he was a wealthy man and the town's largest employer, so there was the expectation that he might use some of that wealth to improve the lives of people in Camajuaní, and he did not defraud that expectation. Every Wednesday when he walked up to the *despalillo* after his trip from Havana, there would invariably be a small queue of people waiting for him outside the entrance to ask him for help in meeting some urgent need: money for a critical medicine, a job, rent money so as to avoid eviction, and so on. He usually helped those he felt were deserving. His notebook has several lists, written at different moments in time, with names of people and money amounts. The lists are headed "defaulted loans." Some amounts were thousands of dollars.

His greatest single contribution to the town's welfare, however, was the expansion and refurbishment of the local public school, located in the center of town, on the highway from Santa Clara. Public schools, especially those outside Havana, received minimal financial support from the government. Lisandro's contribution made a big difference, but it was an ongoing commitment on his part. Whenever the school needed repairs, maintenance, or painting, the principal would contact Lisandro, and he would send over his maintenance crew from the *despalillo* to take care of any issues. To acknowledge his beneficence, the town council issued an official proclamation naming him an "adoptive son" of Camajuaní and naming the school in his honor.[8] It remained "Grupo Escolar Lisandro Pérez" until its name was changed in 1961.

A float passes by the school named for Lisandro Pérez during the annual street festival, *parranda*, to honor Camajuaní's patron saint, San José, March 19, 1947. Photograph by J. Muros, courtesy of Ramiro A. Fernández.

Part of Lisandro's weekly routine was to start his Mondays in the Havana warehouse by sitting down at his desk, taking out a legal pad and a pencil, and writing out longhand and in Spanish a report to General Cigar on whatever he wanted to report on (inventory, the cost and quality of the *vegas,* overhead costs, etc.). He would then fold the sheets, place them in an envelope, put a stamp on it, and mail it to New York. General Cigar had on staff in their main office a translator who would render the report in English and circulate it to the board of directors.

The purchase of Echevarría y Pérez by General Cigar was one of many takeovers of Cuban businesses by US corporations during the first three decades of the twentieth century. Many Cuban historians and writers of the period bemoaned the trend, arguing that Cubans were losing control of their wealth and economy. To be sure, it was a disquieting trend with far-reaching consequences, but the case of General Cigar and its relationship with my grandfather provides an example of how even with US ownership, there was Cuban agency. Lisandro in effect made all the management decisions for the US company that had bought him out. Perhaps it was an uncommon case, but it was probably widespread in sectors of the economy in which the Americans relied on Cuban expertise to maximize the profits from their investments. Even in the sugar industry, we saw how the board of the Cuban American Sugar Company in New York placed entirely in the hands of Menocal and Ernesto the management of their huge investments in northeastern Cuba. The takeover of the Cuban economy by US corporations was real, but these particular cases show how a microanalysis of the broad trend yields nuances in how the process took place.

9

OSCAR AND NANCY

As he lay dying, Colonel Ernesto Fonts y Sterling fretted about the future of his family without him. He did not doubt that his older brothers would provide his wife and sons with the necessary financial support, but what worried him was that Carlos and Oscar would also try to control the lives of Malila and the boys. He wanted his wife to maintain a certain independence, and he wanted Ernesto Jr. and my grandfather Oscar to have the same life-changing experience he had: a military education in the United States so they would learn discipline and, especially, English. The Colonel anticipated, or perhaps he requested, that the government grant Malila a pension that would enable her to move to New York, away from his brothers' meddling, and enroll the boys at New York Military Academy. It was his dying wish, which he expressed repeatedly and urgently to his family in his final days.

Eleven days after Ernesto's death, the *Gaceta Oficial*, the Cuban government's daily publication for all official business, ran on its front page a notice from the Treasury Ministry that President Mario García-Menocal approved a congressional bill granting "María Luisa Acosta, widow of the Colonel of the Liberation Army Ernesto Fonts y Sterling, an annual pension of 2,400 pesos, payable monthly . . . and to each of his minor sons, Ernesto and Oscar Fonts y Acosta, six hundred pesos annually until they reach maturity."[1]

Malila wasted no time in complying with her husband's wish. She vacated the rented house in Vedado and arrived in New York with plenty of time to enroll the boys in New York Military Academy (NYMA) before the school year started in the fall of 1918. The school Colonel Fonts had attended in New York, Mount Pleasant Military Academy, was already in its final years, eclipsed by the NYMA, which was founded in 1889 and quickly became the premier military boarding school in the Hudson Valley. My grandfather Oscar was only fourteen when he was enrolled and therefore could look ahead to several more years at NYMA, but his brother Ernesto Jr. was already sixteen, and he did not stay long in the school. There is no record that he ever graduated. My grandfather's brother had a reputation, which endured even into his mature years, as a hell-raiser. He had little patience for the rigors of a military school.

New York Military was (and still is) located near Cornwall, on the west bank of the Hudson, about sixty miles north of New York City. It was a full boarding school, so Malila sent the boys up the river and installed herself in a residential hotel in Manhattan, the Walton, located at 104 West Seventieth Street, on the southwest corner of Columbus Avenue.[2]

It took a great deal of courage for Malila to uproot herself from where she had been born and always lived, surrounded by family and friends, to comply with her husband's dying wish and live in a strange new place, and not just any place, but bustling New York City. Unlike her husband, who was fluent in the language, Malila spoke barely a word of English. But she was not entirely among strangers at the Walton. She may have chosen to live there because it was managed by Manuel Quevedo; his wife, Fausta; and their adult son, Manuel Jr., Cubans who migrated to New York in 1910. By 1920, when the enumerator R. W. Darling canvassed the hotel for the US decennial census, he or she found thirteen Cuban-born residents at the Walton, including Malila and Ernesto Jr., the Quevedos,

My grandfather Oscar (left) and his brother Ernesto Jr. in their New York Military Academy uniforms, circa 1918. Fonts family collection.

Malila and her sons in their apartment at the Walton, Upper West Side, Manhattan, circa 1918. Fonts family collection.

and two cousins of Malila who followed her to New York and moved into their own apartment: Dolores de la Cruz Muñoz, forty-eight years old and a widow; her unmarried sister, Juana, thirty-eight; and Dolores's son Eddy, twelve years old.[3]

Because he was boarded at the military academy, my grandfather Oscar was not enumerated at the Walton. He did, however, take advantage of every opportunity to visit his mother and brother in Manhattan. Malila would take her sons to museums, theaters, and especially, the opera. One

particularly memorable performance was the Metropolitan Opera's production of *Aida*, with Enrico Caruso in the role of Radamès. The Fonts
boys, however, would attend by themselves their favorite spectacle: the
feats of Harry Houdini, an act Malila was happy to forgo.

The years he spent in New York enabled my grandfather to expand and
diversify the stamp collection he had started during his years in Chaparra.
In Manhattan, Oscar was able to acquire stamps from all over the world by
visiting the many philatelic shops in the city. He had a special interest in
European stamps. My grandfather organized the collection by placing the
stamps into small envelopes that were filed by continent, country, and year
of issue. He was less interested in, or perhaps found too tedious, displaying
the stamps in albums.

Malila and her sons never visited Cuba during the five years they lived
in New York. They returned to the island in 1923, but not before attending
a party hosted by the brother of Dolores and Juana, Malila's cousins who
also lived at the Walton. The brother, Federico de la Cruz Muñoz, also a
cousin of Malila, lived at 603 West 111 Street. His son, Fred, attended New
York Military Academy with Oscar. The party was held on a Sunday to
welcome to New York close friends of Federico's who had arrived the day
before, on April 21, 1923, aboard the *Orizaba* from Havana and were staying
with him during their time in Manhattan. The visitors were Ana Boullosa
(née Zamora), forty-two years of age, and her daughters Isabel, twenty;
Nancy, eighteen; and Consuelo, eleven.[4] Ana's husband, Juan Boullosa,
stayed behind in Havana while his wife and daughters went to New York
to enjoy the many offerings of the city and the hospitality of Federico.

The party that Sunday at the Upper West Side apartment was a festive
affair, with *danzones*, the most popular Cuban musical genre of the time,
playing from the discs in the phonograph. The apartment of the Cruz
Muñoz family was larger than that of Malila's at the Walton, but the living
room was still too small to amply accommodate the dancers. The visiting Boullosa sisters, who knew very few people at the party, were sitting
in chairs on the perimeter of the room when my grandfather Oscar, who

was dancing with another girl, stepped lightly on one of Nancy's feet as he brushed by. He did not turn to apologize. Later, Oscar asked Nancy to dance, but she refused, letting him know that she was upset about what had happened earlier. Oscar apologized but told her with a smile he had stepped on her foot on purpose to catch her attention. The smile from the tall nineteen-year-old must have persuaded her to change her mind, and she accepted the offer to dance.

Ana Boullosa and her daughters returned to Cuba after their vacation in New York. Malila, Ernesto Jr., and Oscar returned later that same year. But Oscar and Nancy stayed in touch and resumed their relationship in Havana. On March 12, 1925, less than two years after they met in New York, my grandfather and grandmother married in the Church of the Angel (Iglesia del Santo Ángel Custodio) on Compostela Street in Havana's colonial district. Oscar was twenty-one years old, and Nancy was twenty.

Nancy's father, Juan Boullosa, was born in 1877 in Havana to immigrants from Santa Cruz de Tenerife in the Canary Islands.[5] He worked for the government as a civil engineer and spent most of his life insisting that he never got proper financial compensation, or recognition, for drafting the plans to expand and modernize the Havana aqueduct. He did make enough money, however, to buy a house on the corner of Juan Bruno Zayas and General Lacret Streets in La Víbora, one of the fashionable residential neighborhoods that was developed at the turn of the century south of the city, just beyond El Cerro. He and his wife, Ana (Anita) Zamora, lived there with their four daughters. The three older ones, Margot, Isabel (Billie), and my grandmother Nancy (whose legal name was Ana Delia, but no one ever called her that), were all born, in that order, less than two years apart from one another. Seven years passed, however, before the youngest one, Consuelo, was born in 1912.

In their younger years, the Boullosa sisters led sheltered lives, seldom venturing outside the house. They were educated at home with a governess and a music teacher who taught each of the sisters a different instrument. My grandmother Nancy played the piano, Margot the violin, and

A young Nancy Boullosa, my grandmother.

My grandparents Oscar and Nancy at their wedding in the Iglesia del Santo Ángel Custodio, Havana, 1925. Fonts family collection.

Billie the harp, and the young Counselo was added to the family ensemble as soon as she was old enough to play the guitar. Juan Boullosa, whom his daughters called *papaíto*, was a meticulous man who loved to follow a strict daily routine. Always home in time for dinner with the family, he and Anita would adjourn after supper to the drawing room where their daughters regaled them with a concert of classical compositions they had practiced that day with their teacher. The entire family would then climb the stairs all the way to the roof to enjoy the night air. La Víbora had a reputation for having a healthy environment, since it was built on one of the highest natural elevations in the city. In the distance, they could see from the roof the lights of the bustling center of Havana.

That sheltered life was disrupted by the surprising decision of *papaíto* to send his three oldest daughters to finish their secondary education at St. Cecilia Academy, a Catholic school for girls established by Dominican nuns in Nashville, Tennessee.[6] For my grandmother Nancy, the change from their sheltered home life in La Víbora to a boarding school in the United States was initially traumatic. It was a very foreign and austere environment, and the nuns were harsh disciplinarians. She was especially struck by the treatment of the school's black servants, who were routinely addressed by one elderly nun with the "N" word. The Boullosas had black servants in La Víbora, some of whom had been with the family since before Nancy was born, but Anita had taught her daughters to treat them with respect. In time she adjusted to the school, in large measure thanks to the support and protection of her older sister Margot.

Nancy was closer to Margot than to any other member of the family. They had similar personalities: soft-spoken, kind, and judicious. The two were confidants, and Nancy, who had a very sensitive and timid nature, drew upon her older sister's strength when she faced adversity, especially in Nashville. In the house in La Víbora, they grew up sharing a bedroom that was always organized and tidy. The other two sisters were very different. Billie and Consuelo tended to be impetuous and undisciplined, more likely to challenge authority and be scolded, and their shared room was usually a mess.

Margot Boullosa, my grandmother's sister. Fonts family collection.

Not long after the sisters returned home from Nashville, Margot, who was eighteen, fell gravely ill with fever, vomiting, and diarrhea. A few days later, she died from typhoid fever. It was the first of several profound losses that my grandmother experienced in her lifetime that impacted her sensitive nature and made her progressively more fragile and dependent. In Oscar she had a husband with the personality of a caretaker who for the rest of his life would handle all the details, great and small, involved in running a household and raising a family. Nancy bore children, nurtured them, and attended to daily household tasks, but Oscar managed everything else and made all the important decisions regarding the upbringing and education of their children.

❋ 10 ❋

LIFE IN HAVANA

The "Dance of the Millions" of the 1920s transformed Havana. The capital was flush with cash, and its residents embraced the modernity that came with the growing economic and political presence of the United States on the island. That modernity had both material and nonmaterial manifestations, shaping styles, consumption patterns, and values. Havana's Americanization took place rapidly in what had always been a city with a port culture, distinctly secular and cosmopolitan with an outward-facing orientation that rapidly adjusted, and even welcomed, whatever the ocean would deposit at the city's wharfs. The most visible sign of that Americanization was the early invasion of automobiles from Detroit that made possible the rapid expansion of upscale neighborhoods such as Vedado, La Víbora, and the neighboring municipality of Marianao, across the Almendares River. Much of the splendid residential architecture that is admired to this day, even if now decayed, dates to this period, as upwardly mobile Cubans sought to display their newfound wealth with mansions that seemed to sprout up almost overnight.

By the mid-1920s, the Pérez and Fonts families were settling into the capital, each constructing a residence that would accommodate a growing family.

THE HOUSE ON G STREET

Lisandro and Amparo had three daughters when they moved to Havana in 1919. The oldest, Rosa Marina, was born in 1910, almost three years after her parents were married in Camajuaní.[1] She was named after her two grandmothers: Rosa Vidal y Caro, Amparo's mother, and Marina Moreno y Montero, Lisandro's mother. As with many of my ancestors, however, who never used their given names, my aunt was always known to the family, and to everyone else, as Mara. About two years later, a second daughter was born, Raquel. Her nickname, among family and friends, was Kela.

When their two oldest daughters were born, Lisandro and Amparo were living in Placetas, the nearest large town to the rapidly expanding tobacco-growing region of Zaza del Medio. Lisandro decided to move there for a few years to establish relationships with the new *vegueros* in that region before moving back to Camajuaní. To attend to her pregnancies and deliveries, Amparo called on the services of Dr. Carlos Enríquez Costa, who practiced medicine in the neighboring town of Zulueta. Dr. Enríquez was a widely educated man who encouraged his young son's artistic talents, sending him to study in Havana and to a summer course in painting at the Pennsylvania Academy of Fine Arts. That son, Carlos Enríquez Gómez, became one of Cuba's most renowned painters, a leading figure of the "vanguardia" generation of artists of the 1930s and 1940s. Lisandro and Amparo urged Dr. Enríquez to relocate to Havana when they did in 1919, auguring for him a very successful practice in the capital. He did so, and he went on to fulfill that prediction, eventually becoming the physician to President Gerardo Machado and his family.[2] He also delivered the rest of Amparo's children, who were born in Havana, including my father.

Amparo had good reason to get the best possible medical attention for her pregnancies and deliveries. She had several miscarriages before Mara was born, and there would be more in the six years that separated the birth of Kela and that of her third daughter, Gisela (Gise), who was born in Camajuaní in 1918. To have her ten children, Amparo reputedly went through twenty-two pregnancies. After Gisela was born, she apparently got this pregnancy thing right. My father, Lisandro Manuel (Tano), the first male and the first of Amparo's offspring born in Havana, was delivered by Dr. Enríquez in January 1920, and his brother, Rubén, was born in November of the same year. Amparito (all her nephews and nieces called her Watty) arrived in 1922, Carlos Humberto (simply Humberto) in 1924, and Baldomero (Lalo), my godfather, named after Amparo's father, followed a year later in 1925. Sergio was born in 1926, and just when Amparo's fecundity appeared finished, she gave birth three years later, in 1929, to María Leticia (Letty) at the age of forty-four. Five girls and five boys. My grandfather always carried with him a small three-ring binder in which he kept notes, reminders, and financial figures. The first page of the notebook had a listing of all his children's names and their birthdays.[3] With that many children, that important information could not be entrusted to memory.

For ten years after moving from Camajuaní to Havana, the family lived in a series of five rented houses before Lisandro decided to plan and construct the house on G Street. All those houses were in Vedado, except for the one in which they lived for the longest time, a spacious home on the corner of Poey and Patrocino Streets in La Víbora, the same neighborhood as the Boullosas. They moved to that house following Dr. Enríquez's advice, so that my father, who was a sickly boy in his earliest years, would ostensibly benefit from the salubrious environment of the neighborhood. The house in La Víbora turned out to be the model for the house on G Street. It had a columned terrace that wrapped around most of the house with a floor plan vertebrated by a central hallway. Lisandro found that the layout was perfect for his growing family, inspiring him to start the process of building a similar house in Vedado, the neighborhood where he wanted to settle permanently.[4]

He found a perfect location on the northeast corner of G and Fifteenth Streets, at the top of a gentle hill that rises from the Vedado waterfront six blocks away. There was a wooden house on the property, one of the first ones in Vedado, which was demolished when construction started early in 1929. Lisandro gave very specific instructions to the architects and engineers of the Frederick Snare Corporation, a New York construction company with an office in Havana. The cost of the lot and the house came to $125,000, which he paid in cash, no doubt from the windfall of the sale of Echevarría y Pérez to General Cigar several years before.

Lisandro, Amparo, and the ten children moved into the house on January 6, 1930. Vedado was still being developed, so G Street was an unpaved, dusty gravel road. The oldest child, Mara, was about to turn twenty, and the youngest, Letty, was an infant. My father would turn ten that month, and he and his brother Rubén were enrolled in the nearby Catholic school for boys run by the La Salle brothers, as were their younger brothers when they became old enough to attend school. Mara had already graduated from the Sacred Heart of Jesus School for girls, where Kela was in her senior year and Gisela was in the elementary grades. Amparito (Watty) was educated at home with a tutor because she could not perform intellectually at her age and grade level. She was a fully functional person and knew how to read and write, but just not with the level of intelligence needed to keep up at an elite school such as the Sacred Heart. There were no other options for her education except to provide her with individualized attention at home. The exact origin or nature of her mental disability was never mentioned, so I never learned of it, but I did know her as very sweet and devoted to her nieces and nephews. She was a special aunt.

Despite living outside the center of the city, no one in the household knew how to drive. Lisandro had his company chauffer, César, who was on the General Cigar payroll. But since my grandfather was very scrupulous about using César and the Buick only for company business, to drive him to and from the warehouse in Havana and on the trips to Las Villas, he bought another Buick for the family and hired a chauffeur, José, who was kept busy driving family members where they needed to go, especially ferrying the children to and from the different schools. The boys' school was nearby, but the Sacred Heart school that Kela and Gisela attended was

The twenty-fifth wedding anniversary portrait of Lisandro and Amparo, with their ten children, in the library of the house on G Street, 1932. Standing, left to right: Letty (the youngest), Mara, Kela, Rubén, Watty, and Gisela. Seated, left to right: Lalo; Lisandro; Amparo;
Sergio (standing next to Amparo); my father, Tano; and Humberto. Author's collection.

in Havana's colonial district and later, when Gisela was in the secondary
grades, in El Cerro.

As my father and his brother Rubén entered their preteen years, they
were beyond the ages when they would go out in the yard or neighborhood to play with their younger siblings under the supervision of Amparo,
the older sisters, or nannies. The La Salle school they attended held classes
on Saturday, but on Sunday they were underfoot in the house and tacitly,
as older boys, became the responsibility of Lisandro. But my grandfather
was already past sixty years of age, with a busy work schedule during the
week, and therefore had no inclination to spend his Sundays doing anything but relaxing and enjoying his new house, or perhaps going to the
Habana Yacht Club to join a game of dominoes. Besides, at that time there

was no expectation that parents were personally responsible for providing their children with entertainment. His solution to the problem posed by the older boys was to pay César out of his own pocket to deal with Tano and Rubén on Sundays. César was single and had no family obligations, so he agreed to earn the extra money by taking the two boys (on public transportation, of course, since the company car was not to be used for that purpose) to where he usually went on his day off: to watch the soccer matches between the different Spanish immigrant associations.

César was born in Galicia, Spain's northwestern region and traditionally one of its most impoverished areas, largely due to a system of subsistence agriculture in which landholdings became increasingly fragmented with each successive generation until it became untenable for the younger male children to stay on the farmstead once they became adults. They had to find a living elsewhere, and Spain's thriving former colony in the Caribbean was a favorite destination. Independence from Spain did not disrupt the migration that had for centuries taken enterprising villagers from the peninsula to the colony to take advantage of the opportunities in the New World, especially during Cuba's Sugar Revolution of the nineteenth century. The Fontses, Lisandro's grandfather, Amparo's father, and Nancy's grandfather had all formed part of that migration flow during the colonial era. Spanish civilians had no reason to leave the colony when it was lost, as the Cuban leaders urged reconciliation and the American occupiers protected the existing property rights. That large and continuous Spanish presence was the foundation for massive immigration to Cuba during the first three decades of the twentieth century. They arrived from all over the peninsula, but especially from the poorer northern regions of Galicia and Asturias. The 1931 census found 257,596 Spanish-born persons living on the island that year. It was by far the largest immigrant group, accounting for 6.5 percent of the total Cuban population and nearly 60 percent of the country's foreign-born population.[5] Some achieved considerable wealth in the former colony, but most became employed in the service sector or as small entrepreneurs.

The Spanish immigrants formed mutual benefit societies and social, cultural, and recreational clubs based on their particular Iberian regions of origin. The *gallegos* built a sumptuous baroque building in the center of Havana to house their club, facing the equally grand, if more staid, club for the *asturianos*. The different regional clubs fielded soccer teams to play one another in hotly contested Sunday matches at the Jardines de La Tropical on the outskirts of Havana. César always attended, not only to cheer for the *gallego* team, but also to socialize. Tano and Rubén would tease him that having them tag along inhibited César's possibilities of hooking up with a young *gallega*. Women were also present among the immigrants from the region and were typically employed as domestic servants in Havana.

Lisandro and Amparo were not devout Catholics. They did attend mass every Sunday morning with all the children at the nearby San Juan de Letrán Church, and they placed their sons and daughters in religious schools. But that was less about religious convictions and more about conforming to the norms of the Havana socioeconomic class they joined when they moved to the capital and built that house in Vedado. Public schools were woefully underfunded and only for poorer people. Catholic schools, of which there were many in the capital run by various religious orders from Spain and France, were the private schools of choice among Havana's upper classes. Mara, Kela, Gisela, and later, Leticia, were enrolled in the Sacred Heart school, which was a top, elite Catholic school for girls, run by the Sisters of the Sacred Heart of Jesus, an order founded by Sister Madeleine Sophie Barat in France in 1800 for the purpose of educating young women. The Havana school was established in 1858 by the sisters from the New York school, located in upper Manhattan.[6]

My grandparents did not realize when they enrolled Kela in Sacred Heart just how much the school would impact their second daughter. Not long after graduating, Kela announced her intention to join the Sacred Heart order and take vows. Her father grieved, and her mother wept. They could not bear the idea that after working hard to provide their children with every comfort and privilege, their daughter would live the austere life of a cloistered nun, without marrying and having children. Lisandro convinced her to postpone the decision for several years until she had experienced more of the world to make sure the religious life was for her: go to parties, date, travel, he told her, in the hope that this was just a passing phase and she would change her mind. Kela followed her father's advice, but in the end, it did not make any difference. She eventually entered the convent and started her novitiate. It was a sad day for her parents.

Lisandro should have known he could not sway his daughter from the decision she had made. Even in a family of assertive personalities, Kela had no rival when it came to acting on her convictions. She was a headstrong and brilliant woman who, after taking her vows, quickly climbed up the hierarchy of the order in Cuba to occupy the directorships of the Sacred Heart schools in Cuba, first in Santiago and later in Havana, by the sheer force of her personality: she was a strict disciplinarian and administrator who allowed no deviation from the strict codes of conduct of the life she had chosen.

Lisandro and Amparo never gave up trying to ease the austerity of her life in the convent, only to be repeatedly rebuffed by Kela. The first Christmas she was cloistered, my grandparents could not adjust to her absence at the family table for the traditional Christmas Eve (*Nochebuena*) dinner and offered to send a plate of food to Kela with all the trimmings. She replied that she could not be singled out in her community for such a privilege unless all the nuns in the convent partook of the food. For years thereafter, Lisandro and Amparo would send to the Sacred Heart convent an entire *Nochebuena* spread (pork, black beans, rice, plantains, etc.) large enough to feed the entire community.

When Kela completed her novitiate in Turin, Italy, Lisandro and Amparo timed a trip to New York so they could sail with Kela on the second leg of her trip back to Cuba, from Manhattan to Havana. Lisandro arranged for José to pick them up at the dock when they arrived. The rules for cloistered nuns required that she go directly to the convent as soon as she disembarked. Vedado is on the way from the harbor to El Cerro, where the convent was located at the time, so Amparo suggested that they stop by the house to visit for just a few minutes. "Your brothers and sisters will be thrilled," Amparo said, "and no one will know." Kela quickly rejected the suggestion with a stern reply: "Mother, I will know."

Sister Raquel Pérez was an extraordinary woman. Fluent in four languages (Spanish, English, French, and Italian), she had a piercing look and an incisive mind and tongue. She was both feared and loved by generations of young women who attended her school. In her last few years (she lived into her nineties), she wrote two carefully researched books, one on the life of her order's founder, and the other on the history of the Sacred Heart schools in Cuba, traveling to France to consult the archives in the order's main convent.[7]

Kela's older sister, Mara, was twenty-eight years old when in 1939 she married a young physician, Rafael Prieto, who was an assistant to one of Havana's most prominent medical doctors. Lisandro and Amparo were thrilled with their new son-in-law, who was lauded in the press as one of the capital's most promising young physicians. The couple moved to a house close to the center of Havana, near Rafael's medical office. They had two daughters, my oldest cousins, Raquel Zita and Marita. My only other older cousin, María Cristina (Cristy), was born in 1947 to Rubén and his wife, Josefina (Josie), who married in 1944, the same year that Kela received her vows. To mark that milestone in Sister Pérez's life, the entire family convened for a family portrait in the Sacred Heart convent in El Cerro, the only place where it was possible to include Kela in the group photograph.

Only a couple of years after that portrait was taken, the family faced a major crisis when Mara's husband, Rafael, was diagnosed with leukemia. Lisandro and Amparo transformed one of the bedrooms of their house into a hospital intensive care unit with all the necessary equipment and staffed by a nurse day and night. His medical colleagues provided him with the best care available. But Rafael succumbed to the disease and passed away in 1947. My cousins Raquel Zita and Marita were seven and five years of age, respectively.

The Pérez family at the Sacred Heart convent in El Cerro, Havana, 1944. Seated, left to right: Gisela, Mara (on the armrest), Mara's daughters Marita and Raquel Zita, Amparo, Lisandro, and Kela. Standing, from left to right: Sergio; Rafael Prieto (Mara's husband); Humberto; my father, Tano; Watty; Lalo; Josefina Pernas (Rubén's wife); Rubén; and Letty. Author's collection.

Lisandro and Amparo convinced Mara to move back into the house with her daughters. The original design of the house included an apartment at the rear of the structure, atop the flat roof. It was accessed by a steep marble staircase that was concealed by a door just off the dining room, next to the kitchen. The original purpose of the unit was to serve as the Havana lodgings of Amparo's sister Aminta (Chicha) and her husband during their frequent visits from Camajuaní. Chicha was the sister who was married in the same ceremony in which Amparo and Lisandro married. Since she had no children (unrelated, one would think, to the fact that her husband's name was Casto, which means "chaste"), Chicha doted on her nephews and nieces, taking to Havana loads of presents for all of them every time she visited. Lisandro disapproved of her generosity, claiming she was spoiling the children.

My grandfather had the apartment remodeled for Mara and her daughters, expanding it to two bedrooms and adding a foyer that served as a sitting area. With her return to the parental home, Mara took on greater responsibilities in managing the household. There was always a certain gravitas about her demeanor that made her siblings accord her a great deal of respect. With widowhood, that deference became even more accentuated. She adjusted to the loss of her husband with an evident stoicism. One of her coping mechanisms was to keep a daily diary, a practice she continued for the rest of her life. Her early widowhood led her to live a well-examined life. I remember her as a wise woman devoted to her daughters, always ready to give her siblings and her nephews and nieces unequivocal advice on any problem, great or small.

The house on G Street was an oasis of peace and stability during one of Cuba's most turbulent eras. The year they moved into the house, 1930, marked the beginning of a period of political violence that enveloped Cuba for several years.

In the election of 1924, the Liberal Party candidate, General Gerardo Machado, an independence war veteran, defeated Mario García-Menocal, who was still the leader of the Conservative Party and was trying to return to the Presidential Palace after leaving it in 1921. Machado benefited from the prosperity that Cuba experienced during his first term in office, enjoying a level of popularity unattained by any of his predecessors. He launched a number of ambitious public works projects, including the construction, at last, of a central highway running the entire length of the island.

Machado was born in, of all places, Camajuaní. He became one of the youngest Generals in the war of independence and served as the mayor of Santa Clara after the war. He and Lisandro had ample opportunity to become acquainted. After his election to the presidency, Machado approached my grandfather with an offer to form part of the slate of candidates that the Liberal Party would field in the next election to represent the province of Las Villas in the senate. Machado knew of Lisandro's deep roots in the region and wanted to run respectable candidates that were untainted by previous political officeholding.

Lisandro may have been tempted, perhaps for a moment, to seize the opportunity to become a senator of the Republic under such a popular administration. But his instincts led him to unequivocally reject Machado's offer. Those were the same instincts that kept him from enlisting to fight in the war of independence and that had always led him to maintain his distance from the political frays and intrigues that came to characterize the Cuban Republic. He did not deviate from the trajectory he had traced for his life: escape poverty by building a successful business and provide a prosperous life for his family. In the precarious political environment of the Cuban Republic, officeholding could well place that life plan at risk.

It did not take long for Lisandro to realize that he made the right decision. As the 1928 elections approached, Machado, using his popularity and control of the Congress, managed to have legislation enacted that kept him in office through an election with no opposition. Even in the context of Cuba's well-established tradition of corrupt elections, Machado's *prórroga* ("extension") of his presidency was so brazen that it immediately stirred up widespread opposition to his regime. Machado's power grab coincided with the 1929 crash and the depression that ensued, plunging Cuba into hard times, so he no longer could count on economic prosperity to buoy his popularity. The labor unions opposed him and so did university students, a new generation unwilling to accept the scandals and abuses of a political system that had frustrated the lofty goals that had driven Cubans to fight for independence from Spain. Strikes and marches were organized, and acts of political sabotage and violence became a daily occurrence in Havana. Machado responded with a brutal repression carried out by a secret police force. Opponents were summarily imprisoned or killed. Student demonstrations were quelled with live ammunition. Almost overnight, Machado went from beloved President to hated dictator.

The situation on the island became so unstable that the US ambassador brokered an agreement that resulted in Machado relinquishing power and leaving Cuba on a plane to Miami on August 12, 1933. Immediately mobs formed in the streets of Havana to exact revenge on members of Machado's government and his associates in Congress by ransacking their homes. Had Lisandro agreed to Machado's offer, the house on G Street would have been a target of the angry mob, and the family would have had to leave the country. As it turned out, the house almost did not escape that fate. A mob searching for the house of a minister in Machado's cabinet who lived on G Street assumed that the stately Pérez home on the corner of Fifteenth was the minister's house and started climbing the iron fence in an attempt to assault the residence. They were waved off by Lisandro and the two chauffeurs, who managed to convince the mob that they were at the wrong house.

Lisandro's unwavering focus on his business built the house on G Street and sustained it through turbulent times. His financial success gave him the option to exercise his good sense and refuse the offer to join the government, in a republic where the exercise of power was ephemeral and fraught with risks. Ernesto Fonts y Sterling did not have that option, as a veteran with few prospects, and consequently had to face the uncertainties and conflicts posed by the fragility of the political system. The house on G Street was emblematic of the stability and prosperity that Lisandro and Amparo had created for their children. All of them always remembered the house as the place that centered their lives as they were growing up.

THE HOUSE ON EIGHTEENTH STREET

Not long after he married, Oscar Fonts started making plans to build a home to accommodate not only the children that he and Nancy planned to have but also his mother Malila and his brother Ernesto. They did not have much capital, but with Malila's pension and the jobs the two brothers landed when they returned to Cuba, the family managed to buy a lot in Miramar in the municipality of Marianao, just across the Almendares

River from Havana. Miramar was the new and upcoming neighborhood, and lots were selling at cheaper prices than in established neighborhoods such as El Cerro and Vedado. The two bridges that were built spanning the river placed the new development just a few minutes' drive from the western boundary of Vedado. After five years of living in New York, Malila and her sons were ready to settle in back home.

Oscar had an avocation as an architect, so he designed the home the family built on a lot on Eighteenth Street, between Fifth and Seventh Avenues in Miramar. Fifth Avenue was Miramar's principal artery. They bought that lot because across the street lived Oscar's cousins, the Valdés-Faulis, related through Colonel Fonts's sister Aurora, who was married to a lawyer named Guillermo Valdés-Fauli. Oscar designed a two-story home that was, of course, much more modest than the house on G Street. The right side of the first floor was the living area: living room, dining room, and kitchen. On the left side were two bedrooms separated by a connecting bathroom, one for Malila and the other for Ernesto Jr. The second floor had three bedrooms and a bathroom, designed for Oscar and Nancy and the children they planned to have.

The Fonts house on Eighteenth Street, Miramar. Author's collection.

Not long after the house was completed, my mother, Nancy (formally Ana María), was born on March 31, 1926. Almost three years later, a boy was born, Oscarito, named after his father.

My grandfather landed a job not long after he arrived from New York in the largest printing company in Havana, P. Fernández y Compañía, which handled all the printing for the Cuban government, producing items such as official reports, statistical publications, and even postage stamps and lottery tickets. The manager of the company, Fabián Urruti-beascoa, an older man of undeniable Basque ancestry given his surname, knew Oscar's father and took it upon himself to mentor the Colonel's son and get him started on a career, especially since Fabián and his wife, Dolores, had no children. Oscar could not afford an automobile when he started the job, and Fabián did not know how to drive, so he gifted my grandfather a brand-new car with the understanding that Oscar would drive him to and from work every weekday. It was a deal, especially since Fabián lived in El Vedado, on the way from Miramar to the company's office on Bernaza Street in the old colonial section. Eventually Fabián retired and Oscar succeeded him as General Manager of P. Fernández. He also got to keep the car.

As a stamp collector, Oscar immediately took to the job of managing the printing company, especially the elaborate process of printing the stamps. He found it fascinating to be involved in the production side, contracting designers, selecting ink colors, deciding on the volume of the run, and overseeing the maintenance of the delicate presses that were dedicated exclusively to printing the sheets of stamps. From his position, it was easy to build up the Cuban component of his collection.

The job at P. Fernández apparently left him with enough time to have a sideline business as an importer of American manufactured goods. Capitalizing on his fluency in English and his interest in the latest trends in products coming out of the United States, he developed contacts with several companies to import their products to Cuba. His most successful venture was the importation of Indian motorcycles, a business that grew

Oscar and Nancy with their newborn daughter, Nancy, my mother, 1926. Author's collection.

out of his relationship with Ralph Rogers, a Dallas businessman who in 1945 bought the Indian Motorcycle Manufacturing Company, at one time the largest manufacturer of motorcycles in the United States with its models the Scout, made from 1920 to 1946, and the Chief, made from 1922 until 1953. Oscar also imported Whizzer bicycle engines that were sold as kits to be assembled and attached to a buyer's bicycle to create a motorized bike.

One of the things Oscar liked most about the import business was hosting the trips of his American business associates to Cuba. Havana was a top tourist destination for Americans, and Oscar, with his sociable nature and penchant for the good life, delighted in showing his friends the best of the city. In this way he built a wide network of friends in the United States, and he traveled there at least once a year, usually taking the hydroplane service from Havana to Miami and then on to New York.

Oscar acquired in the Hudson Valley the pastime of hunting for small game, a diversion that was not too common among urbanites in Cuba. He organized a group of friends to occasionally go into Havana's hinterland and hunt for various types of game birds. He would leave very early in the morning and return late in the evening. His last hunting excursion took place in October 1931 when, as usual, he slipped out of the house in the darkness of the early morning hours while everyone was sleeping. When he returned that evening he found a chaotic scene: nurses and doctors scurrying about and a house full of family and relatives trying to console a hysterical Nancy. On that morning Oscar went hunting, Oscarito woke up with uncontrollable vomiting and diarrhea, the telltale symptoms of gastroenteritis, one of the leading causes of childhood deaths in human history prior to the discovery of antibiotics. That year, more than twenty thousand children under the age of five died in the United States of the ailment.[8] In Oscarito's case, contaminated milk was suspected to be the cause. He did not survive the night.

It was another devastating blow to my grandmother Nancy's fragile character, which had already been affected by the loss of her sister Margot.

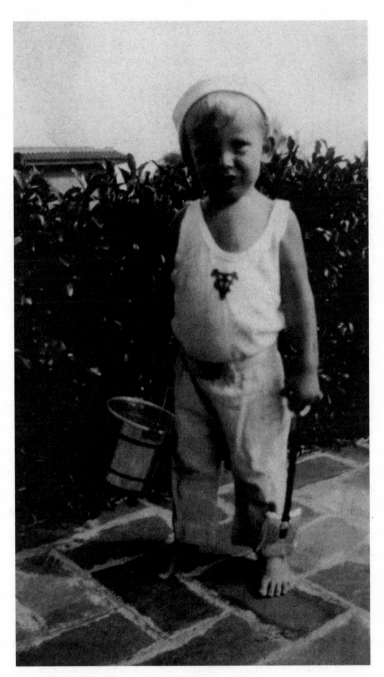

Oscarito, my mother's brother, 1931. Author's collection.

Oscar not only lost his son, but he struggled with a sense of guilt at being unreachable and absent during the hours the tragedy unfolded. He never went hunting again.

Almost exactly a year later, in October 1932, Nancy gave birth to María Luisa, named after Malila. My aunt, however, who would also be my *madrina* (godmother), was given an anglicized nickname, Mary Lou, but it was pronounced in Spanish (mah-ree LOO). When she was born, Oscar could not hide his disappointment that she was not a boy.

One consequence of the death of Oscarito was my grandparents' hypersensitivity to health threats to their children. In September of 1934, for example, at the height of a polio outbreak in Cuba, Oscar decided to relocate the family for two months to a hotel in Miami. They took with them my grandmother's younger sister, Consuelo, as well as Mary Lou's nanny, Gumersinda Álvarez, an immigrant woman from Galicia who would spend many years thereafter in the employ of the family, assuming a major role in raising my aunt.[9]

Almost eight years after the birth of Mary Lou, my grandfather was able to celebrate the birth of a son. My uncle was named Carlos, one of those repetitive Fonts names.

Malila died sometime in the late 1930s, and Ernesto Jr. remained single and living in the house on Eighteenth Street until his late forties when he married a widow much older than he and moved out. Since the house was co-owned by the brothers, Ernesto asked for his share of the value of the house. Oscar could not afford that, so the house was sold, and the family moved to a rented home some ten blocks away. It was while living in that rented home that my mother, Nancy, met my father.

NANCY

My mother was the perfect oldest child: obedient and normative, always following the rules. She also had an innocence and an absence of guile that never left her. It was not until she was in her teens that she finally realized that there is no Santa Claus. As the oldest, she was the center of her father's attention during her early years. Oscar could be a fun parent. He spent a lot of time with his daughter, playing games and building toys. He once constructed a plane that Nancy could wear around her waist as a costume. But Oscar also had inherited some of his father's strictness for following rules and etiquette, especially at the dinner table. His brother Ernesto would sometimes intervene if Oscar was being too severe in his admonishments, but my grandfather would quickly tell him to back off. There was the time that Oscar noticed that his daughter was trimming off the crust from the sliced bread and leaving it on her plate. He said nothing, but the next day when Nancy eagerly opened her lunch box in school, she found it contained nothing but bread crusts.

As Nancy grew older, Oscar started preparing her for marriage. She was enrolled in ballet and guitar classes. The ballet did not go very well, but she became an accomplished guitar player and beautifully sang many Cuban boleros. She also attended a finishing school for lessons in etiquette and deportment. Oscar enrolled her in several courses in haute cuisine offered in Havana by a prestigious Paris culinary school. My mother became an excellent cook, with deep knowledge of many basic cooking techniques. She could whip up a béchamel sauce and turn out some innovative dishes from her kitchen. In the house on Eighteenth Street, however, Oscar saw to it that nothing fattening was served. My mother had a tendency since her early years to be chubby, so weight management was part of Oscar's training program for marriage. My uncle Sergio, my father's younger brother, recalled that the first time Nancy was invited to have dinner at the house on G Street and she was served a dessert of homemade guava preserves with cream cheese, she asked for several servings of it, something that no doubt endeared her to Amparo.

Had she been a different person, perhaps Nancy would have shown some rebelliousness at Oscar's persistent efforts to shape her life, but my mother did not have a rebellious bone in her body. Her compliant and obedient nature made her a star student at the Sacred Heart of Jesus School,

My mother, Nancy, as a teenager. Fonts family collection.

where she was a favorite of the nuns, including Kela. Her academic work and exemplary behavior earned her the Second Medallion of her graduating class, equivalent to the rank of salutatorian. She always told me that she could have won the First Medallion, but that it went to a classmate who eventually took religious vows, so she didn't stand a chance.

The Sacred Heart school graduating class of 1944, El Cerro, Havana. My mother, Nancy, is in the second row, center. Fonts family collection.

Nancy graduated from the Sacred Heart school in 1944. She attended the usual parties and social events in the social clubs but never had a formal boyfriend until she met my father in late 1945. She fell head over heels in love with him. My father could be a charmer. She waited patiently until he finally made up his mind to marry her, more than two years after they met. My mother was totally devoted to him. I remember hearing her singing many times the classic bolero she had dedicated to him, "Toda una Vida" ("An Entire Life") by Osvaldo Farrés:

> An entire life I would be with you
> I don't care in what way, or how, or where
> But together with you.

11

TANO

After three girls and several miscarriages, Amparo finally gave birth to a boy in 1920, ten years after her oldest daughter was born. My father was given his father's name, of course, but he was always called Tano (TAH-know), a nickname whose origin I never learned.

Tano was a skinny, sickly baby, so Amparo devoted herself to his care, preparing special menus for him heavy in proteins and carbohydrates. She carried on with this nurturing regime even during her next pregnancy, which began almost immediately after my father was born. My uncle Rubén was born only ten months after Tano. Eventually, Amparo's efforts yielded the desired result; in fact, my father grew to be the tallest of all her children, about six feet two inches in height. Because of that early intensive care from his mother, however, Tano was always regarded in the family as the momma's boy, Amparo's favorite. My father, in turn, grew up accustomed to being nurtured and attended to by women, a trait my mother would discover after marrying him.

WOODMERE

Tano and Rubén were both enrolled in first grade at the LaSalle brothers' school in Vedado, but when they neared their thirteenth birthdays, my grandfather made the difficult decision to send them to study in the United States. Lisandro knew that Cuba was galloping toward a greater integration with the American economy, something he learned firsthand through the acquisition of his company by General Cigar. American acquisitions of Cuban corporations were occurring in many industries, to the point where US companies started exercising monopoly control over entire sectors of the economy.[1] He wanted his sons to be better prepared than he was for what looked like Cuba's inexorable future. Lisandro never learned English, and he lacked a familiarity with that world up north that was now part of his life but that in many ways was so foreign to him.

It was also an opportunity to give his sons a quality secular education. At the time, religious schools dominated the top tier of private secondary education in Havana. While acceptable for his daughters, he was not convinced of the value of religious education for boys, especially if any one of his sons became as influenced by a Catholic education as Kela was. Giving up one offspring to the Church was quite enough.

Lisandro sought the advice of Bernhardt G. Meyer, the Vice President of General Cigar. Meyer had a son, Max, older than my father, who was enrolled in a private school in Long Island. He not only recommended his son's school, Woodmere Academy, but arranged for the school's director, Horace Perry, to house the two boys in his home. Woodmere was not a boarding school, so Tano and Rubén would live with the Perry family, who had two boys of similar age who also attended Woodmere. It was to be a complete immersion experience in US society and culture.

My father and Rubén spent the first half of 1933 learning English with a private tutor on the terrace of the house on G Street. Linguistically ready or not, they joined their father and their older sister Mara, who was then twenty-three and unmarried and usually accompanied their father on trips, aboard the *Morro Castle* for the trip that would take them to an American education. They arrived in Manhattan on July 1. The following day, a Sunday, they all found themselves in Mr. Meyer's box seats at the Polo Grounds to watch a doubleheader between the Giants and the St. Louis Cardinals. The scene made quite an impression on my father: it was Fourth of July weekend, and the stadium was festooned with red, white, and blue banners, with a capacity crowd of some fifty thousand fans cheering on the Giants. It was exactly what he expected the US to look like. The first game lasted eighteen innings, with Carl Hubbell accomplishing the incredible feat of pitching the entire game, allowing the Cardinals only six hits, no walks, and pitching twelve of the innings perfectly. The Giants won 1–0. They also won the second game by the same score, but my father did not get to see it.[2] My grandfather stood up at the end of the marathon first game and announced he had seen enough baseball for one day, and they all left for their hotel, the MacAlpin, near Herald Square.

After installing his sons in the Perry home on Long Island and enrolling them in Woodmere, Lisandro returned to the MacAlpin with Mara to spend the night before boarding a ship the next day for the return trip to Havana. That night, Mara heard a faint sound coming from the adjoining room that Lisandro occupied. She moved closer to the wall to try to discern it. She was astonished to hear a sound she had never heard before: her father sobbing. My grandfather must have been very convinced of the value of an American education to have made the heart-wrenching decision to leave his thirteen-year-old sons with strangers in a strange place.

The Pérez boys initially went through a difficult adjustment to their new life, which was so different from what they had known. Woodmere was a coeducational school with a student body that was predominantly Jewish, and they lived in a Protestant household. There was more than one unfamiliar world to which they had to adapt. Coming from a religious school for boys, what struck them most was having girls in the classroom. On the first day of class, my father was seated behind a blonde girl with braided double ponytails. Entranced, and without any experience with female classmates, especially blonde ones, he somehow decided it would be appropriate and friendly to tickle her neck. In an instant, the girl swiveled and slapped him across the face.

Eventually, however, they adapted to life in Long Island and stayed there for the five academic years that took them from eighth grade to graduation in 1938, all the time living with the Perrys, whom my father remembers fondly for having treated him and Rubén as part of their family, helping greatly in their adjustment to the new environment. The brothers integrated themselves into the school largely through the sports programs, contributing to whatever success Woodmere Academy achieved in extramural competitions. This garnered them not just acceptance but a certain popularity, especially in their senior year. In baseball, Rubén was the pitcher and Tano the catcher. My father was the center, tallest player, and top scorer on the basketball team. That year Woodmere had an undefeated basketball season and won the conference championship. In the game against Brooklyn Friends on January 18, 1938, Tano scored ten of the twenty-four points that Woodmere put on the scoreboard for the win.[3] The coach for both baseball and basketball was the school's gruff physical education teacher, M. J. "Pop" La Rue, whom my father remembered as a demanding coach. The basketball team's equipment manager was a fellow student who joined Woodmere the third year that Tano and Rubén were attending the school: Rogelito Echevarría, the son of Lisandro's longtime business partner. Rogelio was apparently persuaded by Lisandro that enrolling in Woodmere was a good option for his son.

The boys only went home for the summer months. Not wanting them to be idle, Lisandro would take them with him on his weekly trips to Camajuaní so they would start learning the business. The summers were a busy time with the *escogidas*, so they would be assigned tasks in the *despalillo* or sent on trips to the countryside to pick up the *vegas*. Amparo complained that between school in Long Island and summers in Camajuaní, she barely got to see them. But Lisandro wanted to make sure that New York would not make them forget where the family was rooted.

The 1937–38 Woodmere Academy basketball team. Standing at far left, my uncle Rubén; next to him, my father, Tano; and on the far right, Rogelio Echevarría. Sitting in the front row, Coach "Pop" La Rue. Author's collection.

During his first summer back from Woodmere, when my father was just fourteen, he was wandering around the *despalillo* when he encountered a tobacco leaf that had been dropped on the floor. He mindlessly kicked it out of the way. A few moments later, an employee told him that Lisandro wanted to see him in his office, which was on a mezzanine level that over-looked the entire facility. When he went into the office, his father told him that he had seen how he had treated that tobacco leaf and admonished him that "in this family, we treat a tobacco leaf with respect, because it is what pays for everything: the clothes you are wearing, that big house in Vedado, and that fancy school in New York... don't ever forget that."

My father had good memories of his years at Woodmere. The weekend excursions into the city on the Long Island Railroad were usually to watch a game at Yankee Stadium or at the Polo Grounds. He also remembered fondly the charms of one Peggy Cohen, to whom he may have dedicated the poem "I Dream of You," which he submitted as the text to accompany his senior picture in the 1938 commencement booklet. In the poem, he anticipated his permanent return to Cuba upon graduating and the un-avoidable end of the relationship:

> My time has passed like fleeting clouds beyond,
> To hide into eternity forlorn;
> With me you've shared all joys and sorrow,
> Which will be but sweet vagueness in the morrow.
> Remember yet when we played by the sea
> Building dreams which now abruptly stop?
> Many ecstasies unearned you've given me;
> For this, for all, will I remember thee.[4]

The poem reveals two of my father's lifelong traits. One was the com-mand of English he acquired at Woodmere; he wrote beautifully in the language and spoke it without a trace of an accent. The other was his fond-ness for women.

Lisandro and Amparo attended their sons' graduation from Woodmere. Tano and Rubén returned to Cuba permanently with them on
June 17, 1938, aboard the *Orizaba* of the New York and Cuba Mail Line.[5]
Their classmates at Woodmere were college bound, most of them to Ivy
League schools. But that was never the plan for the Pérez brothers, who
returned home to work for their father. A college degree from a US university seemed a more remote career path than going back to Cuba and
becoming part of the successful world their father had created for the family. The same was true of the younger brothers, Humberto and Lalo, who
followed their older brothers to Woodmere and to the Perry home. Sergio
was the only one of the Pérez brothers who did not study in the US, perhaps because he had a reputation as rambunctious, or perhaps because he
would have had to go alone. The sibling who did graduate from a US university was Leticia, the youngest, who upon graduating from the Sacred
Heart school asked to go to Newton College, a Sacred Heart college for
women in Boston that was later merged with Boston College. She received
a degree in education.

CHORIZOS

Tano and Rubén returned from Woodmere to work for their father in
the tobacco business. Lisandro was trying them out to see which one he
would keep as a permanent employee of General Cigar. He realized that
not all his sons could work for the company, so eventually he made the
decision that Rubén would work for him and placed him on the company
payroll, while my father would manage one of his investments. Because
of his entrepreneurial talents, my grandfather would frequently invest in,
or acquire, businesses that showed growth potential. For example, on his
weekly trips to Camajuaní, he always stopped for breakfast at an eatery
run by an Afro-Chinese family in Colón, Matanzas, and on the return trip
he would usually stop there for lunch.[6] The owners were a hardworking
family that provided great food and service, but the place was small and

run down, so he entered into a partnership and invested to expand and upgrade the restaurant in exchange for a share of the profits.

Lisandro had long had his eye on a plant in Camajuaní that produced Spanish-style chorizos and other types of encased and canned meat products. It was on the edge of the town, on the western extension of the same street where the *despalillo* was located. Its products were sold under the brand name "El Riojano," and it enjoyed a good reputation among consumers in the region. The plant needed some updating, but it already had all the necessary equipment.

My grandfather bought El Riojano in April of 1940 and created a company called L. Pérez y Cía., naming himself as owner and President and my father as General Manager. Tano was barely twenty years old and knew nothing about chorizos, but Lisandro made sure to keep on the payroll the critical personnel who were experienced in carrying out the various steps of the production process. Lisandro was hoping his son would learn how to manage a business on his own. My father was thrilled at the opportunity of living in Camajuaní and enjoying a certain measure of independence.

Lisandro, however, did not entirely leave his son on his own and without supervision. Tano had to render a weekly report on the finances of the business on the days his father was in town. He was placed under the watchful eye of one of Lisandro's most trusted employees: Eulogio Cáceres.

Eulogio was Lisandro's younger half brother, a son of his father, Manuel, and a woman in Remedios that Manuel met after his wife, Marina, died and the children left for Yaguajay. He did not have a long-term relationship with the woman and refused to recognize the child as his. Raised by his mother, Eulogio had a difficult childhood and never finished school. Lisandro came to learn of his half brother's existence only when Eulogio was already an adult, and he took him to Camajuaní and employed him as the overall custodian and night watchman of the *despalillo*. The relationship was never disclosed, but it was undeniable: Eulogio looked like my grandfather's younger twin. In his youth he was angry and irascible, getting himself into fights and usually besting his opponent, which earned him the nickname "El Tigre." One of those fights cost him the full use of one of his legs, and for the rest of his life, he walked with an evident limp. He mellowed with age and grew more appreciative of his half brother's support, becoming Lisandro's loyal confidant and eyes and ears in Cama-juaní. Looking out for my father was something he cherished, especially since Tano loved him and looked up to him as a true uncle, which he was. I remember Tigre, as I called him, as a kindly old man with the simplicity and unpretentiousness of the rural folk of Las Villas.

At first, Tano lived with his aunt Arminta ("Chicha") and her husband, Casto, but they lived on the other side of town, on the hill, beyond the railroad tracks. As Tano learned more of the business and started manag-ing all aspects of the operations, he decided to rent a small cottage just around the corner from the chorizo plant. The work was demanding. Lisandro had not given his son an easy job. El Riojano employed some twenty-five workers. Perhaps the most challenging part was scouring the countryside for the right pigs and beef cattle to purchase at a good price from local ranchers and herding or transporting them to the plant's corral. He then had to book an appointment at the municipal slaugh-terhouse and take the livestock there. It was unlawful in Cuba to com-mercially slaughter animals anywhere but in the local government-run facility, which was staffed by professional butchers and where health stan-dards were presumably maintained. The butchers quartered and pack-aged the meat according to the customer's specifications. Tano would sell the viscera to local butcher shops, since he had no use for them in the manufacture of the chorizos. The days that El Riojano slaughtered, the town knew there were fresh livers, kidneys, and brains for sale at their neighborhood butcher shop.

At the plant, the meat was put through huge grinders and blended with garlic and imported Spanish paprika (*pimentón*). It was then pushed into tripe casings imported from Chicago. The products were canned using a special canning machine, and the tins were packed in boxes for shipment. All the machinery was powered by a huge diesel engine.

My father worked hard to succeed at the opportunity his father had given him, but he also thoroughly enjoyed himself. He remembered his years in Camajuaní as among the happiest of his life. In Havana, he would have been just another young man living in Vedado, but in Camajuaní, he was a big fish in a small pond, the son of one of the town's most prominent businessmen and benefactors and the manager of a manufacturing plant that was the source of income for many families. He owned a horse, a gun, riding boots and pants, and a 1939 green Buick. Tall and fairly handsome, he was no doubt considered a very desirable catch for any of the young women of the town, and he took full advantage of that, dating many of them and accepting all invitations for parties and dances.

For almost five years my father continued to successfully manage the chorizo business and showed no sign he wanted to leave Camajuaní to return to Havana. For a time, he even considered marrying a nice local girl he had been courting. But everything changed abruptly when he was about to turn twenty-five and Isabel Rubio entered his life.

Isabelita, as she was known in the town, was ten years older than Tano. She was tall, elegant, and stylish, a trendsetter in provincial Camajuaní as the owner of a dress shop that stocked the latest fashions from Havana. She was educated, charming, and a great conversationalist. And she was married. Her husband was Alfonso Paz, a house painter who was the first in Camajuaní to use pneumatic spray guns. Alfonso was a taciturn man with a brusque demeanor who shied away from social gatherings. He and Isabelita had no children.

My father had known Isabelita for years. She was about the same age as Tano's older sisters, whom she knew from the days when Mara and Kela were growing up in Camajuaní. Isabelita and Alfonso lived just one block from the *despalillo*, across the street from Vivina, one of Amparo's sisters, and next to Higinio González, the longtime manager of the tobacco stemmery. But it was not until late 1944 that Tano and Isabelita started noticing each other in the *romerías* that were traditional in Camajuaní. *Romerías* were social gatherings of townspeople held on weekend afternoons at a farm on the outskirts where the hosts, which were frequently organizations or businesses, contracted the farmer to roast a pig and serve a spread of traditional food. There would also be live music and dancing. Isabelita started attending these social occasions unaccompanied by her husband, who preferred to work or stay at home.

The cottage by the chorizo factory was the ideal place for the trysts that soon took place between Tano and Isabelita, usually in the late mornings before she opened her shop at noon. In a small town, of course, nothing can long remain a secret. El Tigre became concerned and cautioned his nephew, and he also told Lisandro, who probably thought better of becoming involved in what must have seemed to him like a perfectly normal activity for an unmarried man, taking advantage of the opportunity to have a relationship with an attractive woman like Isabelita, who after all was not young and naive and knew what she was doing.

On February 28, 1945, Camajuaní's daily newspapers reported that the winds of Lent had arrived early in town, kicking up dust from some of the unpaved streets. It was a Wednesday, and Isabelita thought it strange that although it was nearly 11:00 a.m., her husband had not left for work. She was in front of the mirror in her bedroom, putting on makeup and earrings before going to the shop, perhaps planning to make a stop at the cottage. Alfonso came into the room and told her he knew everything and demanded that she stop the affair. She readily confessed, but without remorse, and casually dismissed his demand to end it. Alfonso reached behind his back for a .38-caliber revolver he had tucked in his belt and fired two shots at his wife, killing her instantly. Higinio González happened to be home and heard the two shots, followed by another one. When he rushed next door, he found both Isabelita and her husband dead. Alfonso had turned the gun on himself.

Quickly assessing the situation, Higinio rushed to the *despalillo* to tell El Tigre to alert Tano and get him ready to leave town. Higinio knew that

Isabelita's two brothers were aggressive types who would quickly blame Tano and seek to avenge her death. Eulogio hobbled as quickly as he could to the chorizo plant. Shortly after he got there, Higinio arrived with a car, and they pushed Tano into the back seat. My father was protesting the whole time, not fully realizing what had happened. They drove him to Santa Clara and placed him on the first train to Havana.

Higinio was right: Isabelita's brothers vowed to kill Tano if they ever saw him in Camajuaní. My father did not return to Las Villas for nearly seven years.[7]

My father's permanent return to Havana meant that his career in chorizo manufacturing was over. It also meant that once in Havana, he would have the opportunity to meet my mother later that same year. Tano noticed Nancy at a social event at the Habana Yacht Club but did not have the opportunity to approach her on that occasion. She stayed on his mind, however, and he started making inquiries about her. When he learned she had graduated from the Sacred Heart school, he contacted Kela to find out what his sister could tell him about Nancy. Of course, Kela gave Tano a glowing report on her former star student, which emboldened him to give Nancy a cold telephone call. It took a few phone calls before Nancy agreed to go out with my father, but only properly chaperoned, of course.

Lisandro established another business in Havana that his son could manage. This one would capitalize on Tano's knowledge of English: an import firm. My grandfather named it the International Trading Company and opened an office on Ayesterán Street, not far from the General Cigar warehouse. My father started importing many of those desired American manufactured goods, such as Bell and Howell projectors and Royal typewriters. He also developed a niche market by importing surgical tools and scientific equipment for use in research labs and medical schools. He seemed to have achieved enough success in the business to embolden him to finally propose to my mother.

By the time Tano and Nancy married on Valentine's Day in 1948 in Santa Rita Church in Miramar, Lisandro had situated his sons in gainful

CRONICA HABANERA

ELEGANTE BODA EN SANTA RITA

NANCY FONTS Y LISANDRO PEREZ Jr.

Photograph that accompanied the newspaper story of my parents' wedding, 1948.
Author's collection.

occupations. My father was at "La Internacional," as he liked to call it, Rubén and Lalo were on the General Cigar payroll, and Humberto was at work keeping the accounts in La Tabacalera, the insurance and benefits company for tobacco workers that Lisandro helped to establish. Sergio, the only son to undertake university studies, was finishing a business and accounting degree at the University of Havana. Once he had a college degree and was marketable, he had employment choices beyond working at the companies his father controlled or in which he invested. Lisandro offered him a job, but Sergio, always the most rebellious of the Pérez boys, told his father that he did not pay enough and that he had a better offer elsewhere. To this, Lisandro answered, "You are an adult."

The year 1949 would have both good and bad tidings for my grandfather. The good news was that his first grandson would be born in February. It would not be until August that he would experience a much less fortunate event.

✳ 12 ✳

BIRTH AND DEATHS

The Anglo-American Clinic was just eight blocks from the house on G Street. I was born there in the early morning hours of February 23, 1949. My grandfather Oscar had predicted that I would be born on that exact day. Foreshadowing my binational existence, he intuited that I would arrive between George Washington's birthday (February 22) and the day Cubans commemorate the start of the war of independence in 1895 (February 24).

The name of the clinic was no doubt meant to appeal to the growing number of *americanos* in Havana. The building itself was a Vedado mansion that had been converted into a medical facility that was favored by many of the capital's obstetricians as the venue for delivering babies. My mother's doctor, however, was not present when I was born. When Nancy went into labor, my father drove her from their apartment in Miramar to the clinic and left her in the care of the nurses while he hurried off in the middle of the night to fetch the doctor, who lived nearby. They did not make it to the clinic in time. My mother had a short labor, and the nurses on duty were the ones who delivered me just after midnight.

That night, my father did not wait long to take the short ride to the house on G Street to wake up Lisandro and tell him that he now had a male grandson, the next Lisandro. It was a Wednesday, the day of the week that my grandfather would customarily leave for Camajuaní for his weekly business trip. That Wednesday he postponed the trip upon learning the news, and he, Amparo, and my father had an early breakfast, announcing the news to each of my aunts and uncles as they entered the dining room to eat their morning meal. José the chauffer was asked to ready the Buick for the visit to the clinic.

Apparently, Lisandro was quite taken with his new grandson. I once saw a picture (now lost) of him bending over my crib, grinning at me. But I have no memory of my paternal grandfather. Less than six months after I was born, he walked out of the house on G Street and got into the back seat of the Buick for the short trip to a surgical clinic in Vedado. He was seventy-seven, still working every day as he had done all his life, and healthy, except for the ailment that in time would also afflict my father, my uncles, and me: an enlarged prostate.

Lisandro had long endured the symptoms. On one occasion, my father accompanied him on a horseback trip to a remote *vega* in Zaza del Medio. Lisandro had made that trip every year for more than fifty years during the *escogida* to complete the purchase of this particular *vega*, which was accessible only by horse and ox cart. The *veguero* was one of the best and most faithful of Lisandro's suppliers, one who coincidentally shared his first name: Lisandro Prieto. Every year since my grandfather was a young man and getting his start in the tobacco business, Prieto always sold his *vega* to him. They had come to trust each other unquestionably. Lisandro trusted the quality of Prieto's *vega* without inspection. The *veguero* trusted the fairness of the price that Lisandro would set, without ever discussing it. That type of personal relationship with the *vegueros* had always been the key to Lisandro's success, and his relationship with this *veguero* in Zaza del Medio was the most lasting and emblematic of those relations. When my father suggested to Lisandro that he should forgo the difficult trip because of his worsening prostate condition, my grandfather would not hear it. It was a personal, not business, relationship, and he had to show up, despite knowing that the trip would be sheer agony. My father recalled that on the way to the *vega*, and back, Lisandro would try to raise himself up on the stirrups to avoid the pain of his scrotum hitting the saddle with every stride of the horse.

Lisandro arrived for his surgery on that August day in 1949 at the brand-new Centro Médico Quirúrgico. The building's architect was Max Borges, who had designed the dramatic Tropicana nightclub. When it opened in 1948, the Centro won the gold medal from the national association of architects for its modern design, a worthy example of the emerging midcentury style that had started to predominate in the capital. It was a facility built exclusively for surgeries and staffed by Havana's most renowned surgeons. Lisandro would be getting the best care, and the surgery itself was not complicated. He expected to be back at work the following week. The only concern with this procedure was the formation of blood clots during recovery. Safe anticoagulants were still in the nascent stages of development. The traditional treatment was to prescribe absolute postoperative immobility. But some of the doctors at the Centro were aware of the growing medical literature that suggested that, on the contrary, the patient should be ambulatory as soon as possible after the surgery to prevent clots. The debate between the doctors was won by the traditionalists, and absolute bed rest was ordered after the successful surgery. In the early morning hours on Saturday, August 13, while still recovering at the Centro, a blood clot reached Lisandro's lungs, and he suffered a pulmonary embolism, dying instantly.

The following day, on page ten of the *Diario de la Marina*, Havana's leading daily, six paid death notices appeared announcing the passing of Lisandro. One was placed by the family and the rest by the business entities with which Lisandro was affiliated: the General Cigar Company of Cuba, La Tabacalera Insurance Company, Echevarría y Pérez, the Association of Wholesalers and Growers of Tobacco, and the International Trading Company. The notices invited those who wished to pay their respects to go to 309 G Street on Sunday, August 14, and to accompany the body that same day at five in the evening to its interment in the Colón necropolis.[1]

What better place to hold the wake than in the house on G Street, which Lisandro built and which was more spacious than any funeral home?

The casket, surrounded by candles and flowers, was placed in Lisandro and Amparo's bedroom, just off the main living room. The widow and her sons and daughters sat on chairs along the walls of the bedroom. Guests arrived throughout the day, expressing their condolences to the family and then pausing for a few silent moments by the casket before moving on to sit or stand in the living room, the foyer, the hall, or the library to engage in muffled conversations with other mourners. Servants passed around refreshments. As the day wore on, the house became crowded with visitors. Those who felt especially close to Lisandro would come early and stay all day and then join the caravan to the cemetery. Despite the short notice, many of the mourners had made the four-hour trip from Camajuaní, Remedios, Cabaiguán, Placetas: people who had known, worked for, or done business with Lisandro most of their lives. Cars were parked all along both sides of G Street and up and down Fifteenth.

Everyone except my aunts Kela and Letty was there. Letty had just arrived in Boston for the start of her senior year at Newton College, and the family decided that she should not make the trip back and miss classes. Besides, it would delay the funeral, which Amparo insisted should be a quick one; she did not want the body to linger for days either in the house or in a mortuary with strangers. Kela, however, was less than fifteen minutes away, cloistered in the Sacred Heart convent and school in the Cerro neighborhood. My father asked Kela's superiors at the school for a dispensation so that his older sister could join them for the funeral. Kela always had an equanimous and stoic presence that would have greatly comforted her mother. But the nuns flatly refused. My father was stunned by the response. He had not anticipated the severity of pre-Vatican II restrictions on cloistered nuns. He insisted to no avail. True to her vow of obedience, Kela remained silent.

Lisandro's death served to instill in my father two convictions that accompanied him throughout the rest of his life. One was a lack of confidence in medical doctors. The other was a disdain for Church authority.

Although his death was sudden and unexpected, Lisandro had, characteristically, planned for the eventuality. Shortly after moving to Havana and knowing he would spend the rest of his days in the capital, he persuaded his business partner, Rogelio Echevarría, to join him in another sort of partnership, an eternal one: they jointly purchased a lot in Havana's Colón cemetery and built a mausoleum that they and their families would share. United in business and in death.

Colón is properly a necropolis, not a cemetery. It's an impressive place: a 136-acre city of the dead made entirely of stone and marble, with numbered streets and avenues. Some of the mausoleums are literally works of art in their architecture and statuary. The Pérez-Echevarría mausoleum is located on one of the wider arteries of the necropolis, on the same avenue as the Fonts family gravesite. It is a stone edifice about fifteen feet in height and in the shape of a small church, with a pitched roof and a

The Pérez-Echevarría mausoleum, Colón necropolis, Havana, 1979. Photograph by the author.

cross at the top. Its iron front door gives access to a room about twelve feet in both length and width, with a high ceiling and marble walls and floor. There are two parallel crypts, one along the right wall of the room and the other along the left wall. The one on the left was for the Pérezes, the right one for the Echevarrías. Each crypt has enough depth for four stacked coffins. There is also a central crypt with stairs that lead to a small enclosure at the lower level with numerous niches lining the sides. Following the practice at Colón, after sufficient years elapse after the burial, the remains in the coffins are transferred to urns and placed in the niches. This maximizes the space in the tombs and is one reason that the Colón necropolis has remained contained within its original walls after more than a century of burials.

Lisandro's body was not the first one to occupy the mausoleum. Rafael Prieto, Mara's husband, had already been buried there, and there had already been two burials on the Echevarría side. One of those was Rogelio himself, who passed away in 1938, when my father and Rubén were finishing up their senior year at Woodmere. Rogelio had died suddenly while he and his wife, Elvira, were vacationing in Europe. Lisandro asked his two sons to make the trip from Long Island to the pier in Manhattan where Elvira was arriving on a ship carrying Rogelio's body. The boys were to accompany her and see to her needs while she waited to sail to Havana on the next ship from New York. The other Echevarría buried in the mausoleum was Rogelio's oldest son, Rogelito, who had also attended Woodmere and died only a couple of years after his father, barely in his twenties, of an aggressive sepsis.

She was only sixty-six years old, but Amparo gave up on living after her husband's death. She even fretted when her daughter Gisela tried to comb her hair and apply some makeup on her face. The administration of the household now fell primarily on Mara. With the exception of Kela, Rubén, and my father, the rest of the Pérez children still called the house on G Street home, in addition, of course, to Mara's two young daughters. Gisela, with her boundless energy and efficiency, was probably in charge of most day-to-day details, but Mara was not only the oldest but commanded the respect that made her the obvious person to head the household.

For years after Lisandro died, my father would stop by G Street every weekday morning on his way to La Internacional to visit with his mother. Once I was able to walk and talk, my father, at Amparo's insistence, would drop me off at G Street in the morning and pick me up in the afternoon. I was told that Amparo enjoyed spending time with me. I was her first grandson, and I liked to talk and listen.

But the days I spent at G Street were not just for my grandmother's benefit. Shortly after I turned three, my mother was pregnant for the fourth time, after having lost two pregnancies since I had been born. This fourth one, in 1952, progressed well, and my brother, Victor, was born in December of that year. With a history of delicate pregnancies and then a new infant, my mother probably welcomed my day trips to G Street.

Those days spent with my grandmother served to anchor me at the house where my father had grown up, creating in me a true sense of belonging to a family beyond my immediate one, in a house with a grandmother, uncles, aunts, and cousins. It was there during those daily visits, when I was three and four years old, that my earliest memories are situated. Many of those memories are shrouded in a gauzy haze, more tactile than visual or auditory. I remember the feeling of the thick embroidered cloth that covered the armrest of the lounge chair where my grandmother would recline in her bedroom as I sat alongside her on the ottoman. I would stroke my grandmother's forearms and feel the softness of her skin, which was taut and smooth until I reached the elbow, which was all wrinkly. She would laugh when I tugged on the wrinkles.

My memory sharpens as I grow a bit older, and I remember the grapes she prepared every day just for me, which she kept on a covered dinner plate in the refrigerator. She had peeled every one of them and cut them in half to remove the seeds. Midmorning she would take the plate out of the refrigerator and place it in front of me, along with a spoon and a cloth napkin. I remember the scene in which I learn where the grapes come from: "El Chino José," as he had done for many years, enters the house through the back door with a huge, flat wicker basket he would carry on his head, lowering it onto the large table in the kitchen where I am sitting eating my peeled and seedless grapes. My grandmother starts selecting from the many offerings of fruits and vegetables in the basket. Before she is finished, and anticipating one of her choices, José raises from the basket a beautiful bunch of plump purple grapes, and smiling at me, exclaims in heavily accented Spanish, "And the grapes, for the little grandson!" The arrival of José with his basket became for me one of the highlights of those days at G Street. One Christmas, José gave me a small, red cardboard box wrapped in cellophane and labeled with indecipherable but fascinating letters. I was told it was tea, but I was not sure what that was (Cubans drink tea only when they are sick or nervous). I never opened the box, keeping it as a relic in a drawer for years after that, occasionally taking it out and gazing at the writing.

By the time I met José, the Chinese had already established a large presence in Cuba. In the mid-nineteenth century they arrived as contract laborers to replace the Africans in the waning years of the slave trade. There was a second wave during the initial decades of the twentieth century, with many settling in Havana and opening small businesses engaged in selling, buying, and providing personal services. Many adopted, or were given, Spanish first names. The Cuban capital came to house one of the largest Chinatowns in the Western Hemisphere. I learned from my grandmother that, as was the case with most of his compatriots, José had arrived in Cuba alone, without his wife and children, leaving them behind in Canton until he could make enough money to send for them or perhaps to rejoin them in China as a returning prosperous merchant. I imagined how sad it must be to live without any family, and I was glad that in some way I was helping José by eating the grapes.

Amparo's unwillingness to live finally manifested itself in a bleeding ulcer. The doctors were unsure if surgery would cure her, but she made the decision for them: no operation. It was during her final days that I

experienced my first continuously running memory, that is, not in images or scenes as before, but as in a film: a lengthy sequence of unfolding events. It starts in the Jardines de La Tropical, built at the turn of the
twentieth century as the gardens of a brewery in what was then the southwestern outskirts of the city. I am at some child's birthday party. I cannot
recall whose party it was, probably because I never knew the child's name.
My childhood weekends were occasionally taken up by large birthday parties for children I did not know but to which I was invited only because
the family of the birthday boy or girl was an acquaintance of my family.
It could have been, for example, the child of someone who had gone to
school with my mother, or the grandchild of one of my grandparents'
friends or business acquaintances. The birthday parties of Havana's upper
classes were usually elaborate affairs in large venues such as the Jardines
de La Tropical, with plenty of food and entertainment, and they therefore
had lengthy guest lists appropriate for grand events.

I do not recall which adult accompanied me to La Tropical on that afternoon in November 1953. I did not have a nanny, so one of my parents,
almost always my mother, would take me to birthday parties. But she was
not there that day, for reasons I would learn later. I must have tagged along
with the parent or nanny of another guest.

There were plenty of rides at the party, and I was having a fun time
when I saw José, the chauffer, drive up in the black Buick. He got out,
spoke to someone, took me by the hand, and said, "Your *abuelita* wants
to see you." He sat me in the back seat and drove off in the direction of
Vedado.

José parked the car near the back of the house on G Street and took
me in through the back door that led to the kitchen. My father was waiting for me in the dining room. He took me by the hand and walked me
down the central corridor of the house to the last bedroom on the left, my
grandmother's room. As I entered the room, I saw that my mother and all
my uncles and aunts (except Kela) were there, standing around the bed.
There was a heavy silence in the room, eerily unusual for a gathering of my

father's family. As my father led me toward the bed, the circle of persons around it opened and I saw my grandmother, with her head propped up by a pillow, and in her right arm was a needle that was attached by a thin tube to a large glass jug hung upside down on a metal stand by the far side of the bed. I was suddenly aware that I was the only child in the room and the center of attention. Amparo managed a smile as she waved me closer and said in a weak voice, "Come, give me a kiss." My father released my hand, and I clambered onto the near side of the bed and gave her a kiss on the cheek. She took my hand and squeezed it. It was but an instant. As my father led me back toward the door, I glanced at the lounge chair and the ottoman in the corner.

Amparo died on November 3, 1953. The funeral was identical to Lisandro's: the wake in the house, the coffin in the bedroom, the interment in the Pérez-Echevarría mausoleum in Colón, and Kela absent, cloistered in the Sacred Heart convent, to my father's renewed chagrin. I did not attend. Young children did not attend funerals in my family. A few weeks later after her will was read, my father handed me what she had bequeathed to me: her wristwatch, possibly her most personal item, one she always wore and that I remembered well from our sessions at the easy chair. It was a simple gold watch, with a patent leather strap, and on the face were thin, delicate black hands and roman numerals. My father told me not to brag about it to my cousins because I had been the only grandchild to whom she had left one of her personal possessions.

☀ 13 ☀

AN (AMERICAN) CHILDHOOD

When I was a newborn, my parents did not have the budget for both a nanny and a housekeeper, so my mother made the choice to take care of me, leaving the cooking and housework to someone else. Nancy took on the role of mother with her characteristic assiduousness. When she was pregnant with me, she applied the so-so English she learned at the Sacred Heart school to a careful reading of what was then the baby care book that was breaking sales records in the United States, Benjamin Spock's *The Common Sense Book of Baby and Child Care*. I am sure my grandfather Oscar gave it to her. He would have found it in the English-language paperback and magazine store adjacent to the Minimax supermarket in Miramar that sold all things American and that he frequented to buy Holsum sliced bread, canned beets, and other uniquely American goods and magazines, such as *Life* or the *Saturday Evening Post*. He would have recommended to my mother that she follow Dr. Spock's book. Surely, the way Americans raised their offspring had to be superior to the coddling, the *malacrianza*, with which Cubans raised so many coddled and undisciplined children. That my mother followed Dr. Spock's baby book has always led me to believe that, in terms of how I was nurtured, I am a true American baby boomer.

Nancy and Oscar's twenty-fifth-anniversary portrait, taken at a photographer's studio, Havana, 1950. Standing, left to right: my uncle Carlos; my father, Tano; my mother, Nancy; and my aunt Mary Lou. Seated on the armrest: Oscar. My grandmother Nancy, seated on the couch holding me. Author's collection.

Nancy's confidence as a competent mother was badly shaken when I was just a few weeks old. She was bathing me in the bathroom of our Miramar apartment, in one of those portable baby bathtubs in use at the time that consisted of a rubberized canvas that held the water and had a drain plug in the bottom. The canvas was mounted on foldable metal cross-legs that were high enough so that an adult would not have to stoop. The devices were known as "bathinettes," the trademark of their manufacturer, the Baby Bathinette Corporation of Rochester, New York, which sold its products in Sears and Roebuck stores, including the one in Havana, which opened in 1942 and was the retailer's first store outside the United States.

As Nancy told it, I was all lathered up when I slipped out of her hands like a bar of soap and fell headfirst from a height of almost four feet onto the tile floor. My mother swore that I fell with such force on my head that I bounced off the floor. Hysterical, Nancy rushed me to the office of my pediatrician, Dr. Manuel Pérez-Stable, who stroked the top of my head, flashed a light in my eyes, and declared me without injury, assuring my mother there would be no long-term effects. "Babies are made of rubber," he said.

Maybe it was that fall, combined with Dr. Spock's advice, that made me a very well-behaved child. My good behavior was one reason that even when I was able to walk, a nanny was not hired and there were no concerns that I would be an unwelcome handful when I was taken to G Street to spend the day with Amparo. Nannies were regarded as an absolute necessity for well-to-do parents who had the luxury of not having to bother with the day-to-day tasks of raising young children. In Cuba, the word for a nanny was *manejadora*, from the verb *manejar*, to handle, as in a situation, or to steer, as with an automobile. A *manejadora* was a handler, a steerer, of children. My brother gave a clear indication early in his life that he needed to be steered, and he had a nanny not long after he was born.

LAFAYETTE

Another consequence of my good behavior was that my parents felt confident about placing me in kindergarten when I was only four years old. They chose a private school not far from where we lived in Miramar: Lafayette School, located on Quinta Avenida, the broad boulevard that connected the Havana suburb with the city. Its location was not my parents' main reason for choosing it, but rather that it was an "American" school. That meant that it catered to the large American colony in Havana and to Cubans, such as my parents, who wanted their children to learn English and gain a familiarity with the culture of the country that played such a prominent role in their lives.

Lafayette would turn out to be the only school I attended in Cuba, from kindergarten through the seventh grade. Most of those years the school was in a large two-story house on Quinta Avenida in Miramar. The building had originally been built as a residence, probably around the 1920s or '30s, but by the early '50s, it had been acquired by a married couple, Gerald and Natalie de Berly, the owners of the school. Almost every room in the house had been turned into a classroom to accommodate grades one through six. The kindergarteners were in the former garage, which had been remodeled into a spacious classroom with an adjacent small playground. I don't know if there was another location for the upper grades, or if they even had upper grades, but I don't recall seeing any big kids while I attended Lafayette at the house on Quinta Avenida.

Natalie de Berly (née Heller) was an American expatriate with a degree in education from a US university. I remember her as a tall and elegant woman in her late thirties or early forties, with a ready smile for all students. She oversaw the academic side of the school while her husband was the disciplinarian and businessman. He was an imposing man: older and even taller than his wife, balding but with a heavy mustache, and always impeccably dressed. He spoke gruffly and with an accent. Making him

In my *guajirito* (peasant) costume, ready to play the *claves*, circa 1953. Author's collection.

even more formidable was his prosthetic left hand. Mr. de Berly would walk like a specter down the hallways, swiveling his head to survey everything around him, usually wearing his suit coat like a cape over his shoulders, without introducing his arms. I never knew for sure what his background was, but the word around the school was that he was Austrian and a veteran of some European war in which he had lost his hand. I am sure he was probably a much nicer man than he appeared and he just cultivated a fearsome image so he could be a more effective disciplinarian. A teacher's threat to send a student to his office was a great deterrent to misbehavior at Lafayette.

Lafayette was evidently a successful enterprise for the de Berlys. By the time I started fourth grade, the school moved to a sprawling two-story building that the de Berlys had built in the La Coronela neighborhood of Marianao, in the rapidly expanding semirural suburbs southwest of the city. It was near the neighborhoods where Americans lived. The other leading private schools had already relocated to this area: Belén Jesuit School, the Sacred Heart of Jesus School (which relocated from El Cerro), and Ruston Academy, also an American school. The new building had space to house classes from kindergarten through twelfth grade.

I loved the new building. It had three wings of classrooms intersecting one central hallway, with outdoor patios between the wings. Connecting the two floors were exterior ramps instead of stairs. The school had a gym with a full-sized hardwood basketball court, a cafeteria, science labs, student lockers, a large athletic field, and a public-address system that transmitted announcements from the school's office to every room in the building. It was in every way a modern midcentury American school building, complete with a lending library, something totally new to me. Lending libraries were extremely rare in Cuba, even in schools, and there were no public lending libraries, except for one that was established in the early 1950s in the city of Matanzas by a descendant of nineteenth-century Cuban émigrés to the United States, a woman who had grown up in Providence, Rhode Island, appreciating the value of public lending libraries.

Her ancestors were originally from Matanzas, and in their memory, she dedicated her sizable inheritance to building and operating a lending library in that city. It became known throughout Cuba because of its unique concept: *matanceros* could borrow books and read them at home. The de Berlys's intent to have Lafayette replicate an American school, including having a lending library, was a boon to me. Once I learned the system, I was constantly exercising my library borrowing privileges.

I did not appreciate at the time that Lafayette was not a typical school. It was not until after I left Cuba that I realized that bilingual schools were by far the exception, especially in the United States. During most of the school day classes were taught in English, and not just literature, grammar, and spelling, but also mathematics, science, and world and US history. There were roughly the same number of Cuban students as there were American students enrolled in those classes. For the rest of the day, the students were split into two different curriculum tracks. The Cuban children attended classes in Spanish, along with any American student whose parents opted to have them take those classes. The rest of the American students, the vast majority, remained in courses taught in English. Classes in Spanish included literature and grammar (not spelling, of course, since Spanish is a phonetic language), Cuban culture, history and geography, and "morality and civics." The de Berlys hired certified American teachers to teach at Lafayette. The La Coronela building even had a few small apartments for single faculty members who were brought in from the United States. The classes in Spanish were taught, of course, by certified Cuban teachers.

The curriculum favored instruction in English because it was, after all, a school primarily for the children of American families living in Cuba, and for those of us who were there to learn the language. The school was accredited in the United States, and we used the textbooks widely in use at the time in American schools. In mathematics, I recall that each year we had a textbook that was commonly used in the United States for the next higher grade, following the practice in Cuban schools (and, I believe, in most of the world) of utilizing a more demanding math curriculum than what was usually offered in elementary schools in the US.

My favorite subjects were history and the social sciences, subjects that I received in double doses: in English and in Spanish. It was, I now recognize, a curious duality, an exposure in elementary school to contrasting historical narratives. I remember well the hefty US history textbook we read in sixth grade, which covered the Vikings to the Korean War with scant mention of indigenous populations and Columbus. The book emphasized wars and expansionism, including the Spanish-American War. I remember the teacher well: Miss Tetzeli, an attractive redhead in her late twenties or early thirties who was covered in freckles and always fashionably dressed, down to her high heels. She would walk into the classroom with a swagger, ready to champion American greatness, imperialism, and historical invincibility.

That same year, my Cuban history and geography teacher was Sra. Valdés, a no-nonsense older woman and a nationalist who always seemed to exude defiance, as if repulsed by the foreignness that surrounded her at Lafayette. She imparted impassioned lessons about the island's great struggle for independence, the richness of Cuban culture, and the heroism of Martí and Maceo. I remember that once in geography class she made the argument that Cuba stood on its own continental shelf and was therefore entitled to be regarded as the sixth continent.

Sra. Valdés's nationalist pedagogy was part of a midcentury shift in Cuban education. There had long been a concern that Cuban civic culture was being deformed by the considerable number of foreign teachers, especially the many Spanish priests in Catholic schools, who were not educating Cuban children in the values that supported strong nationhood. To address this, the convention that drafted the 1940 Cuban constitution inserted an extraordinary provision that required that all courses on Cuban history and culture taught in both public and private schools throughout the island had to be taught by Cuban-born teachers using textbooks written by Cuban-born authors. Sra. Valdés and textbooks such as Leví

Marrero's *Geografía de Cuba*, which I treasured, could not have been more nationalist.

During any given school day, therefore, I was exposed to the conflicting discourses of Americanism versus nationalism that have long dominated so much of Cuban political discourse. Far from being confused, I thrived on it. I relished the national pride that Sra. Valdés instilled in her students in an almost conspiratorial way, for it was largely just us Cubans in her classes, and she taught in the language we spoke at home. But I was also thrilled to learn about that other place that I knew had such a large presence in my family's history but that I had not visited, and to learn about it from a teacher who was the United States incarnate: a stylish and leggy redhead who looked and walked like she belonged in those Technicolor American films that my mother would take me to see at the Rodi, Trianon, or Miramar movie theaters.

On Fridays, the entire school would line up by grade on the athletic field, and we would sing "The Star-Spangled Banner," the Cuban national anthem, and the Lafayette school song (in English), which had a very catchy tune. I always kept that tune in my head, and decades later as

Friday assembly at Lafayette School, 1956–57. Two flags, two anthems. Lafayette School Yearbook.

I watched a college football game on television, I was startled to hear it again. It was the University of Notre Dame fight song, with "La-fa-yette" replacing "No-tre-Dame."

I developed friendships with both my Cuban and American classmates, but my closest bonds were within the group of Cuban students, simply because we attended Lafayette year after year throughout the elementary grades and we spoke Spanish among ourselves. The Americans tended to be more transient, their families in Cuba only for the length of their corporate or diplomatic assignments. There were exceptions. The one I remember best was Susan Murphy, a chubby and jovial brunette who was in the same class as me during all the years I was at Lafayette and who spoke Spanish like a Cuban, which for all practical purposes, she was. Susan's father was an executive with McCann-Erickson de Cuba, a subsidiary of a New York advertising firm. The Murphys chose to have Susan take full advantage of the bilingual and bicultural experience that Lafayette offered. She joined the Cuban students in the Spanish language classes and tended to hang around with us instead of with the Americans.

The American students that filed through Lafayette during all those years gave me a glimpse of what life may have been like in that country during the 1950s. In Havana, American families tended to live in their own enclave, re-creating the world of suburban America. Bobby, for example, would sometimes bring to school a bag with an extra pair of shoes that he would place in his locker. He once explained that after school he would go directly to something called "tap classes." Greta was a spunky, pony-tailed girl who at an end-of-the-year dance showed the rest of us how to dance to "Rock around the Clock" by Bill Haley and the Comets. And then there was Ann Morehouse, who enrolled for the first time when I was in third grade. Her father was Vice President of Bethlehem Steel's Cuba operations. Although I had met many Americans since my kindergarten year, I had never seen anyone quite like Ann. I could not avoid staring at her the entire day I first saw her. Her hair, cut in a perfect pageboy, was very straight and so blonde that it was practically white. She had huge blue eyes and very pale skin. When she came in after recess from playing in the Cuban heat, her shirt was sweaty, and her cheeks were hot pink.

One year, perhaps in the fourth grade, I was invited to an after-school party at the home of one of my American friends. I showed my mother the written invitation, and she knew what to do. She took a piece of an old bedsheet, draped it over me, and cut out some holes so I could see. I was to wear the sheet to the party, so she put it in my school bag. After school, as planned, the mother of the party's host loaded several of us into a wood-paneled station wagon, and we were off to a house in the neighborhood where many Americans lived.

At the party we played several organized games, the most memorable of which consisted of trying to capture, with only one's mouth, several float-ing apples in a small tub full of water. No one was successful, and the whole game seemed to me to be an exercise in humiliation. As the sun was going down, we were given empty bags, we put on our costumes, and we again piled into the station wagon. We were driven to several houses where Ameri-can families lived. At each one we would get out, enter the house briefly, have candy tossed into our bags, and then get back into the station wagon and move on to the next house. It seemed rude to pay such a rushed visit to those nice people who had given us candy.

What I remember most about that evening was feeling totally baffled. My mother must have explained to me what was going to happen, but I am sure I was unable to process and retain in my mind something so devoid of any context within my experience.

POLITICAL SUNDAYS

Once the children of Lisandro and Amparo started marrying and moving away from the parental home, the family instituted the tradition of hav-ing everyone convene at the house on G Street every Sunday for lunch. By the time of Amparo's death in 1953, all the boys had married except for the youngest, Sergio, who would marry a few years later, as would Leticia.

Mara was still living at G Street with her two daughters, and Gisela and Amparito, who would remain single, were also living in the house. But on Sundays, everyone was there, except, of course, for Kela, who by this time was cloistered in Sacred Heart's new school in the same neighborhood as Lafayette.

I remember Sunday lunches at the house on G Street as boisterous affairs, especially by the time my brother and my male cousins, five in all and younger than I, became old enough to run and tumble around the house's terrace and gardens, getting their best Sunday clothes dirty despite the admonitions from the nannies. I considered myself too old to be involved in their rowdiness, so I usually sought instead the company of my cousin Cristy, Uncle Rubén's daughter, who was slightly older than I.

But my real preference on those Sundays at G Street was to hang around with the adults in the living room and the dining room, where the action was even more raucous than among the young children. Almost without exception, Lisandro and Amparo's children were a strong-willed and opinionated bunch, a disposition they each developed growing up with the complex interpersonal dynamics of large households, where assertiveness is a necessary trait. Argumentativeness was the lifelong default mode of my father and his siblings, and nowhere was that more evident than during those Sunday lunches, when almost all of them assembled. By the time the platters of rice, beans, pork, chicken, plantains, and the like were brought out from the kitchen to the dining room under the supervision of Mara and Gisela, the sparring was already well underway.

With the increasing precariousness of Cuban society, there was a lot to argue about. Fulgencio Batista's coup d'état in 1952 had ended a constitutional order that had been both democratic and corrupt. Of the two, corruption was the one that survived the coup, and in earnest. Batista headed a government that was unconstitutional and increasingly dictatorial, and the influence of the United States accelerated and became pervasive. One Cuban novelist called the 1950s "those American years," but it was more than that: it was a decade of contradictions. The long-standing ills of

the Cuban Republic came to an inevitable climax: stark socioeconomic differences, especially between cities and the countryside; widespread corruption with both foreign and domestic origins; the selling of Cuba to a
wide range of US interests, both licit and illicit; in short, the breakdown
of a republic that had ostensibly been founded half a century before to
advance the tenets that José Martí had laid down for the Cuban nation:
social justice and sovereignty. The contradiction between ideology and
reality became untenable in the 1950s for many in the middle and upper
sectors of Cuban society, especially urban professionals, who lived their
lives as progressives and cosmopolitans but found themselves governed
by a military dictatorship, no better than a "banana republic," with their
capital city turned into a playground for Americans. Cubans thought of
themselves as better than that. Havana was a thoroughly modern city, with
a rising middle class with high aspirations and awash in American cars and
other consumer goods. Yet the country had a monocultural economy, an
impoverished peasantry, and a military ruler.

My father embodied those contradictions. Educated in the US, fluent in
English, favoring an American school for his children, and making a living from importing American manufactured goods, he was nevertheless a
nationalist and an anti-imperialist. He was a proud member of the Partido
del Pueblo Cubano, known as the Ortodoxo Party, founded in 1947 by
a charismatic and populist leader named Eduardo Chibás. Chibás was a
senator and a member of an elite Havana family. He became the leading
opposition figure to the Auténtico Party that ruled Cuba, constitution-
ally, from 1944 to 1952. The *auténticos* had defrauded the trust that many
Cubans had placed in them to champion the progressive constitution that
had been enacted in 1940 and to lead Cuba, finally, into a new era of true
sovereignty and social justice. Chibás became the voice of that frustration,
using his fiery rhetoric to expose the moral decline of the *auténtico* governments. His death in 1951, from a self-inflicted gunshot, left a vacuum in his
party, but the *ortodoxos* nevertheless presented a full slate of candidates for
the 1952 elections, and they had every expectation that the voters would

give them control of the government. Among the *ortodoxo* candidates was my father, who was running for the congressional seat that represented Camajuaní. He was banking on his father's name recognition in the region to help him win. For the first time since the fatal incident involving Isabel Rubio, he returned to the town, campaigning and renewing his contacts with many of the citizens of Camajuaní.

We will never know if the *camajuanenses* would have elected him because the elections were never held, preempted by Fulgencio Batista's coup as the country came under military rule. My father, of course, became an ardent anti-Batistiano after that, and although he was not, to my knowledge, active in the efforts to oust the new self-proclaimed "President," his *ortodoxo* affiliation placed him on a list of the regime's opponents. Whenever the climate became tense in the capital or when security was tightened in anticipation of a major event or a visit by a foreign head of state, the police would round up everyone on the list and hold them in precinct stations throughout the city, releasing them after a few days.

It became routine. Batista's security forces were apparently not good at keeping their dossiers up to date, because they always went to pick up my father in the middle of the night at the house on G Street and not at our apartment in Miramar. His sister Mara would then telephone him as the officers waited. He would drive from our house, surrender himself, and be placed in a police van for the ride to the station. He was never harmed, but my mother always became understandably alarmed and would call her father to see if Oscar knew anyone who would intercede for my father to make sure he remained safe. It was not an unwarranted concern, especially after 1956, when the regime's repression intensified and stories circulated about detainees who were not seen again.

Naturally, these experiences served to make my father heap even greater scorn on the Batista regime than what he unloaded on the Catholic Church and the medical profession. And the best place to voice his strongly held opinions on the sorry state of the government and the direction of Cuban society was in the privacy of the house on G Street, on Sundays among his siblings. Some of them, especially Leticia, echoed his views. But the counterpoint to his arguments was usually voiced, with equal vehemence, by Rubén.

Uncle Rubén had a stern and formal demeanor. He would come to the Sunday family reunions at G Street impeccably dressed in a suit and a tie, a perfectly ironed and starched white shirt with cufflinks, pleated pants, shined dress leather shoes (usually wingtips), and with a simple gold chain attached on one end to a belt loop on his right side with the other end disappearing into his right pants pocket. His black hair was sheened and completely combed back. He was perhaps the most handsome of all the children of Lisandro and Amparo, women included.

Rubén exuded an air of authority that may have been either the cause or the consequence, or both, of succeeding Lisandro as the head of all General Cigar operations in Cuba. In many ways, that made him the head of the family after Lisandro died. Although my father was the oldest male, born barely eleven months before Rubén, my grandfather had anointed my uncle as his successor, recognizing in him the attributes necessary to successfully run the family business. He was disciplined and organized, with a compulsive work ethic and strong administrative skills, capable of tightly managing a complex organization such as the General Cigar Company of Cuba. And Rubén had one other trait, which my father clearly lacked but was indispensable in dealing with corporate headquarters in New York: Rubén was unabashedly pro-American. He was comfortable with, and indeed favored, the growing cultural, economic, and political influence of the United States in Cuba. He and his wife, Josefina (Josie), had a lifestyle that was more American than Cuban. Their circle of friends included many Americans, they drank Scotch and smoked American cigarettes, and Josie was an avid reader of the latest American best-selling novels, such as *Peyton Place*.

What I remember most about Rubén, and which, in a single gesture, encapsulated so much about him, was the way he would greet me every Sunday. Upon arrival at G Street, my uncles and aunts would shower me (as well as my cousins) with hugs and kisses; so many that I had to frequently wipe the wetness from my cheeks. But Rubén would come up to me, extend his hand, and in English, say, "For the woman, the kiss; for the man the sword." I was eight or nine years old, but despite the severity of his words and the firmness of his handshake, my uncle did not intimidate me. I liked Rubén, maybe because I knew he was not only my father's closest brother but also his lifelong friend.

It was a bond forged during all those years Rubén and my father grew up as close companions, especially at Woodmere, where they relied on each other as they adjusted to that entirely unfamiliar world of Long Island. But they were two very different men, and they came out of their student years in the United States with opposite political views on what was best for Cuba. My father's nationalistic and anti-Batista views clashed with Rubén's advocacy for a strong pro-American government that would ensure stability and continued US investments. Those were the recurring themes of the heated discussions among the siblings during those Sundays in the house on G Street, with Rubén and my father leading the never-ending debate.

My Sundays did not end at G Street. Sometime after lunch, my father, mother, brother, and I would head to the home of my grandparents Oscar and Nancy for dinner. Compared to the rowdiness of the Pérez's lunch, dinner with my maternal grandparents was a much more subdued and intimate affair. We were rarely joined by my aunt Mary Lou and my uncle Carlos, both of whom usually had other plans on Sundays. At those dinners, political discussions were infrequent, perhaps because they were potentially conflictive. Oscar was in many ways similar in his politics to my uncle Rubén; he was an admirer of the United States and of things American. Not surprisingly, Rubén and Oscar were good friends, perhaps closer than Oscar was to my father, which was not very close at all. Aware of his son-in-law's strongly held views, Oscar avoided discussing politics with him.

One Sunday dinner, however, Oscar unwittingly sparked a rare contentious exchange with my father. It was over mashed potatoes, and I remember it well because I intervened in it. Oscar liked to be self-sufficient in the kitchen and not depend on any hired help to cook, so he was a fan of American convenience foods. It was a time when US corporations were turning out a plethora of time-saving food products and appliances designed to make housework easier and, as with all American products, notably automobiles, they were readily available to the middle and upper classes in Havana.

That Sunday, Oscar proudly unveiled his latest find from the aisles of the Minimax Supermarket: French's Instant Mashed Potatoes. He extolled its virtues: easy preparation and amazingly similar in taste to the real thing. *"Estos americanos son algo serio"* ("These Americans are something else"), he said, as he placed a bowl of it on the table. My father grumbled. He said he found the taste artificial and went on to predict the doom of the small Cuban farmer if everyone in the country preferred some laboratory-produced import over the potatoes produced by the Cuban *campesino*. The Nancys tensed up. This time Oscar, although calm, did not remain silent, insisting that the future belonged to time-saving American innovations that would eventually make it unnecessary to have live-in domestic help. Besides, wasn't my father involved in importing American goods? My father countered that it was one thing to import manufactured goods that Cuba did not produce, as he himself did in his business, but quite another thing to replace with imports the few commodities Cuba produced plentifully, such as starchy roots. Rejoinder followed rejoinder, and things were starting to escalate when I blurted out, impatiently, "It's just mashed potatoes!" Oscar and my father stared at me and both burst out laughing. Argument over and I was relieved. I was used to, and in fact enjoyed, watching my father argue with his siblings, but not with Oscar. There was no upside to that; they were the two most important men in my life.

With time, I came to appreciate the nuances of my grandfather Oscar's pro-Americanism. Despite his affinity for so many American things, rooted in a nostalgia for his years in New York, he had a very firm identity as a Cuban, which was perhaps traceable to a sense of pride in his father's service on behalf of Cuban independence. He was by no means an American wannabe. Oscar always referred to Americans in the third person (*"estos americanos"*), and despite all the positive things he saw in their culture, he sometimes voiced reservations about what he considered to be the banality of American popular culture. For example, he could not figure out why Americans liked the humor of Jerry Lewis, which he regarded as unbearably puerile.

EL COUNTRY

Oscar was forced to sell the house on Eighteenth Street when his brother Ernesto married, moved out, and demanded his share of the value of the house. Having to move from Eighteenth Street was one of Oscar's biggest disappointments. He had designed that house, and despite the pall that fell on it with the death of Oscarito, it also housed the childhood memories of his other children.

The family lived in a succession of rental homes in Miramar in the late 1940s while Oscar designed another house. Miramar had become popular and expensive, so he bought a large lot farther out, in the same semirural suburban area where Lafayette was located and where many American families lived. The area was generally known as El Country Club because it was near the social club of that name, popular among Americans and with the most renowned golf course in Cuba. Cubans referred to the area simply as El Country.

On that lot, Oscar built his new dream house, a two-story midcentury with modern lines. Its most prominent interior feature was a large living and dining area that had a long wall of exposed gray bricks. The wall had a fireplace and a mantel in the center, and Oscar decorated the wall with two collections of curiosities he had acquired over the years. On the left part of the wall, he mounted his antique gun collection, which included, he told me, the same model pistol that John Wilkes Booth used to kill President Lincoln, a .44-caliber, single-shot Derringer. On the right side of the brick wall was an array of small, oval-shaped black picture frames with ink drawings of every one of the Fonts ancestors, going back to Torredembarra and arranged chronologically on the wall from top to bottom like a genealogical tree.

The entire living room was framed in the back by a continuous set of glass doors that opened the area to a terrazzo terrace that led to the expansive backyard with an impeccable lawn. The kitchen was off the dining room and had a breakfast area (not typical of Cuban houses). Through the kitchen one could access the two-car garage on the side of the house.

A freestanding staircase next to the front entrance that spiraled in front of a curved wall of glass bricks led to the second floor, which had a foyer, four bedrooms, three baths, and a small kitchen perfect for late-night

The Fonts house in El Country, rear view. Fonts family collection.

snacks or even a light breakfast. Nancy and Oscar occupied the master bedroom, located in one of the corners of the floor. The adjoining master bathroom led to a second, very small bedroom, where Oscar slept on occasion, mostly afternoon naps. It had only a twin bed, a dresser, and a night table. The other two bedrooms, each with a bathroom, were occupied by my uncle Carlos and, in the one on the other corner, by my aunt Mary Lou. By the time the family moved into this house, early in 1950, my mother was already married.

Inside and out, the house looked no different from an upscale home in suburban America, complete with a manicured lawn, exposed brick, glass doors, and a fireplace. Oscar apparently became enamored with brick-framed fireplaces during his years in the Hudson Valley. There was also a fireplace in the house on Eighteenth Street.

I loved spending time in El Country (as we all referred to the new house) with my grandparents, especially Oscar. My grandmother Nancy was a sweet woman whom I loved very much, but as she aged, she seemed somewhat aloof and distracted. I now recognize that she may have already been in the initial stages of the dementia that would cripple her in subsequent years. Oscar, on the other hand, was a lot of fun, and he paid a lot of attention to me. Not only was I well-behaved, which he greatly valued, but I showed a lot of interest in whatever he wanted to show me or talk about. And Oscar would have a lot of interesting things to show me, and I was always genuinely captivated by it all. I would look wide-eyed at the Derringer, as if it had been the very gun used in Ford's Theater.

Oscar was a bon vivant with a penchant for the finer things in life and for intellectual and artistic pursuits. He read, smoked cigarettes incessantly, loved fine dining and Scotch, had an untiring sense of humor, and was a charmer with women of any age. He was not a rich man, but he appeared to be. For him, money was something to be spent in the enjoyment of life. His car, the one I remember, was a black 1955 Cadillac Fleetwood.

Included in his design for the house in El Country was a small room that served as a wet bar, with an open side that had a counter facing the terrace in the backyard and with a back door to the kitchen. He painted the inside of the bar a dark yellow and then drew on the wall, freehand and using only jet-black paint, a stylized row of cancan dancers, emphasizing the uplifted skirts, the hosiery, and the high heels. When he showed it to me he told me how he had been inspired by the paintings of a French dwarf and went on to tell me how much fun that dwarf must have had, hanging out in dance halls and saloons.

One of the best things for me about visiting El Country was that Oscar had all kinds of interesting reading materials. For me, this was a boon because in our apartment in Miramar there were no books at all, except for my school textbooks, although we did receive plenty of news media. My father subscribed to the *Diario de la Marina* and *Avance*, two of the city's leading dailies, as well as the weekly magazine *Bohemia* and the Latin American edition of *Time* magazine. I would read all of them. I would pick up the *Time* from my father's nightstand, since he read it before going to sleep. My early exposure to the press is one reason that early in my life I became keenly aware of current events, especially what was going on in Cuba.

But my grandfather Oscar had books and interesting magazines, all of them American. Some of the books were large, richly illustrated art history books, with a special emphasis on the Renaissance. He also had a collection of the *Life* photography books of World War II. The magazines were *National Geographic* (a favorite of mine), *Life*, *Look*, and the *Saturday Evening Post* with those Norman Rockwell covers.

One time while I was visiting him at El Country, he placed before me on the dining room table what I recognized as a checkers game board, so I assumed we were going to play that game, which I had learned at school. But then he opened with some flourish a box that contained wooden enameled pieces with green felt bottoms, some black ones and some the lighter color of the wood, and announced that it was time I learned how to play chess. While he set up the board and showed me how each piece moved, he told me that he had not played in a while because he had no one to play with, but that when he was younger, in the 1920s, he frequented a chess club in Havana. In fact, he said, one time he was one of about thirty players who played a simultaneous match against the world champion, José Raúl Capablanca. Oscar lost, but there was no shame in that because Capablanca, my grandfather boasted, was the best chess player who ever lived. He had me take the set home so that I would practice moving the pieces but admonished me to take care of it because that was the same set he used to play Capablanca. We played a few games after that, but if he was expecting to discover a prodigy, I surely disappointed him.

I saw my grandfather Oscar every Sunday afternoon and evening, but on some Saturdays he would pick me up in the Cadillac to accompany him on errands around Havana. We would go retrieve something in his office at the printing company, or go to the post office, or go shopping for American groceries and magazines at the Minimax. Sometimes we would lunch at El Carmelo, a popular but informal restaurant in Vedado where he would always run into a lot of people he knew. El Carmelo had great Cuban sandwiches, *medianoches*, and shakes. They also had a magazine and paperback bookstand inside the restaurant. When we finished eating but before he got the check, he would tell me to go pick a book and he would have the waiter put it on the check.

A couple of times Oscar took me to one of his favorite haunts: La Casa de los Trucos ("Tricks") on Obispo Street. It was a crowded emporium of everything for the practical joker: whoopee cushions, hand buzzers, fake plastic vomit or dog poop, nose and eyeglass disguises, extra hot chewing gum, exploding cigars, and so on. These were all products well-known in the US and sold in similar stores in American cities. The visit to La Casa de los Trucos was not for my benefit but for his; he loved to buy something there to try out on friends and family. One time he bought a complete set of dinner glasses that had a raised floral design. The design concealed that in one of the glasses, just below the rim, there was a row of tiny holes. When his sister-in-law Consuelo, Nancy's youngest sister, joined the family for dinner one evening, it was the perfect opportunity to bring out the glasses, making sure Consuelo got the trick glass. He had been discreet; no one else at the table was in on the practical joke. Consuelo was a perfect target. She tended to be histrionic, but Oscar underestimated her reaction, especially since she was sensitive to any sign of aging. She discreetly wiped with her napkin the first few sips that dribbled on her chin, but as more water dribbled out, Consuelo stood up in a panic and yelled, "*Dios mío*, Oscar, call a doctor! I have facial paralysis!" Revealing the trick immediately, my grandfather was rebuked by the Boullosa sisters for his incorrigibility. He acted contrite, perhaps even sincerely.

Some Sundays I would accompany Oscar and Nancy to mass, usually at an imposing church on Quinta Avenida called Jesús de Miramar. My grandmother, with the lace veil covering her hair, as was the custom at the time, would lead me by the arm to a pew in the front, clutching in her hand the small missal she used in her First Communion, with its deteriorated mother of pearl cover held in place by a rubber band. She would open the missal carefully so that the pages, all in Latin, would not fall out. Nancy would follow the mass by mouthing the Latin words. When the part came to remember the deceased and pray for their eternal life, she would turn her head toward me so that I would whisper with her the names of her most dearly departed, never forgotten by her after all the years: her young son and her older sister. "Oscar Fonts Boullosa and Margot Boullosa Zamora" we would whisper together. My grandmother insisted on saying their full names so there would be no confusion, she told me, as to which Oscar and Margot up there were being remembered. My grandfather Oscar did not sit with us. He would stand in the back of the church, in the company of other men, so that he could sneak out frequently during the mass to smoke a cigarette.

Most Sundays I went with my mother to mass at Santa Rita, also on Quinta Avenida, the church where she married my father. I don't remember my father ever joining us. It became clear to me that going to mass was for women and children.

EL YACHT

I never went to a summer camp as a child in Cuba. My summer camp was the Habana Yacht Club. As far back as I can remember, I would be at "El Yacht" almost every day in the summer, involved in one of several recreational activities offered there. Baseball and swimming were the two I favored. I was good at the second but not so good at the first.

The Habana Yacht Club, founded in 1886, was Havana's most exclusive social club, the place where Havana's upper classes preferred to socialize. There were other similar clubs, and many families frequented clubs besides El Yacht, such as El Vedado Tennis Club, the Country Club, the Biltmore. That there were so many exclusive social clubs in Havana by the 1940s and 1950s was a testament to the growth and levels of consumption of the city's upper sectors, the *gente conocida* ("known people"), as they called themselves. El Yacht, however, was at the very top in terms of prestige and exclusivity.

Even before my parents married, both the Pérez and Fonts families were members. I don't remember going to any other club, except for a couple of times when I spent the day at the Miramar Yacht Club, by invitation of one of my closest classmates at Lafayette, Eugenio Abravanel. Eugenio was the son of a Turkish-born Sephardic Jew named Isidoro who owned a textile factory in Havana. Eugenio's mother was American. It never occurred to me at the time that perhaps the Abravanels went to the less prestigious Miramar because they were Jewish immigrants and were not admitted as members at the Habana Yacht Club. Maybe they preferred the Miramar Club. I don't know. But if the Habana Yacht Club was exclusive enough to reject the President of Cuba as a member, as happened with Fulgencio Batista—a man of color and a former army sergeant, son of a cane cutter but President of the republic nonetheless—it probably also excluded Jewish families. I did not encounter any problems when I reciprocated Eugenio's invitations and would take him for a day at El Yacht, as a guest, of course.

At my age, El Yacht was not a place to socialize and rub elbows with the elite but a place to have fun. It had great facilities. Its principal building was a massive two-story structure directly on the Miramar waterfront, with its own beach (private, of course). The club's complex included a swimming pool, a restaurant and several bars, a large open area with a bandshell for concerts and dances, squash and tennis courts, a small bowling alley, a baseball field, and locker rooms for boys, girls, and toddlers (the latter with their nannies, of course). The men's and women's locker rooms, massage rooms, saunas, and salons to play cards and dominoes were on the second floor of the main building, but only adults were allowed, so I never went up there. Scattered around the property were kiosks that served snacks, sodas, and fruit juices. They served the best ham croquettes I have ever had, two to an order, on a small plate with a lime wedge. I just had to sign the check and write on it my family's membership number. My father would get the bill at the end of the month. I don't think I ever abused the privilege, because I do not remember my father complaining about receiving too many *croqueta* bills.

From about age five to eight, my mother would take me to El Yacht and enroll me in a variety of activities. The earliest I remember were the swimming classes. I also took classes at El Yacht in the two great Cuban sports: baseball and boxing. Both were taught by retired pros. Perico (I never knew his full name) was the cantankerous baseball coach with no patience for little kids like me who could not hit the softly lobbed balls he would pitch to them. "Look at the ball and wait for it before swinging," he would scream. I was a better fielder than hitter.

The boxing classes were taught by Johnny Cruz, a former Cuban lightweight professional boxer whose career lasted until 1937. He was best known for having lost the fight, in six rounds in 1927, in which Eligio Sardiñas (Kid Chocolate), arguably the best Cuban boxer of all time, made his professional debut. Unlike Perico, who seemed to hate what he had been reduced to doing after retiring from professional sports, Johnny seemed genuinely content with passing on his skills to a group of clueless six- or seven-year-old boys in shorts and sporting boxing gloves. Already in his fifties, Johnny always had a bounce in his step as he strode toward his pupils, clad entirely in white: a white golfer cap, a white tightly fitting T-shirt that showed that he was still in great shape, long well-pressed white pants, and white shoes. Even his skin was white, unlike most Cuban professional boxers. Johnny taught us how to punch, counterpunch, jab, and defend our faces. Most of the class, however, was spent doing conditioning exercises: push-ups, jumping jacks, and other calisthenics. Looking back, I think the main purpose of the classes was to give an aging boxer a job.

While I was engaged in all these activities, my mother would join her friends in a breezy outdoor seating area in El Yacht that was shaded by almond trees, or she would play canasta with them on the second floor of the clubhouse. Her friends were usually women who had gone to the Sacred Heart school with her and who, invariably, were also members of El Yacht. Those were the few opportunities my mother had to stay in touch with those lifelong friends. My father disliked dining out or attending the many nighttime social events held at El Yacht, so my parents rarely went out in the evenings, something that could not have pleased my mother. It's not that my father was entirely unsociable, but after having spent most of his youth either in Woodmere or in Camajuaní, he did not have a wide circle of close friends (as my mother had), among the *gente conocida* in Havana, and he probably inherited some of his father's disdain for the pretentiousness of the Havana upper classes.

At about age nine I became much more independent in the summers, going to El Yacht on my own, without my mother and my brother, Victor, and his nanny. I was also sovereign in deciding the activities I wanted to pursue. Boxing was out. I stayed in baseball despite my poor hitting, which became demonstrably worse as I got older and played in the next age bracket where the games were fast pitched. I was usually on the bench, and when I went in, in the later innings, it was always in right field. But I loved the game enough to stay with it.

I also enjoyed swimming and, occasionally, bowling, when I could round up some friends after the baseball game to go to the nearby alley. They had smaller bowling balls for children. The task of setting up and sweeping the pins and returning the balls was done by a crew of black boys, not much older than I, who sat on a small platform with their legs dangling just above the pins.

To get to El Yacht on my own I walked two blocks to Quinta Avenida and hopped on a public bus that ran west along Quinta for about three miles directly to the door of El Yacht. It was not unusual for me, or for Havana boys of my same age, to wander unaccompanied beyond their immediate neighborhood. On my Schwinn bicycle, I would pedal on the sidewalks of a well-sized swath of Miramar, going as far as La Copa, Miramar's largest shopping area.

Despite the exclusiveness of El Yacht, there was never any need for me to present identification at the front door. The two uniformed doormen, longtime employees, could somehow distinguish members from non-members. Privacy on the ocean side of the club was secured by twin piers that flanked the property, running from the beach out to the sea for about one hundred yards. The piers were massive and made of concrete, with a lower level that had arches secured to the ocean floor and a level above it that served as a wide promenade and sitting area covered by awnings. Pacing along that promenade one could always find the paunchy, middle-aged, and well-tanned *Sargento*, a reputedly former member of the Cuban navy who wore the semblance of a naval uniform and cap as he stood at the ready to shoo away with his gruff voice any intruders from the neighboring beaches.

On many a Saturday during the summers I was invited to have lunch with Oscar and Nancy in the club's main dining room. On those days I would take to El Yacht a bag with a nice change of clothes, and after baseball or swimming, I showered in the boys' locker room, dressed, combed my hair, and made sure I was in the restaurant by 1:00 p.m. At that time, Oscar entered the restaurant from the adjoining bar carrying a glass with a fresh shot of Pinch Scotch. My grandmother Nancy met us there from wherever she happened to be socializing with her friends, and we were reverentially shown to our table by Rufino, the tuxedoed and haughty maître d'. It was always the same table, in the corner of the room by the open doors that led to the terrace. It was the best table in the restaurant, and that was no accident. Every Christmas, Oscar would give Rufino one hundred pesos (equivalent to one hundred dollars), a gratuity that was no doubt unmatched by any of the restaurant's patrons, most of whom were probably much wealthier than my grandfather. But Oscar insisted on living well and spending the money necessary to do so, especially on something as strategic as the best table in the restaurant at the Habana Yacht Club. He may have been the poorest man in the room, but he always had the best table.

It was a circular table, and I would be seated between Oscar and Nancy, facing the dining room. It was fine dining, with a tablecloth, linen napkins, water goblets, and silver flatware engraved with El Yacht's logo. Oscar valued table etiquette, something he learned from his father Ernesto, and those lunches were opportunities to teach his pliant grandson all the rules: napkin on the lap, good posture, no elbows on the table, no loud conversation. If your grandmother gets up from the table, as well as when she returns, we stand and help her with the chair. Similarly, if a lady approaches our table to greet us, we stand and remain standing. She is going to ask us to please sit down, but we don't, not only because we are not supposed to, but also because if we remain standing she is likely to depart sooner than if we sat.

At those Saturday lunches my order was always the same: a ground beef steak wrapped with a strip of bacon, mashed potatoes, vegetables, and for dessert, flan. Sometime between the main course and the flan, the three of us would get up and walk across the dining room to briefly pay our respects to an elderly couple who always seemed to be there on Saturdays: Tío Carlos and Tía Juanita. Carlos was an older first cousin of my grandfather, the only offspring of Oscar, the brother of Colonel Ernesto, the man who had refurbished that beautiful colonial house in Domínguez Street in El Cerro where before the war Colonel Fonts had met Malila, his future wife and cousin of Uncle Oscar's wife. Oscar was, of course, the namesake of my grandfather, and Tío Carlos was named after his uncle Carlos, the autonomist and lifelong bachelor who was a brother of Oscar and Ernesto. In turn, Tío Carlos was the namesake of my own uncle Carlos, my mother's younger brother. It could be confusing.

Tío Carlos and Tía Juanita, who had no children, always sat by themselves at the same table, which was probably reserved for them by Rufino not because Tío Carlos gave him as generous a gratuity as Oscar gave Rufino, but because he was the President of the board of directors of the Habana Yacht Club. Carlos had a reputation, at least with my grandfather, for being tight with his money. "He has a lot more money than his father had," Oscar once explained to me during lunch in a hushed voice, "because of his marriage to Juanita, who inherited all her family's considerable fortune." Yet Carlos led a miserly life, almost never leaving that drafty old house in El Cerro. Of Carlos's father, Oscar, my grandfather would say, "Now *that* one knew how to live: a fine dresser, lavish vacations in Europe, membership in all the leading social clubs, the latest automobiles . . ." My grandfather, of course, was referring to his uncle Oscar. That well-lived life that my grandfather admired ended abruptly in 1931 when Uncle Oscar shot himself in the head with a small pistol in that beautiful house. The dispatch from Havana for the *New York Times* attributed the suicide to an incurable illness.[1] The story that was told in my family is that after extensive dental work he suffered such intolerable pain that he lost his mind and, in a fit, reached for a gun in his desk drawer and shot himself in front of his wife.

TITI-BILLIE AND BERNARDO

My grandfather Oscar was not the only one with interesting books in his house. My great-aunt Isabel Boullosa, the sister of my grandmother Nancy, also had plenty of books and many other interesting things. I did not see her frequently, but my occasional day-long visits to her house were unforgettable. I looked forward to them, and she enthusiastically welcomed me for the same reason Oscar spent time with me: I marveled at every story she would tell and the things she would show me.

Everyone in the family called Isabel "Billie," and my mother called her "Titi-Billie." She was a petite woman in her early fifties, not attractive, but vivacious, and she always seemed to speak with an excited tone. Titi-Billie lived in an old house in Vedado with her husband, Bernardo, a surgeon, and their youngest son, a teenager who was called Sonny (pronounced in Spanish SOH-nee). To this day, I don't know if that was his real name. Their house was cluttered and rapidly deteriorating, but they seemed oblivious to the disorder and decay. They lived a bohemian existence; home maintenance was not their forte, and I never saw any servants in the house. It was in that house that I had my most intense exposure to that surrealism that has always characterized so much of Cuban existence, a magical world that defies belief. Recounting it here would appear to be a work of fiction.

My father would drop me off at Titi-Billie's house in the morning and pick me up late in the afternoon. Upon entering it, I was greeted in the living room by a large polar bear rug, complete with the head, its mouth set in a roar. On the wall above it were two oil paintings, one of Titi-Billie when she was a young woman and the other of a bullfighter, reputedly her oldest son, Bernardo Jr. (simply called Junior), who lived in Spain and was, indeed, a bullfighter.

I would spend most of the day with my great-aunt in her studio, a windowless den off the living room that was lit only by a couple of lamps that shone over desks filled with books and papers. It was there that Titi-Billie, fluent in both English and French, was engaged in her interminable life project: translating into Spanish the complete works of Marcel Proust. She would tell me what a great writer Proust was but that I should wait a few years to read him. Titi-Billie also wrote poems, and she would read them to me. Some were in print, and that impressed me.

In one corner of her studio, leaning on a chair, was a large pedal harp, leftover from the days the four Boullosa sisters formed a quartet and played for their parents. Unlike her sister Nancy, who had abandoned the piano, Titi-Billie continued to play her instrument. She would move over to the corner, sit on the chair, lean the harp on her lap and shoulder, and regale me with a passionate performance of a classical composition, her eyes fervently closed as her fingers glided gracefully across the strings. We had our routines. Sometime during the day, I would invariably say, "Titi-Billie, dance the Charleston!" She would place a 78 rpm disc on an ancient record player and would move her feet as lithely as when she was a young woman in the Havana parties she attended with her sisters. My grandmother Nancy always said that of all her sisters, Titi-Billie was by far the best dancer.

I was fascinated by it all, and time would fly in that old Vedado house. More than once, Titi-Billie would suddenly realize, horrified, that it was almost time for me to be picked up and she had not served me lunch. Sonny would be summoned from his room, where he usually spent the entire day, given a few coins, and dispatched to the Chinese takeout down the street for some fried wontons.

My life was ordered and predictable, but the days at Titi-Billie's house were wonderfully chaotic, giving me a glimpse into a life seemingly unencumbered by the quotidian and devoted instead to intellectual pursuits, literature, and the arts, all with the touch of magic imparted by my great-aunt's eccentricities. But Titi-Billie was not the only eccentric in the household. Her husband, Bernardo, contributed in his own way to the house's charm.

Bernardo Diez-Burgos was a surgeon wholly dedicated to his profession. He was frequently not in the house when I visited because he worked long shifts at Havana's largest public emergency hospital. His passion was trauma surgery, and he would sometimes recount in gory detail some of his most memorable emergency surgeries. He was short and stocky, with a full head of silver hair and a round face with a ruddy complexion. Tío Bernardo exuded contrariness and always seemed to speak loudly, frequently shouting, a habit perhaps acquired from commanding emergency room staff. Titi-Billie was frequently a target of his loud outbursts, usually when he would return home tired from a long shift only to find that there was no meal waiting for him while his wife was absorbed in Proust. Titi-Billie, of course, was unperturbed and oblivious to his reprimands. It was as if she did not hear him at all. I sensed that their marriage had long been over and that they merely coexisted in that house, each pursuing their different passions.

Despite his gruff demeanor, Bernardo was always available to everyone in the family for medical emergencies, big or small. If I was going through a bout of vomiting and diarrhea, my mother would immediately call her uncle, and Bernardo would show up at our house with a large glass jug filled with a clear liquid, tubing, a needle, and a small wooden board and bandages to immobilize my arm, which I could not move for hours until the jug drained completely into my veins. I am sure that my mother's concern was rooted in the memory of her little brother Oscarito dying of dehydration from an uncontrollable bout of gastroenteritis. Bernardo had his own memories of a daughter, about Oscarito's age, who also died of the same devastating ailment. Although I was born in the age of antibiotics and Bernardo prescribed them, both he and my mother had learned to take no chances with symptoms that had so swiftly taken those two children. I have always wondered how those tragic deaths, many years before I was born, must have changed the lives of my grandparents Oscar and Nancy and the lives of Bernardo and Titi-Billie.

Bernardo performed all surgeries on members of my family. He was apparently a believer in surgery as the first recourse for treatment. If any one of us had a lingering intestinal disorder, Bernardo would summon them to his operating table and remove their appendix, even if it had not been the cause of the ailment. We didn't need it anyway, he reasoned, and all it can do is give us trouble. Besides, the operation was free. I can't think of a single member of my mother's family who was alive at that time who managed to keep his or her appendix, including me.

Bernardo's drastic medical remedies were not limited to surgeries. When as an adolescent his son Sonny seemed to have developed a sideways tilt in his head and shoulders, his father determined that the problem originated in a clavicle that needed to be straightened, so he placed Sonny's head and shoulders in a hard plaster cast, leaving only his face uncovered. The poor boy was a sight. At a time when American science fiction had spread to Cuba, with tales of Martian invasions, Sonny apparently decided to make the best of it by attaching a small antenna above his head. I don't know how long he was in the cast, but I do remember that when he showed up at my birthday party in El Country, my friends stared at him wide-eyed.

On those days when he was home and not on duty at the hospital, Bernardo relaxed in a woodworking shop he had set up in the garage, away from Titi-Billie and Proust. One day he managed to cleanly sever the little finger of his left hand with an electric saw. The cut was so swift that he did not realize what had happened until the finger was completely detached. As expected of a trauma surgeon, he calmly applied himself a tourniquet, cleaned and bandaged the wound, and then looked around on the floor amid the sawdust for the finger. After rinsing it, he placed it in a glass of water. As he headed for his car with the glass in hand, he yelled to Titi-Billie, who may or may not have heard him, that he was going to the hospital. The reattachment attempt by his colleagues was unsuccessful. This happened before I was born; I always remember Bernardo with a stumpy little finger. He would tell me that even with nine fingers he was a better surgeon than those eminent colleagues of his who only operated on wealthy patients in private hospitals.

Bernardo was an unrelenting critic of private medical practice in Cuba and the inequalities in the availability of medical care. He was true to his principles, never establishing a private practice and devoting all his time to the public emergency hospital, where medical care was free.

During one of my visits to Titi-Billie's house, I wandered off by myself and spotted in a corner of the house's courtyard what looked like a small automobile covered with a cloth tarp. The tarp was dirty and full of leaves. Curious, I took the tarp off and discovered an MG Roadster. Much of it was rusted, and the leather seats were cracked and torn. I climbed in and was having a great time pretending to be in an auto race when Titi-Billie rushed toward me, scolding me for sitting in the car. As soon as I climbed out, she immediately covered it with the tarp and admonished me never to go near it again. It was the only time I ever saw her upset, and I was sorry I had caused her some obvious distress.

When I got home that day I told my mother about the incident. Nancy reluctantly recounted the story of the MG, a story that explained why Bernardo Jr. was living in Spain. About three years before, when he was about twenty years old, Junior was driving the car on Twenty-Sixth Avenue toward the traffic circle in front of the Havana Zoo. As he rounded the circle, he ran over a girl, about twelve years old, who died instantly. The child, who was mentally handicapped, was apparently so excited about visiting the zoo that she broke free from her parents' grasp and ran into the street, directly into the path of the MG. The police investigation into the incident, presented at a court hearing, absolved Junior of any fault. The girl's father, however, maintained that Junior was speeding and that he was being cleared of responsibility because he was from a well-to-do family. At the hearing, he threatened to avenge his daughter's death. Bernardo immediately shipped Junior off to Spain where, after working a few odd jobs, he did indeed become a bullfighter. After the accident, the MG was retired to the courtyard and covered, never to be driven again.

CHRISTMAS

Christmas was a big deal at the house on G Street. My aunt Gisela handled all the arrangements in the big house in Vedado, taking advantage of the high ceilings to put up a very tall Christmas tree in one corner of the foyer, facing the entrance. In one of the living rooms she would labor for weeks, starting in November, to construct on a row of tables against the walls a rambling nativity scene that took up the entire room, an extravaganza with dozens of figurines (shepherds, lambs, peasants, donkeys, angels, the Three Kings and their camels, Joseph, Mary, and Jesus) carefully arranged on a faux landscape of rocks, trees, lakes, a waterfall, and a starry blue sky, with the stable, of course, in the center. Friends and neighbors were invited to drop by and view the completed masterpiece, which Gisela tried to keep fresh by making some modifications to the previous year's scene.

We had a simple nativity scene in our apartment in Miramar. My mother put all her effort into decorating the Christmas tree. We always bought our tree in the nearby grocery store, El Bickford, located just on the other side of the small park on the corner of our block. The trees, of course, were imported from the United States. Although my brother and I were supposed to help, Nancy usually took on the project singlehandedly, and the day the tree was delivered from El Bickford, usually three weeks or so before Christmas, she would not go to bed until she had finished decorating it. Victor and I would wake up the next morning to a completely dressed tree. My mother was a perfectionist in everything she did, and the tree was always flawless. The intermittent lights covered the tree uniformly, the balls were always hung in just the right places, and every branch, even the smallest twig, had a few carefully placed thin aluminum "icicles." Nancy learned to decorate the tree from her father. The tree in our Miramar apartment always looked similar to the one Oscar would put up, also singlehandedly, in one corner of the living room in El Country, next to the brick wall. He also used aluminum icicles.

It was in the Miramar apartment that Victor and I would find on Christmas morning the presents from Santa Claus. Virtually all the kids we knew also received their presents from Santa Claus. We were aware that other children in Cuba, and in other countries, received presents from the Three Kings on the morning of the Feast of the Epiphany, January 6. But our parents, eager to dispel any expectation of double-dipping when it came to holiday presents, explained that the Kings delivered presents only to poor boys and girls, because those children had not gotten anything from Santa.

The year before Santa left me the Schwinn bicycle under the tree, he brought me a *carriola*, a scooter, the type with handles on a vertical pole perpendicular to a flat board with wheels underneath, on which you place one still leg while you propel yourself with the other leg pounding the pavement, not unlike the devices that are used today in many cities and campuses to get around. Mine was a flaming *carriola*, made of a brightly colored metal, with plastic handles and rubber white-walled wheels. It looked great, although it took quite a bit of legwork to build up some speed. One day, as I pushed my *carriola* on a well-paved side street in the nearby neighborhood of Almendares, a working-class neighborhood not far from my house, a group of shirtless dark-skinned boys whizzed by me in their own *carriolas*, looking back at me with triumphant, almost mocking grins. They had the fastest *carriolas* I had ever seen, made with two rustic boards and a wooden handle, all nailed together somewhat haphazardly but with ball-bearing wheels, probably taken from old roller skates, attached to the bottom of the horizontal board. In seconds, they disappeared down the street. Those *carriolas* were obviously not presents from the Three Kings, and certainly not from Santa, but they were a lot faster than my fancy scooter.

The Christmas routine was always the same every year. A couple of days prior to Christmas, my mother would start the preparations for the *Nochebuena* meal, the Christmas Eve dinner. That dinner was held at the home of Oscar and Nancy in El Country, usually a small Fonts family affair with a few guests. My mother would cook all the dishes in our apartment in Miramar, and then early in the evening of December 24, we would carefully place them in our Buick and transport them to El Country. There was roast pork, black beans, white rice, yuca smothered in *mojo*, and fried plantains. Drinks and desserts were up to Oscar. The aroma in the Buick during that twenty-minute drive was unforgettable. The black beans were the mainstay of the menu. Their preparation took three days, and my mother followed the recipe Oscar had taught her, the recipe that had reputedly been developed by his father, Colonel Fonts. My mother in turn taught me the recipe, and I have cooked them every *Nochebuena* for the past forty or so years. The recipe and its story are in the appendix to this book.

Arriving at the home of Oscar and Nancy on Christmas Eve was like walking into an American Christmas card: the tree, stockings hanging on the mantel of a lit fireplace, Bing Crosby or Nat King Cole or Rosemary Clooney singing Christmas favorites on the High Fidelity record player, and my grandfather Oscar making eggnog. Only the language spoken and the food gave away that the scene may not be taking place in the United States. Around the tree were the presents for Victor and me from the Fonts family, but they could only be opened after dinner.

On Christmas Day, after opening the presents from Santa Claus in our apartment, we would head to G Street for lunch with all the uncles, aunts, and cousins. There were wrapped gifts for all the children under the huge tree, gifts that Gisela had purchased. Gise was always very practical, so she would always give us clothes, much to our collective disappointment. Except for the decorations and the presents, the Christmas Day lunch was not much different than the usual Sunday lunches at G Street.

It was around Christmastime that we would pay a visit to Kela, who was cloistered at the Sacred Heart school. By the time I was old enough to remember those visits, the nuns had already moved the school to a beautiful building in El Country, only a few blocks away from the Fonts residence and not far from Lafayette. It was a massive, rambling structure, at least three stories high, with open balconied corridors surrounding internal patios.

My visits to Kela were always filled with apprehension. Upon our arrival, the nun at the door would summon Kela, and we would be shown into a seating area next to the entrance foyer with open doors that faced the interior of the building. We could see Kela coming from quite a distance down the corridor, and she was a frightful sight for a small boy: completely covered in a flowing black habit from the top of her head down to just barely above her laced black booties. Her hands and her face, tightly framed by a starched white fabric, were the only indications that inside that black specter was a human being. Kela was always

The grandchildren of Lisandro and Amparo at a birthday party, Havana, July 1955. Seated on the floor, left to right: Rafael (Humberto's oldest); Rubencito (Rubén's youngest); Carlos (Humberto's second); and my brother, Victor. I am standing at the left, and Martica (Lalo's oldest) is standing in front of me. Sitting in the center are Mara's daughters, Raquel Zita and Marita, with the former holding Hilda María (Mayía, Lalo's youngest). Standing at right is Cristy (Rubén's oldest), and standing in front of her is Héctor (Humberto's youngest). In subsequent years, eight more cousins were born, children of Lalo, Sergio, and Letty. Pérez family collection.

enthusiastic and energetic, so she practically galloped down the corridor toward us, her habit and the long rosary attached to her waist both swaying rhythmically from side to side. I was the first one she would go to, her face moving closer to mine until she was grabbing the sides of my head and planting a kiss on my forehead, all the while expressing surprise, in her booming voice, at how big I had grown since she last saw me.

When I was older and already in school and no longer intimidated by her appearance, I nevertheless continued to be apprehensive about going to see her. Tía Kela was disappointed that, with the pretext of having me learn English, my father enrolled me in Lafayette and not in a Catholic school. During our visits, she would insist that I speak to her in English, as a way of testing if attending the secular American school was worth the loss of a religious education. Since she was fluent in the language, any error or hesitation on my part was met with a quick disapproving glance toward my father, who was unmoved by his sister's admonishments, unlike my mother, who cringed at any sign of displeasure from Kela. Tía Kela was already a nun and a teacher at Sacred Heart during the years Nancy attended the school, so Kela remained for my mother an authority figure, to be defied only at one's peril. Even years after marrying my father, it never occurred to my mother to treat Kela with the familiarity of a sister-in-law. Anyway, my mother probably agreed with her that I should have been in a proper Catholic school, like Belén or La Salle.

HOLLYWOOD

I am sure that no child my age in the United States saw as many American movies as I saw in Havana in the 1950s. My parents were fans of Hollywood, but they differed in the genres they liked, so they rarely went to the movies together. My father liked war and Western movies, so those are the ones I saw when he would take me to the theaters that tended to show them: the Trianon and the Rodi on Línea Avenue in Vedado or the Acapulco in Nuevo Vedado. Those movie outings with my father were less frequent, however, than the ones with my mother, who never passed up an opportunity to see an American musical.

Moviegoing with my mother was usually a day-long affair on any weekday I did not have school. In the morning, we would take a taxi from a stand a block away from our apartment that would take us to the bustling center of Havana. That section of the city, now called Centro Habana, was the principal shopping district, full of the modern department stores that had sprung up in the 1940s and 1950s emulating their counterparts in the United States. The largest and most upscale of all was El Encanto, inspired by Macy's in New York. Its multiple floors, connected by escalators and elevators, was the mecca of consumerism in Havana. It even replicated Macy's original centralized cashier system, with pneumatic tubes containing customer payments that were sent to a central room where all the money was handled. It was in El Encanto where I would go with my mother to buy the uniforms for the upcoming school year.

During these outings, purchases were usually minimal. My mother was mostly a window-shopper. Typically, these excursions were just opportunities for her to get out of the house. I always accompanied her because she would not have ventured alone into the city. She was young, tall, fair, and pretty and would have attracted quite a bit of unwelcomed attention from men, especially along the wide covered sidewalks that bustled with foot traffic and vendors of all types. And it would have been totally unseemly of her to have ventured into a movie theater by herself, even in the middle of the day. I was aware that in many ways I was her bodyguard, her protection from if not all *piropos*, at least from the more aggressive or suggestive lines or approaches that would have been inappropriate to direct at a mother with her child.

By lunchtime we had found our chrome stools at the soda fountain counter at the Woolworth's across from El Encanto. The Cubans called the store "el ten-SEN," a corruption of "ten-cent," derived from the Woolworth's five-and-dime marketing phrase. The Woolworth counter was identical to those in American cities. I would usually order an Elena Ruth, presumably named after the lady who invented it in Cuba: a sandwich with ham, cream cheese, and strawberry preserves on a sweet roll. I would down that with a vanilla shake.

After lunch, it was movie time, a marathonic undertaking. I do not know what the practice was at that time in movie theaters in the US, but in Cuba, one would get for the price of admission a lesser movie (a *relleno* or filler), cartoons, the newsreel, and then, finally the feature presentation. It was a full afternoon affair.

The musicals I saw with my mother that are foremost in my mind are the classic *Singing in the Rain*, *The Glenn Miller Story*, *Rose Marie*, and *The Eddy Duchin Story*, the latter with Tyrone Power and, most memorably for me, Kim Novak. Nancy would always buy at the theater's concession stand the ten-inch vinyl record of the movies' soundtracks, which I would replay countless times at home on the Philips Hi-Fi.

FROM A CLASSROOM WINDOW

In the early afternoon of Monday, October 29, 1956, we were taking turns in my third-grade class reading aloud in English about maple syrup in Vermont. For a Cuban child, it was one of the most exotic chapters in our geography textbook, illustrated with color photographs of a father and son in heavy coats and with pails in hand, trudging from tree to tree across a snowy landscape, emptying the contents of cans attached to the trunks of trees. Our teacher, a thirtyish tall and slender American woman with somewhat disheveled light brown hair, followed along in her book, occasionally correcting a reader's pronunciation as she absentmindedly stroked the heads of her students as she paced up and down the aisles between the school desks.

That school year the third graders met in my favorite classroom at the old Lafayette School on Quinta Avenida in Miramar (the last year before the move to La Coronela). It was a second-floor corner classroom with tall windows that allowed the room to be flooded with the light of the afternoon sun. I always sat near the window so that I could let myself daydream as I gazed out over the traffic on Quinta. On that October day something besides sunlight came in through that window: the beginning of the end of the Cuba I knew.

At first, the noise could have been just a series of backfires from a motorcycle or car. But as the loud popping sounds continued and intensified, it was clear that we were hearing something we had not heard before. We could tell the sounds were not originating in the vicinity of

My third-grade class at Lafayette, Quinta Avenida, Miramar, 1956–57. I am seated on the floor, the last one on the right. Lafayette School Yearbook.

the school, but they were not coming from far away. They were not faint echoes but distinct staccatos. The reader stopped reading. We all looked at the teacher, who had raised her head and eyes from the textbook and was looking around the classroom and beyond the window, apprehensively. A tingle went up my spine. Calmly, the teacher asked those of us near the window to move to the other side of the classroom and sit on the floor. The sounds multiplied. After several minutes, someone from the office came up (perhaps Mr. de Berly), asked us to form a single file line, and led us down the main staircase to the large reception area on the first floor, where all the doors had been closed and the windows shuttered. We were joined there by the other students who were also in the classrooms on the exposed side of the building. We all sat on the floor and waited for the sounds to end, a wait that seemed endless. After that, we were picked up by our parents, and we went home.

The incident started my career as an avid news consumer. That evening, I joined my father and mother in front of the radio to find out what had happened. We talked about it. The following day, I scoured the newspapers that arrived at the house. Something was going on, and it had scared me, and I wanted to know all about it. Whatever was happening in Cuba, it was now happening to me.

The story behind the gunshots started the previous Sunday, the twenty-eighth. Up until then, Havana had experienced few incidents of political violence, even though Fulgencio Batista had already been ruling (unconstitutionally) for almost five years. Back in 1953, Fidel Castro and his group had attacked the military barracks in Santiago, in eastern Cuba, far from Havana. They were subsequently imprisoned and later released as part of a general amnesty. In 1956, Castro and his group were in Mexico, organizing the expedition that would land in eastern Cuba later that year, in December. Havana was relatively quiet.

That Sunday in October, however, marked the beginning of a violent campaign to oust Batista centered on the capital and carried out by university students. To accomplish their goal, they took a page from the playbook of a prior generation of students who had been successful in ousting the dictator Gerardo Machado in 1933: sporadic acts of violence, especially the assassination of top officials of the regime, with the intention of fomenting chaos and destabilizing the government. That Sunday night, two students wearing sports jackets, which concealed the guns tucked into their belts, arrived at the Montmartre Cabaret and Casino in Vedado with the intention of assassinating a close friend and adviser to Batista who was a habitual gambler and a regular at the casino. But the intended victim did not show up. The two disappointed would-be assassins were leaving the casino when an elevator door opened and they came face-to-face with Colonel Antonio Blanco Rico, the head of Batista's military intelligence services. Not wanting to waste the evening, the students took out their guns and fired into the elevator, killing the Colonel and injuring three of his companions, two of them women, before fleeing from the scene and disappearing into the Havana streets.

The brazen attack shocked the capital, and the security forces launched a citywide dragnet. The following morning, a group of armed men, sought by the government for their political activities, entered the Haitian embassy seeking political asylum. The police immediately assumed the group included the two assassins (it did not). The Police Chief decided to storm the embassy around two in the afternoon that day, Monday the twenty-ninth, just when we were reading about maple syrup in Vermont. The Haitian embassy was located on Seventh Avenue, on the same city block as our school on Fifth Avenue. Ten people were killed, including the Police Chief who had led the attack.

After that, the shootings and bombings became more frequent. I followed it all closely in the newspapers and on the radio. My parents repeatedly admonished me to stay away from any packages in public places. I developed a heightened political consciousness, an apprehension about my safety, and a keen awareness of my surroundings. Perhaps this is why I have such sharp memories of that time in my life. It may also be why I have always eyed with suspicion abandoned packages and disliked the sound of fireworks.

That same school year, a little more than four months after the attack on the Haitian embassy, I was still assigned to the same desk by the large window of the second-floor corner classroom at Lafayette. It was a Wednesday, March 13, 1957, just after lunchtime. I don't remember what we were covering in class, and I did not hear any shots, but I knew something was going on when I spotted through the window a convoy of military trucks filled with soldiers speeding down Quinta Avenida toward the center of the city. I surmised they were coming from the Columbia military garrison, which was located just beyond the Miramar suburb.

I turned on the radio as soon as I got home. It was another armed attack, but this time by the university students who had decided to try to assassinate Batista by storming the heavily guarded Presidential Palace. It was a full-fledged assault on a building in the center of the city, too far for the shots to be heard in Miramar. Another group of students had taken over the twenty-four-hour radio news station and transmitted an announcement that Batista had been killed. But he had not been killed. The assailants had made their way to his third-floor office before they were repelled by the army and police.

The Havana press I read at home, especially the weekly magazine *Bohemia*, featured photographs of the carnage: young men lying on the streets in pools of blood. My great-uncle Bernardo, the trauma surgeon and husband of Titi-Billie, happened to be on duty at the hospital where most of the wounded were taken, especially the bystanders caught in the cross fire. "I got to sew together a woman's liver," he told me, gleefully. Bernardo enjoyed his work immensely. It was a red-letter day for him.

In the days that followed, the security forces hunted down the students who had survived the attack. In one notable incident, the police stormed an apartment where four of the leaders had been hiding, killing all of them on the spot. Again, the press printed all the gruesome images. I remember one picture in *Bohemia* that showed a police officer standing next to a blood-covered stairway in the apartment building.

The failure of the attack on the palace decimated the anti-Batista student movement. The assassinations and acts of sabotage in the capital continued, however, eventually carried out by an urban underground movement linked to Fidel Castro and his group, which had established an armed foothold in the eastern mountains.

VEDADO APARTMENTS

The turmoil of 1957 was mirrored in the unsettling transitions that both the Pérez and Fonts households experienced that year. It was the year when both families would move out of the houses I had always known.

The move out of the house on G Street was inevitable. Once Leticia, the youngest, married, followed by Sergio a few months later, the remaining residents of the house were Mara, her two daughters, and my two aunts who remained unmarried, Gise and Watty. A house built for a family of twelve was clearly now too large. The decision was made to rent out the house and for my aunts and cousins to move to a spacious four-bedroom, two-bath apartment they found on Twenty-First Street between L and M Avenues, in what had become the heart of Vedado. Just a block away, the imposing thirty-story Havana Hilton Hotel was under construction, next to the complex that housed Cuba's principal radio and television stations. The apartment was on the top floor of a modest four-story building built in the 1930s.

Initially the house was rented to the Spanish embassy to serve as the residence of the ambassador. The next tenant was a private school whose director saw the practicality of a floor plan with all rooms opening to a central hallway.

The house on G Street was rented unfurnished, so on an agreed-upon day and time, all the children of Lisandro and Amparo, except for Kela, met at the house to divide up the furnishings in a sort of round-robin process. Each of the nine siblings would take turns, by age order (the oldest first), selecting an item and going through as many rounds as necessary until all the possessions of their parents had been distributed and the house stood empty. My mother remembered what her father had told her after that dinner between the in-laws in 1947, and she advised her husband to prioritize the two paintings by Armando Menocal: "The most valuable things in that house," Oscar had said. Tano snatched up the two paintings (they were grouped as a lot) in the first round.

The dispersing of the furnishings was a sad affair, dismantling a house that had been the bedrock of the family for nearly thirty years and the most evident representation of the fruits of Lisandro's lifelong work ethic. There was little left now of his financial legacy, except for the rent from the house and other assets that easily dissipated with so many heirs. The company that he built had long ago been sold to General Cigar.

Mara and Gisela insisted on continuing the tradition of hosting the Sunday lunches, but they were not quite the same in the new apartment. My rowdy younger cousins had limited space in which to play, and the political arguments between the siblings seemed louder in the smaller living room. We all missed the house on G Street.

As the violence in the capital intensified, my grandfather Oscar did not feel the family was safe living in the relatively isolated exurbs. He was probably also growing tired of the commute. The house in El Country was sold in late 1957, and the family moved to a brand-new apartment on First Avenue, between A and B Streets, right on the Vedado waterfront. Unlike the apartment in the older and shorter building that the Pérez sisters had just occupied, the Fonts apartment was in one of the new-generation luxury high-rise buildings that sprouted up in the 1950s in Vedado to accommodate the demand for housing in what had become Havana's most desirable area. With the addition by midcentury of movie theaters, restaurants, stores, and hotels, Vedado in effect became the center of modern Havana, and the burgeoning upper levels of Cuban society wanted to live there, creating the demand for upscale apartments. The modern residential towers mingled in the same city blocks with the stately mansions that had been built decades earlier when Vedado was created as an upper-class suburb. In order to build on the relatively small lots in what had been originally planned as an area for single-family homes, the new apartment buildings were narrow towers with upwards of a dozen floors, typically with one apartment per floor. Taking advantage of Vedado's waterfront location, most of the towers had balconies with ocean views.

The apartment building that Oscar and Nancy moved into was larger than most in Vedado, an impressive fifteen-story structure with four residential towers connected at the lobby and uppermost levels. Imitating condominium development in the United States, the building offered amenities on the upper floors: a rooftop pool, a bar, a game room, and spaces for social events. The lobby had a luxurious look, pushing gaudy, with polished black marble on the floor and walls. It housed upscale stores and even a small theater. The lobby was large enough to serve as a showroom during the building's inauguration for several models of the latest to come out of Detroit: the Ford Edsel. The ill-fated automobile made a splashy appearance in Havana at the same time as in the major markets in the United States, and the capital city's expanding upper and middle classes were always eager to snap up whatever was the latest consumer trend to come from the north. Our next-door neighbor in Miramar bought one and showed me all its innovative accessories, such as push-button transmission.

Oscar and Nancy's apartment had three bedrooms, a large living and dining area, and occupied the entire twelfth floor of tower B, one of the two towers facing the ocean. It had a long balcony enclosed with glass jalousies that made a whistling sound on windy days. Gazing out, one could see only the ocean. The building was close to the waterfront, and the apartment was high enough so that one had to look down to see any land at all. The enclosed balcony was a continuation of the living room, which on one side had a long windowless wall. As soon as he moved in, Oscar started on his project for that wall, painting a huge mural with a panoramic view of Mount Fuji in soft pastel colors, with a lake in the foreground and framed by cherry blossoms. It took him several months to finish it.

* * *

The political violence I witnessed was the capstone of a childhood that until that point had been happy and carefree. But it was clear to me that there were changes coming to the life I had known. It was not so much a foreboding as it was uncertainty about the future. Cuba was now entering a period in which one had the sense that anything could happen. Change was coming for sure, but at the time, we had no idea just how drastic and transformative that change would turn out to be.

✳ 14 ✳

NEW YEAR, NEW CUBA

Despite the escalation of the violence throughout 1958 and the uncertainty I felt, on the surface my life continued unchanged: Lafayette, baseball, lunches with my grandparents at El Yacht, Sundays at the new Vedado apartments. But I became acutely aware of what was going on in Cuba. Not only did I immerse myself in the daily press reports, but I closely followed the intensification of the family political discussions. My grandfather Oscar and my uncle Rubén were predictably wary of any political upheaval. My father and his sister Leticia welcomed the possibility that at last a revolution might come to Cuba. I tended to see things as my father did, perhaps because I was captivated by the idealism of young people willing to sacrifice their lives to get rid of a dictator and usher in a new and better society.

Christmas that year was like any other Christmas. My mother cooked the beans and the pork, and Santa Claus still managed to get himself to Cuba. New Year's Eve, however, was not a typical one. Unlike previous years, when my parents went out to celebrate without my brother and me (New Year's was one of the few occasions when my father would accede to my mother's wishes to go out), in 1958, we all went to a family celebration at the home of my great-aunt Consuelo, my grandmother Nancy's youngest sister. She was divorced and living with her daughter Candy in a modern apartment on the Miramar waterfront.

It was a tense evening. As midnight approached, the music on the hi-fi was replaced by the news on the radio that Santa Clara was about to fall to the rebel forces led by Ernesto "Che" Guevara. It was quiet, even somber, in Consuelo's living room. What was supposed to be a festive countdown to the new year was muted by a feeling of apprehension that change was indeed coming, and it was coming not through a negotiated transition, as happened when Machado was deposed in 1933, but through a full-fledged armed conflict that was ominously making its way to Havana. Even for those like my father, who wanted to see the end of Batista's rule, a military confrontation in the capital was a sobering prospect.

But it did not take long to find out there would be no fighting in Havana. The following morning, January 1, I woke up to the sound of the radio coming from my parents' bedroom. I quietly made my way there, found the door open, and peeked in. My parents were sitting up on the bed listening to the excited voices coming from the radio. My father looked up at me and simply said, "The man left." No further explanation was needed. I was not yet ten years old, but I was as politically conscious as any adult. I knew the meaning and import of my father's words.

We spent that entire day at home listening to the radio. Our neighborhood in Miramar was quieter than usual. But in the center of Havana, mobs celebrating Batista's departure roamed the streets, sacking casinos and the homes of known collaborators of the regime, occasionally encountering some pockets of armed resistance from those who supported Batista and had not managed to escape the country. The mobs also took the opportunity to destroy parking meters, which had only been recently installed and were despised by everyone. But the bit of news of that day that captured my imagination was that Boy Scouts were on the streets directing traffic and providing the only semblance of order on the streets. Given the climate of unrest, it was a courageous display of public service, but it was also unsettling to realize that at that moment uniformed boys were the only semblance of order and authority. Batista's sudden departure had created a power vacuum that could only be filled by the rebel forces that were days away from the city. I experienced something I have never experienced since then: the feeling of living in a place where there was essentially no government, no one exercising authority and preserving order.

The only possible stabilizing influence in the country, the rebel army led by Fidel Castro, rolled into Havana on January 8. That night, at the conclusion of his triumphal entry into the city, Castro spoke from a lectern at Camp Columbia. My father and I sat before the television set to see and hear him. White doves fluttered around Fidel and perched on his shoulders. The new leader pledged to embark on the revolution that had long been postponed, the revolution that progressives had advocated for decades, the revolution that would restore power to the people, end corruption, assert Cuban sovereignty, and usher in a new era of peace and justice.

Fidel Castro was not proposing anything other than what my father had always supported: a Cuba for Cubans and the end of injustice, inequality, and corruption. The revolutionary rhetoric that night was neither ominous nor menacing. Advocating for revolution had never been radical in Cuban political discourse. In the nineteenth century, José Martí labeled his movement revolutionary, and generations of leaders that followed him fell woefully short of the ambitious agenda that Martí had established for the Cuban nation. Movements that were said to be revolutionary fell into complacence, corruption, and business as usual, defrauding the people who aspired for true change. But on that January 8, a victorious leader who had just seized power committed himself to the difficult task of making sure that this time it would be different. This time there would be a true revolution. When Fidel finished, I saw something I had never seen before: my father's eyes welled up with tears.

But not everyone in my family welcomed the prospect of a revolution. From the very beginning, my grandfather Oscar and my uncle Rubén, those committed pro-Americans, viewed the new order warily. They knew, as did everyone else in Cuba, that at the top of the agenda of a government that professed to be revolutionary had to be the most sacred of José Martí's tenets: the attainment of sovereignty. The rampant Americanization of the economy and its consequences for the political order had reached a climax in the 1950s, and radically reversing that trend had long been an integral part of Cuban revolutionary discourse throughout the republic. If this was to be a true revolution, then a confrontation was looming.

Although my daily life did not change much, 1959 was an eventful year for me, starting with two new experiences that originated with Oscar and Rubén: my first trip to the United States and my firsthand introduction to the tobacco business.

FLORIDA

During the first few weeks and months following the triumph of the revolution, those who had in any way been associated with the Batista regime left Cuba, including my aunt Mary Lou, my mother's younger sister, and her husband, Eduardo Rodríguez. They had married the year before, when Eduardo was a pilot in the Cuban air force. Although he was a professional career officer, it would be a matter of time before revolutionary tribunals would hold accountable those who had served in the military forces that supported Batista. Since the revolution had not yet affected the long-standing travel connections between the island and the US, Eduardo was able to leave for Miami, and Mary Lou followed him on the regularly scheduled ferry from Havana to Key West, taking with her their 1958 green Ford Fairlane and Mary Lou's dachshund, Chorri.

My mother's other sibling, my uncle Carlos, was already in Florida, sent there by my grandfather Oscar in late 1958 to complete his senior year of high school. Ostensibly, the decision to send Carlos abroad was an academic one. He was such an unruly youngster that he had been expelled or withdrawn from practically every private high school in Havana (he even did a brief stint at Lafayette), and he needed to complete his secondary education. But it was not just Carlos's schooling that Oscar wanted to address by sending him to Florida. In the turbulent climate that predominated during the closing years of Batista's rule, young men were involved in violent activities against the government, and given Carlos's penchant for getting himself into trouble, my grandfather lived in dread that his son would be wittingly or unwittingly swept up in the repression unleashed by the regime. I remember the many times that an anguished Oscar, unable to locate Carlos, would call my mother to see if she had heard from him.

My grandfather called on an old friend, Fred Aufford, with whom he had done business years earlier, and asked him if he and his wife could take in Carlos during the year it would take my uncle to graduate from the local high school. The Auffords lived in Lake Wales, a sleepy town in central Florida with a large retiree population, just the place where my uncle could concentrate on finishing secondary school and staying out of trouble. Carlos enrolled in the all-white Lake Wales High School, where he was the only student in his graduating class with a Spanish surname. Despite his heavily accented English, Carlos seems to have adjusted well to the school. It helped that he was an outgoing and tall eighteen-year-old who had inherited the Catalonian good looks that generations before had enabled the Fonts to marry well. The rhyming quote under his senior picture in the Lake Wales High School yearbook reads, "Every woman's heart grew bigger when she saw his manly figure." Carlos was elected President of the Spanish Club and joined the school's chapter of Future Farmers of America.[1]

I was thrilled when my grandparents Oscar and Nancy invited me to go along with them on a trip to Florida to visit Mary Lou and Carlos during Easter Week, which in 1959 fell in late March. I had never been on a plane or outside of Cuba, and I quickly needed a passport. My father called on an old acquaintance from his Ortodoxo days, Roberto Agramonte, who was the foreign minister in the new revolutionary government. Agramonte, a lawyer and sociology professor, had been the Ortodoxo candidate for President in the never-held elections of 1952. Like so many members of that initial 1959 cabinet who were part of the old political establishment, Agramonte would not last long in his position, eventually exiling himself to Puerto Rico, escaping from the very government he had served and supported. With the newly minted expedited passport my father and I picked up at the ministry, we went to the US embassy, where a relative of my grandfather Oscar who was a US citizen and an employee of the consulate promptly stamped it with a US tourist visa. Revolution or not, things could get done if you knew the right people. I was all set to go to the place that had already been part of my life through my education at Lafayette.

Oscar, Nancy, and I boarded a National Airlines propeller plane at José Martí International Airport for the short flight to Miami. We stayed at the Alhambra Hotel in the downtown area, since there was no room for us in the small studio apartment (known in Miami as an "efficiency") where Mary Lou and Eduardo lived near Hialeah Racetrack, on the (then) outskirts of the city. The Alhambra Hotel was around the corner from that very American icon of the time, a Howard Johnson's restaurant, where we took most of our meals, from American breakfasts to shakes, hamburgers, and club sandwiches. Everything seemed so different, so clean, so American.

Visiting his children was not the only reason Oscar made the trip. In fact, the main purpose may well have been to do what historically many Cubans had done since early in the nineteenth century: protect themselves from the frequently volatile political and economic climate of Cuba by placing funds in a US bank. The day after we arrived in Miami, I accompanied Oscar and Nancy as we walked a couple of blocks to the Pan American Bank, where Oscar opened an account and deposited a sizable portion of his liquid assets. Oscar's misgivings about where Cuba was headed would prove to be financially invaluable to the family.

After a couple of days in Miami, Oscar, Nancy, Mary Lou, Eduardo, the dachshund, and I piled into the Fairlane and headed north on the two-lane

US 27 highway to Lake Wales, about two hundred miles away. The colors of Miami gave way to a bleak landscape with sleazy motels and drive-up burger joints. Only during the last portion of the drive, as we headed into the rolling hills of the citrus belt, did the terrain become interesting, with orange groves only a few feet from the highway. My grandfather took the opportunity to note that, unlike what would happen in Cuba, nobody in the United States would think of pulling the car over to pilfer fruit from the trees. Oscar would never pass up a chance to point out the ways in which he felt that there was greater respect in the US than in Cuba for property rights and political institutions.

We stayed with the Auffords, who had ample space in their rambling midcentury home, located by a small, placid lake complete with a pier and a rowboat, a setting I was not likely to ever see in Cuba. The Auffords themselves were right out of the Norman Rockwell *Saturday Evening Post* covers I had seen in Oscar's house. On the night of Good Saturday we saw Lake Wales's leading annual event: an open-air performance of the Passion of Christ. Despite the depiction of the sufferings of Christ, I saw it as just a play that did not come close to the frightfulness of the Good Friday *Santo Entierro* (Holy Burial) procession that would slowly and mournfully make its way down G Street to the sound of a slow-beating drum. On Easter Sunday we stood around the most important landmark in the Lake Wales area, the Singing Tower in Bok Gardens, a 205-foot-tall carillon that on that day would play a special concert to mark the Christian observance of the resurrection.

The trip to Florida was an incredibly enriching experience for me. The United States, albeit Florida, was now an actual place, not just a world that existed only in the classrooms and textbooks in Lafayette School or in the many interesting things and books in my grandfather's house. To have traveled, even if only for a week, and have acquired a glimpse of that place would prove helpful and reassuring when I embarked on my next trip to the United States; the one that, contrary to expectations, turned out to be a one-way journey.

PLACETAS AND CABAIGUÁN

Just as Oscar was apprehensive about the new order in Cuba, so was my father's brother Rubén, who as President of the General Cigar Company's subsidiary in Cuba started taking precautions to minimize losses should the government eventually move toward confiscating American-owned companies. Early in 1959 Rubén started accelerating the pace of the company's operations. Commitments to buy the crops of the *vegueros* had to be fulfilled, the tobacco had to be at least minimally processed and transported to the warehouse in Havana, and then it all had to be shipped promptly to New York. In the event of the nationalization of the company, there could be no inventory left in the processing plants in Las Villas or in the warehouse in Havana.

I am not sure why, as a ten-year-old, I was sent to Las Villas to "help out" my uncle Rubén during that frenzied summer of 1959. I suspect that my father shared his father's sense that it was a good thing to regularly take one's children out of the orbit of Havana's modernity and consumerism, away from the private schools and social clubs, and expose them to that world with more traditional values and simpler living, the place where our family was still rooted, lest the bright lights of the capital should lead anyone to lose sight that it was the tobacco leaf from the soil of Las Villas that had made everything possible: the house on G Street, the membership in the Habana Yacht Club, the education in the United States. So during the summer of 1959, my usual recreational activities at the yacht club were interrupted by a month-long "internship" in the tobacco business.

I was placed under the supervision of my godfather Lalo, one of my father's brothers. Lalo was a nickname; he was named Baldomero, after Amparo's father. Rubén and Lalo were the only two of Lisandro's sons who by 1959 still worked in the family business. But unlike Lisandro, who made his money with General Cigar on a commission basis, my two uncles were employees of the company, with Rubén heading all the operations in Cuba and his younger brother Lalo reporting to him as the supervisor of many of the operations on the ground in Las Villas. As my grandfather had done, Rubén lived in Havana, making weekly trips to Camajuaní. But Lalo and his family had relocated to the town of Placetas to be closer to the day-to-day operations in the region. It was with Lalo and his wife, Marta, and my two younger cousins, Martica and Hilda María (Mayía), that I lived during my sojourn in tobacco country.

Although Martica and Mayía have recently assured me that their father was quite capable of displaying anger, I never saw that side of my godfather. I remember Lalo as a soft-spoken, easygoing, and reserved man, not in the least argumentative or authoritarian; in other words, he was quite unlike all the other children of Lisandro and Amparo. His wife, Marta, was an engaging and funny lady, with the raspy laugh of a smoker. I felt comfortable in Placetas.

Although Lisandro had chosen Camajuaní as the center of his operations because of its rail connections to Havana and all the towns in the region, Placetas, located about twelve miles to the southeast of Camajuaní, was closer to the region around Zaza del Medio, where many of his best suppliers, including Lisandro Prieto, cultivated their *vegas*. With time, the company's facility located in the nearby town of Cabaiguán grew in importance as it was processing a progressively greater share of the tobacco grown in the region and was upgraded to serve as both an *escogida* and a *despalillo*.

My "internship" was based in Cabaiguán. The days would start in Placetas at five in the morning with a quick breakfast of Kellogg's Corn Flakes, *café con leche*, and buttered Cuban bread, after which Lalo and I would take the Central Highway in his 1957 Nash Rambler for the half-hour drive to Cabaiguán. The first time I walked into the large *escogida* and stemming plant in the town, a group of older *despalilladoras* on the large main floor stopped removing stems from the leaves and got up to greet me with hugs and caresses. They had worked there most of their lives, and they kept saying to each other, "This is the grandson of the old man," as they pointed to a large, framed picture of my grandfather hanging prominently on a wall of the large room, overlooking the rows of women busy at their benches, as if still supervising their work.

I was also greeted with affection by a fiftyish man by the name of Antonio Barquín, who had been hired as a young man by my grandfather and had spent almost his entire life in charge of all the operations at the Cabaiguán facility. As with the Spanish immigrant Higino González, who was Lisandro's manager in Camajuaní, Barquín was one of those lifelong employees in a key position, men on which my grandfather had placed all his trust and was rewarded in turn with unwavering loyalty. It was a business based on noncontractual interpersonal relationships, and Lisandro had built solid ones over many years, from employees to *vegueros*, who retained genuine affection for him, even ten years after his death. As Barquín shook my hand and welcomed me as his newest "employee," I could tell he was visibly moved by meeting the grandson who carried the same name as the old man.

Aside from those moments that served to make me aware of my legacy in that place that seemed so different and far from Havana, what I remember most about Cabaiguán was the pervasive aroma of tobacco and the incessant rain. Not only did I become accustomed to the pungent aroma, but I came to appreciate its different nuances. The rain, however, was another matter. It was not like the afternoon thunderstorms that suddenly swept in from the ocean and drenched Havana for several intense minutes. Rather, it was the unrelenting, day-long drizzle of the rainy season. It was more than an inconvenience, it was a crisis, for it threatened to upend Rubén's tight timetable for the completion of the *escogida*. Every day except Sunday we were scheduled to go out from the town to a different *vega* and pick up the entire crop, which the *veguero* had harvested months before and hung in neat bundles arranged in rows inside his curing house. We would take two trucks, one covered with a canvas to transport the personnel and some supplies, and the other a sort of tractor trailer with side doors in which we would stack the bundles of leaves. To get to the *veguero*'s property, and especially once we entered it, the trucks had to lumber over unpaved roads, and in most cases no roads at all, to get as close as possible to the curing house to efficiently transfer the leaves onto the truck. The rain softened the ground, and there was the danger that the trucks would get stuck in the mud.

The days when the rain would ease a bit and we knew that the *vega* for that day was accessible, we would venture out and do the scheduled work. But on those days when the rain intensified, we would stay in Cabaiguán, and the entire schedule for the *escogida* was pushed back yet another day. Rubén was under a lot of pressure to move the tobacco through the process as quickly as possible. He traveled from Havana and called a meeting in a small house in Placetas that the company owned to house visitors. I remember hearing from the adjoining room raised voices, mostly Rubén's. Lalo came out of the meeting downcast, but the result was that from that day forward we rarely missed going out to the *vegas*, taking greater risks with the trucks and getting ourselves soaked.

The days at the *vegas* were long and labor-intensive. We had to form a line from the curing house, where the bundles had to be unhung and weighed, to the truck, briskly passing the bundles from man to man on the line. Loading an entire *vega* would take us until the early afternoon. Only after all the work was done and the *veguero* was paid according to the set price by weight did we have lunch, which the *veguero*, by tradition, would serve in his home to everyone who had worked that day. Invariably, lunch would be either a whole roasted pig that was slaughtered for the occasion or arroz con pollo. I remember those lunches fondly, usually sitting at the table with the *veguero*'s wife and children and having some of the most delicious meals of my life. But then, it may have been that I was starved almost to the point of faintness; it had been many hours since that early morning breakfast in Placetas. Of course, the day was not finished after lunch. We had to unload the truck when we got back to Cabaiguán.

I especially enjoyed the days when the rain forced us to stay in Cabaiguán because I was given a task that I was told was very important. The floor of the big room was full of women sitting at their desks stemming (*despalillando*) the leaves. The usual routine was for them to pick up a bundle from a window just off the main floor, take it back to their worktables, and destem each of the leaves. When they were finished, they would re-bundle the leaves, place a tag on the bundle that identified the woman who had done the work, return it to the window, and pick up another bundle. The tag was important, of course, because *despalillar* was piecework, remunerated according to the amount produced. The tag also enabled the supervisor to inspect the quality of the work and address any issues directly with the employee.

Normally the women would pick up and drop off the bundles themselves, but since I was available and utterly trustworthy, they were given the option of having me run the errand to and from the window, summoning me by simply raising their hands. The women appreciated the service because it maximized their time. While I was going to and from the window, they could use the restroom or get a snack. They always rewarded me with a sweet smile, frequently with a pat on the head, or a piece of candy or gum, or even better, a kiss on the cheek and a "*gracias, mi amor.*"

On the final day of my stay in Las Villas, my father arrived in Cabaiguán from Havana to pick me up. It was a Saturday, payday, the day Barquín would call out each employee's name and hand her or him a small brown envelope with their pay in cash. The last name he called out, much to my surprise, was mine, the old man's name. The *despalilladoras* clapped and cheered. Inside the envelope were two five-*peso* bills, which I suspect had been contributed by Lalo or my father. It was an immensely proud moment for me.

The visit to Florida gave me a window into what was to be. The visits to Placetas and Cabaiguán gave me a window into what had been, the true foundation of the house on G Street and the family that lived there.

✳ 15 ✳

STAMPS

With the end of that eventful summer of 1959 came the start of sixth grade. Everything appeared unchanged at Lafayette, but it was clear at the very outset of the school year that the world around us was changing. On September 14, students and teachers boarded buses to attend a massive outdoor gathering at the Columbia military complex for a ceremony marking the conversion of the huge garrison into a school, an event meant to signal the new government's commitment to education for all Cuban children. All schools, both public and private, were urged by the government to attend. The de Berlys complied, but I surmised from Mrs. de Berly's expression as she herded us into the buses that she was not pleased with the disruption of the school day and, perhaps even more troubling for her, with the possibility that the new government was going to be hostile to private education as it sought to universalize educational opportunities.

The event seemed interminable. We had to stand in the sun as various government officials spoke, culminating in a speech by Fidel Castro himself in which he urged the assembled students to study "because we have yet to make the revolution . . . you are the ones who are going to do it, but you need to study in order to make the revolution . . . the child who does not study is not a revolutionary."[1]

In that same month of September 1959, during a Sunday visit to Oscar and Nancy's apartment, my grandfather took me aside and said, "Come, I want to show you something." He led me to a piece of furniture in the foyer that had always been a mystery to me. I had first noticed it when it was on the second floor of the house in El Country but had never known what it was. And it was noticeable: a large rectangular wooden chest, about four feet wide, three feet high, and not much more than a foot deep, mounted on four spindled legs, its entire front elaborately carved with the heads of fierce lions. The entire piece stood about six feet high. Oscar told me it was called a *bargueño*. *Bargueños* are intricately carved wooden furniture that for centuries have been manufactured by the skilled craftsmen of the town of Bargas (hence the name) in the region of Toledo, near Madrid.

Intrigued, I watched as Oscar, slowly and somewhat ceremoniously, as if to heighten my curiosity, grasped the small lion heads that were on each side of the lower portion of the chest. As he pulled on them, two square pieces of lumber attached to the lion heads slid out from the chest to a length of about a foot parallel to the floor while remaining rigidly attached to the *bargueño*. He then inserted an old-fashioned skeleton key into the lock located in the top center of the chest, releasing the entire carved front panel that was attached to bottom with hinges. Oscar carefully swung the panel down until it rested on the protruding pieces of wood. I peered inside and saw what looked like a hundred small drawers. The *bargueño* was a secretaire.

Oscar started opening a few of the drawers. Most contained little brown envelopes full of postage stamps. The envelopes had a country's name and a year written on them. Other drawers were crammed with loose stamps, some of which would fall out when you opened the drawer. I had heard Oscar talk about his stamp collection, but I had never seen it. He told me that he had been collecting stamps since he was a boy but had never dedicated any time to organizing them and placing them in albums where they could be displayed. Oscar proposed that I help him do that, that it would be our project. Maybe some other ten-year-old might have thought the proposal a huge bore, but Oscar knew his grandson. I was thrilled.

Every Saturday and Sunday in October 1959 we would meet in his apartment, poring over piles of stamps laid out on the same glass-top dining table where he had taught me to play chess. Using a magnifying glass and tweezers to hold the stamps, Oscar would teach me about perforations, watermarks, color differences, and the many exceptions and imperfections that made a stamp either valuable or next to worthless. Some of the stamps were faded and brittle, from countries that no longer existed. Others were large and colorful. Many were still affixed to a torn piece of envelope. We made little headway in organizing them, usually just placing them back in the same envelope where they had been stored for decades. It seemed like an endless undertaking.

The project with his grandson may have been a way for Oscar to distract himself from the many troubles that were weighing heavily on his mind. Two of his offspring were outside of the country with an uncertain future. Mary Lou was effectively an exile in Miami, and Carlos had enrolled that fall at the University of Florida in Gainesville. Oscar knew that his son was not a dedicated student, so there was no telling how long that would last. Cuba was moving in the direction he had feared, with the state assuming a more authoritarian character marked by a growing anti-American rhetoric. But he was facing his most immediate challenge at the printing press he had managed for many years, P. Fernández y Compañía, the contractor for the printing of government publications, documents, stamps, and lottery tickets. As the new regime moved toward nationalizing many critical aspects of the country's production, control over the printing of official materials had to be a top priority. A government official was assigned to be at the plant, looking over Oscar's shoulder at every aspect of the operation. Oscar was especially distressed by the plan to move the printing presses from the company's plant on Bernaza Street to the building of the Ministry of Communications. He tried to convince the officials that the presses, especially those that printed the stamps, were so delicate that they were originally assembled on-site and that any move would damage them. His objections were overruled, and he was eventually stripped of all authority in the management of the company. It was a humiliating turn of events for him.

When my mother, father, Victor, and I joined Oscar and Nancy in the apartment in Vedado to celebrate my grandfather's fifty-sixth birthday on Saturday, October 31, 1959, he seemed downcast as he recounted all those things that were troubling him. I was successful in lightening his mood by reporting to everyone on our "progress" in organizing the stamp collection. At the end of the evening, Oscar walked us to the elevator and waved goodbye through the small round window on the elevator door.

Three days later, on Tuesday, November 3, just as I was sitting down for dinner with my parents and Victor in Miramar, the phone rang. My brother, as he usually did, rushed to answer it, but he hung up after only a few seconds. "It was just some lady crying," he said. "I couldn't understand what she was saying." The phone rang again. This time my mother answered. She could barely understand what my grandmother Nancy was saying, but when she hung up, she turned to my father and said, "We have to go; something has happened to Papi." Victor and I were left in the care of the maid.

The following morning, my father woke me up to tell me Oscar had died. Victor and I were to get dressed, but not in our Lafayette uniforms. We were not going to school. During the days of the wake and the burial, my brother would be staying with Uncle Rubén and Josie, and I would be spending that time with my aunts Mara, Gisela, and Amparito in their Vedado apartment.

I did not fully assimilate the news until I was dressed and heading out with my father and Victor to our respective destinations. We did not get into our Buick, which had been left with my mother, who had spent the night with my grandmother. Rather, I climbed into the front passenger seat of the Cadillac, Oscar's Cadillac, which my father had driven home sometime during the night. I had sat so many times in that seat as Oscar drove to the many places he would take me, like El Carmelo and La Casa de los Trucos, humming absentmindedly and holding in his right hand both the steering wheel and a cigarette. Not seeing him in the driver's seat made his absence real.

Oscar had arrived from work that Tuesday evening tired, my grandmother recounted later. He was not hungry, so he asked her to fix him a bowl of Cream of Wheat as he headed to the bathroom. My grandfather never came out of that bathroom. He suffered a massive brain hemorrhage.

At fifty-six, he may have been young enough to have survived the problems that besieged him if it had not been, perhaps, for the thousands of cigarettes he had chain-smoked since his teenage years in the Hudson Valley. I had grieved the loss of my grandmother Amparo, but I was much younger when she died. At the age of ten, I could fully weigh the loss of Oscar and understand that he was irreplaceable. I had learned so much from him. I was his favorite pupil, but now that education that I so valued, and still value, had suddenly ended. This early encounter in my life with sudden death, that you could go to the bathroom and not come out, gave me a respect for the fragility of life that I carry to this day. Added to my sense of loss was the realization that my grandfather had left me with an unfinished project.

Carlos traveled from Gainesville for the funeral, but Mary Lou, of course, could not. My grandfather was buried in the Fonts family plot at the Colón necropolis, with his father, mother, his young son Oscarito, and his uncles Carlos and Oscar. After the burial, which I did not attend, I was picked up from my aunts' apartment where I had spent several days, and I joined my mother, my grandmother, and my uncle Carlos in a somber return to the apartment where Oscar had lived and died. Before anyone could live there again, one daunting task had to be done: the bathroom had to be cleaned. There was blood, by this time dry, all over the floor. Carlos immediately took the initiative, and I, as the other male in the group, volunteered to help. We finished quickly, without saying a word.

My grandmother Nancy had lost more than a husband; she had lost her caretaker, the partner who took care of everything, handled every detail of daily living. She had a dependent personality. Emotionally, she became very fragile. This was the third, and most insurmountable, loss in her life. First, her close sister Margot and then Oscarito, her son. My mother took on the task of singlehandedly emptying the apartment and having her mother move into a unit that had just become vacant directly downstairs from us in Miramar.

It was not an easy move. When Oscar and Nancy downsized from the house in El Country, a great number of possessions were stored in a spare room in the Vedado apartment. My mother had to make the decision to dispose of many things. There were boxes and boxes of *National Geographic* magazines and stylish hats my grandmother had worn in the 1920s. And then there was a small trunk, in the back, under all the boxes. It looked old and had rusted hinges. I was there when my mother opened it and gasped. It was full of the clothes of the child that had died nearly thirty years before, all neatly pressed and folded as if ready to use, including the little sailor suit and hat that Oscarito had worn in a photo taken shortly before his death (see p. 171). There was also a teddy bear and a few other toys. My mother never knew of the existence of this trunk, and at that moment she was upset that it had been left up to her to dispose of something so dear, yet something that should have been discarded long ago.

There was something, however, that was not thrown away. Not long after the funeral and before the apartment move was underway, my grandmother gave me the key to the *bargueño* and told me to take everything inside: "Your grandfather meant for you to have that collection. You worked on it." I suddenly had a tremendous sense of responsibility for a valuable legacy. Armed with boxes and manila envelopes, I spent an entire day carefully emptying the *bargueño*. If the many little drawers of the secretaire had given the stamps a semblance of order, all of that was lost, and the collection was now a veritable mess.

I took the stamps home but was not sure what to do with them. I had never seen an organized collection. My mother arranged for me to meet a friend of Oscar, one of Cuba's foremost philatelists, so he could show me his collection. She knew of him because on repeated occasions he had tried to convince Oscar to sell him all those stamps that were now mine. His name was Ricardo Moreyra, and he had a day job as an engineer-architect, but his true occupation was philately. One afternoon, my mother and I arrived at the appointed time at his residence, a beautiful midcentury home in El Country that he had recently designed and built. A servant ushered us to a living room that featured a freestanding terrazzo stairway that led to the second floor. Within minutes, a short balding man in his fifties smoking a pipe descended from the stairway. As soon as he spotted me, Moreyra started laughing heartily. As he approached, he pointed at the ten-year-old in front of him and between laughs asked my mother, "*This* one? *This* is the one who has Oscar Fonts's collection?"

We followed him up the stairway to his study, or rather, to his philatelic temple. It was a beautifully furnished windowless room with, he told us, temperature and humidity controls. There was a large empty wooden table in the center, and one of the walls had a built-in bookcase full of thick albums. Moreyra and I sat at the table while Nancy occupied an easy chair in a corner. The collector started pulling down albums, opening them, and placing them on the desk. They were beautiful. The stamps were meticulously mounted, only a few to a page. He pulled out a magnifying glass from a drawer, and we started making our way through some of the albums as he made observations about the stamps. In many cases, there were what appeared to be duplicate stamps mounted next to each other. He told me to look at them closely. Sure enough, they differed in some minute detail, usually an imperfection that made one stamp rare and valuable and the other of little value. "That is why," Moreyra advised, "you must carefully examine every item in the collection, but especially the Cuban stamps. Your grandfather oversaw the printing of them for many years. I am sure he placed in that collection quite a few imperfectly

printed rare stamps." I left Mr. Moreyra's house both excited and apprehensive. I felt even more acutely the responsibility that I had assumed
when Oscar died.

The next day, my mother and I went to a philatelic store in Centro Habana. She purchased for me a world stamp album that was more than four
inches thick and both volumes of the 1960 edition of *Scott's Stamp Catalog*.
A few days, later a truck delivered a secretaire that my father bought. It was
made of metal, not wood, but was more functional than the ornate *bargueño*. It stood about a foot taller than I, with two lockable double doors in
the front. Inside it had a pull-out work area and many drawers of different
sizes. I was set and threw myself into the task of organizing the collection
of Oscar Fonts.

Although there were many transformations occurring in Cuba in the
first few months of 1960, my immediate world continued unchanged,
except, of course, that there were no more Sunday dinners or Saturday
lunches with Oscar and Nancy. The Sunday lunches at my aunts' apartment were still being held, I was attending Lafayette, and I could still go,
if I wanted, to swim and play baseball on weekends at El Yacht. But I had
no time for leisure. I had a stamp collection to organize. Virtually all my
waking hours outside of school were spent seated in front of my new secretaire, sorting stamps, looking them up in the catalog, and affixing them to
the album. What was especially time-consuming was soaking and separat-
ing the many stamps that were still affixed to torn pieces of envelopes.

My obsession with organizing the stamps distracted me from what was
going on in Cuba. I stopped listening to the news on the radio or reading
the newspapers that arrived daily in the house. Only the most sensational
events managed to catch my attention, such as the March 4 explosion of
La Coubre, a French cargo ship that was being unloaded in Havana harbor. The ship was carrying a huge supply of Belgian-made armaments and
munitions that had been purchased covertly by the Cuban government.
More than eighty people were killed (mostly dockworkers), and about
three hundred others were injured.

I did not hear the explosion. That afternoon, I was far away in an air-conditioned classroom in the new Lafayette building, but the next day the newspapers featured the pictures of the dead and mutilated bodies. It was reminiscent of the days of the anti-Batista struggle. At the funeral for the victims, Fidel Castro delivered a blistering speech blaming the US Central Intelligence Agency for the blast. Pledging that the "revolution will not cower, will not retreat," he used for the first time the words that would become a slogan for the revolution: "¡Patria o Muerte!" (Homeland or Death).[2]

The explosion of La Coubre was an inflection point in the radicalization of both the rhetoric and actions of the government. Henceforth, there was an escalation in the conflict with the United States as well as in the measures intended to assume greater control over the nation's economy and society. The government became increasingly authoritarian. The promised elections were postponed indefinitely. The leadership was committed to bringing about a revolution that would redeem the long-postponed agenda of sovereignty and social justice that José Martí had envisioned for the Cuban nation. That, however, placed the government on a collision course with Washington and, internally, with those at the top of the country's economic and social institutions.

As that process of radicalization started unfolding during 1960, a progressively greater share of the upper sectors of Cuban society became alienated from the pervasive changes the government was implementing. Many who had welcomed the revolution found that at some point those changes crossed the line between the progressive changes they were willing to support and what they considered too radical, radical enough to have, in the Cold War era, the whiff of "communism." Where that line was drawn was different for different people, but when it was crossed, emigration was the typical response.

For my uncle Rubén, who from the very beginning regarded the new order warily, that line was crossed early. As the President of a US subsidiary company in Cuba, he developed an exit strategy that anticipated the nationalization of the company. After that frantic *escogida* of the previous summer in which I had participated, he had a massive inventory in the warehouse in Havana. Early in 1960, he personally sought permission from Ernesto "Che" Guevara, who had been named Economic Minister of the government and President of the National Bank of Cuba, to ship all the tobacco in the warehouse to New York, alleging that it was necessary to make space for an even larger *escogida* later that year. Guevara agreed, perhaps looking ahead to that promised larger inventory that would be available when the government planned to initiate a broad nationalization of almost every sector of the Cuban economy.

It was a ruse. Rubén had no intention of doing another *escogida*. As soon as the last *tercio* of tobacco had been shipped in May to New York, he met with the company's lawyer in Havana to dissolve the General Cigar Company of Cuba. The lawyer looked at him grimly and said, "You will have to leave the country." My uncle already knew that. That night, in the backyard of his house in Miramar, he, Josie, and the children gathered in the backyard around a bonfire and burned the company's records. The following day, Rubén was on a flight to Miami, and Josie and the children followed him the next day. Only my father and mother knew of the plan.

Unlike Rubén, my father had always held nationalistic and progressive views, so he had welcomed the revolution, embracing many of its policies, including the nationalization of US corporations. But the departure of his brother had a demonstrative effect on him. It was one thing to abstractly embrace a political program but quite another to face the possible personal consequences of that program. With Rubén and his family gone and the prospect of a greater radicalization of the regime, it became increasingly apparent to Tano and Nancy that their world was changing in ways that were unpredictable and alarming. Perhaps Oscar had been right: this was "communism," a haunting prospect in a Cold War world. That same month that Rubén left, a leading Havana daily newspaper was closed by the government.

Throughout the summer of 1960 there were growing indications that the world that my parents knew—that I knew—was being dismantled. The nationalization process went beyond just foreign-owned companies and started including Cuban-owned firms. But even more unsettling was the rumor that the government would extend its control beyond the economic sector to the nation's private school system. That raised the specter of state control over family life and "communist indoctrination" of children. Compared to many other families we knew, we had relatively little to lose economically. Even before the revolution, Tano had closed the office of La Internacional on Ayesterán Street and continued the business from an office he set up in one of the bedrooms of our home in Miramar, a rented apartment. We did not have sizable assets or property we stood to lose through the total nationalization of the economy that many feared. But to my parents, Cuba was shaping up to be a place in which one would not want to live.

I was aware, of course, that my parents were contemplating leaving the country. My grandmother Nancy left that summer to join Mary Lou and Carlos in Florida. Through a contact in the cargo business at the Havana airport, my mother had started surreptitiously shipping out to Mary Lou a lot of valuables, such as the two Menocal paintings, silverware, and even pieces of furniture. The political climate in Havana was tensing up in palpable ways. We could hear the marching feet and the shouted orders of a contingent of *milicianos*, the government's new volunteer military units, parading in the middle of the night in the streets of Miramar. My parents always seemed to be in a worrisome mood and evidently chose not to communicate much of their plans to Victor and me so as not to upset us. With increasing tension on the island and in my own home, I became even more focused on the stamps. I buried my head in the piles of stamps and envelopes that Oscar had left me.

The 1960–61 school year opened at Lafayette with an appearance of normalcy; the impending nationalization of private schools had not yet taken place. I was now in *Secundaria Básica I*, the equivalent of seventh grade.

There seemed to be fewer American kids enrolled, but the bilingual and bicultural curriculum, and the school's American atmosphere, remained in place. We even heard the radio broadcast, through the school's public-address system, of the walk-off homer by Bill Mazeroski, in the seventh game of the World Series, that gave the Pirates the title over the Yankees.

Sometime in mid-October, around the time of Mazeroski's homer in Pittsburgh, my parents announced we were leaving the country. Victor and I would go first, followed by my mother a couple of weeks later, and then my father. The priority was to get Victor and me out as soon as possible. The rumor was that following the nationalization of the private schools, the children were going to be sent to schools in the Soviet Union to be brainwashed with communist propaganda. Thousands of Cuban parents, acting on the rumor, started sending their children to Miami as part of what became known as Operation Peter Pan, a coordinated effort with the support of the US government that brought to this country more than fourteen thousand unaccompanied children who were received by several charities and housed either with host families or in facilities in southern Florida until their parents could leave Cuba. Although Victor and I were leaving without our parents, we were not part of the operation, since we would be met in Miami by Mary Lou and Carlos.

When I learned we were leaving, my first question was, "What about the stamps?" "I don't think we can take them," my father said. The conduit through the airport that had enabled my mother to ship many things was no longer operational. I was devastated. I had worked so hard for almost a year to organize those stamps, and I was far from finished. Abandoning them meant I would fail the task that Oscar had given me.

Gisela, my father's sister, came to the rescue. Gise, who carefully crafted those elaborate nativity scenes, who kept all the closets in the G Street house carefully organized and labeled, the aunt who lived by the motto "A place for everything, and everything in its place." She called me up when she learned of my disappointment and instructed me to reduce the collection to its essentials, in other words, the stamps themselves. I had to tear out the pages of the album where I had already mounted stamps (the rest of the brand-new album is not going) and combine stamps in smaller envelopes into larger envelopes; everything replaceable, such as the catalogs, unused mounts, or magnifying glasses, had to stay. It took me a couple of days to essentially disorganize what I had organized. Once I had finished, Gisela showed up in the Miramar apartment with a cloth tape measure and methodically arranged the condensed collection into a neat, flat, rectangular pile on my bed so she could measure its dimensions. The following day she returned with a small suitcase she had managed to find while scouring the stores in Havana armed with her tape measure. It was the perfect size: small enough to carry onboard the plane, but large enough to fit all the stamps, without an inch to spare.

It was October 29, 1960, almost exactly four years to the day that the reading on maple syrup in Vermont was interrupted by the sound of gunfire coming from the nearby Haitian embassy. My three aunts—Mara, Gisela, and Amparito (Watty)—waved goodbye from the driveway of our Miramar apartment as the Buick pulled away, headed for the airport. My father and mother took Victor and me through the check-in process for our flight to Miami on Pan American Airways 422. After tearful embraces from our parents, my brother and I found ourselves in the *pecera*, or fish tank, the glass-encased departure gate for passengers only, just the two of us surrounded by anxious strangers. We waited there for nearly three hours. The authorities were investigating a passenger who might not have been allowed to leave. I wondered, Will they inspect my suitcase and take the stamps? Finally, we were called to board the flight. I clutched Victor's hand with my right and the suitcase containing the stamps with my left, and we walked across the tarmac to the plane's stairs, boarding the flight that marked the end of my life in Cuba.

EPILOGUE

As normally experienced, sense of place quite simply *is* . . . and the thought that it might be complicated, or even very interesting, seldom crosses our minds. Until . . . we are deprived of these attachments and find ourselves adrift, literally *dislocated*, in unfamiliar settings. . . . On these unnerving occasions, sense of place may assert itself in pressing and powerful ways. . . . It is then we come to see that attachments to places may be nothing less than profound. . . .

—Keith H. Basso, *Wisdom Sits in Places*

My father, my mother, my brother, Victor, and I left Cuba for Miami on US tourist visas, as if we were going on extended vacations, with every intention of going back home once Fidel Castro was overthrown. Surely, given the history of US influence and meddling in Cuban affairs, Washington would not allow the Cuban government to consolidate itself and drift into the Soviet Union's sphere of influence, not in the middle of the Cold War. Relying on the US to step in and "fix" things had a well-established precedent among elites during the Cuban Republic, as we have already seen in earlier chapters. Starting in 1960, those who became dissatisfied with the revolution or felt threatened or were persecuted left the country in droves expecting that the Americans would do something. It was a realistic expectation, and it was almost met. It was not for lack of trying that the United States was in the end not able to oust Castro and his government. Efforts to reverse the course of the revolution by the US included sponsoring an invasion of the island, the Bay of Pigs debacle, in April 1961.

My family may have left with tourist visas and with the illusion of returning, but apparently both governments knew what was coming better than we did. The US converted our tourist visas into refugee visas, and the

Cuban government regarded our departure, and those of the thousands leaving at the time, as definitive; in fact, that is exactly what they called it: *salida definitiva*. After my father left our apartment in Miramar for the last time, bound for the airport, an official came and sealed the front door. It was now government property, and the government would allocate it to another family.

I did not share my parents' expectation that we would be going back. I settled into my desk in the seventh-grade class of a Miami school less than a week after having sat at a similar desk at Lafayette, the only school I had ever attended. I remember thinking, this is not going to be temporary, so I better adjust to it. I was thankful that I had learned English at Lafayette and was ahead of my new classmates in math, spelling, and even US history.

I had an extraordinarily rich childhood in Cuba. A large network of family and relatives living in the same city and whom I saw frequently, my early interest in family history, the sense of legacy represented by the house on G Street or in Oscar's stamp collection: all these and other experiences led me to develop what psychologists call a "strong intergenerational self," often seen with children who know that they "belong to something bigger than themselves."[1]

This book is the best evidence that I never lost that strong intergenerational self, despite my dislocation from the place and the dispersion of my extended family. Only a few family members stayed in Cuba, while the rest left for either Miami, New York, Spain, or Puerto Rico. Returning to visit the island was not possible for twenty years. Faced with that distance from the people and the place that had nurtured my sense of belonging, I willed myself to remember that place and time and the people close to me who inhabited them, which is why I retain such a sharp memory of my childhood in Cuba, much sharper than the memories of my subsequent childhood years in the US.

When in 1979 the Cuban government allowed those who had left to return to the island to visit, I jumped at the opportunity, going back twice that year. It was, of course, a joy to again embrace those who still lived there: Kela, Gisela, Watty, Letty (and her children, my cousins), and my great-uncle Ernesto, Oscar's brother.[2] But the most transcendental moments of the trip were the re-encounters with the places. Despite appearing smaller than I remembered them, visiting them had a profound impact on me, for these were the places in the memories I had nurtured in my mind: the house on G Street, the house in El Country, my apartment and neighborhood in Miramar, Lafayette, El Yacht. To occupy those spaces again, if only momentarily, was to overcome the time and distance that had separated me from them. My childhood memories, which had been frozen in time, were refreshed and enhanced by seeing with adult eyes the places where they took place.

Re-creating those childhood memories during my visits to Cuba has not been difficult, given that so many of the places of my childhood, like my memory, have also remained frozen in time. Cuba's institutions, of course, were totally transformed by the revolution; its political, economic, and class systems bear no resemblance to what had existed before. Yet with limited investment in physical infrastructure, the places have remained virtually intact, albeit much decayed. Sometimes even the people have remained in place.

The best example of this is the incident that occurred during a return visit years ago, when I decided to enter and look around the warehouse my grandfather had built in Havana, on the corner of Luaces and Bruzon Streets. The warehouse and offices from which Lisandro, and later Rubén, ran the operations of General Cigar became the principal Havana facility of Cubatabaco, the government-run tobacco company. I knew it would be difficult to venture inside, because the Cuban government keeps fairly tight security over tobacco facilities, but I decided to give it a try. As soon as I walked in through the front door, I immediately realized that everything was exactly as I remembered it: the wooden reception counter on the left, the desk inside the reception area, and in the far corner, the large freestanding safe with "General Cigar Company of Cuba" written on it. I imagined that Rubén had no doubt emptied that safe and locked it before he left and that it had not been reopened in thirty years. The security guard, in an unwelcoming tone, asked if he could help me with something. I remembered that my grandfather had hired, forty years before, a trustworthy young man everyone called "Vicentico" as the night watchman of the building, and that he lived in a small apartment on the second floor of the facility. Knowing how so many things have remained surrealistically unchanged in what is otherwise a totally changed environment, I decided to chance it: "I'm here to see Vicentico. Is he in?" Without batting an eye, the guard turned to someone in the office and asked, "Is Vicentico in?" Someone answered that he had just stepped out but should be back soon. "Do you mind if I wait for him?" I asked. The guard nodded, and that was all I needed to casually roam a bit and peer into open doorways. The inner office was also identical to how I remembered it, as well as the courtyard surrounded by two floors of stacked *tercios*. Waiting for Vicentico, who was not expecting me and probably would not remember me, was probably not a good idea, so I told the guard I would come back later (which, of course, I did not).

Not everything that is frozen in time is in Cuba. In all the years since I left—a lifetime—I have not taken a single step toward what my grandfather Oscar and I proposed to do more than sixty years ago: organize the stamp collection and mount it in albums. I have added to it substantially, but that just means there are even more envelopes stuffed with stamps. I regret not having kept Gisela's suitcase as a souvenir, but it became so worn from the many moves throughout all these years that it was falling apart and was thrown out.

I still regard the stamp collection as I did when I was ten years old, that is, as a priceless legacy, but also as an overwhelming and endless task that I once undertook but ended up having to undo all the progress I made when the most life-changing event I have ever experienced intervened. Unlike Sisyphus, I have not mustered the determination to start rolling that boulder uphill again, especially when other more pressing tasks have taken up my time, such as earning degrees, teaching, researching and writing, directing academic departments and research centers, and of course, spending time with family. Writing this book was one of the tasks that, at this point in my life, remained to be done. Now that it is finished, I intend to put my shoulder to that boulder and fulfill the obligation I owe my grandfather Oscar.

New York City

December 2022

ACKNOWLEDGMENTS

At the core of this book are the family stories I have been depositing and nurturing in my mind for an entire lifetime. My first debt is therefore to those who shared those stories with me, most of whom are long dead but are remembered every day: my mother, Nancy, and my father, Tano; my grandfather Oscar; my uncles Humberto and Sergio and my aunts Mara, Kela, Letty, Gisela, and Watty; and Sergio's wife, Mari Pedroso. Fortunately, not all my cherished family sources have passed. As I write this, my aunt and *madrina* Mary Lou Rodríguez née Fonts, my mother's sister, is still, at age ninety, providing me with material, as well as motherly advice (which despite my age I can still use, even if I don't always follow it). "Yeye," as I called her as soon as I was able to talk, is the source of most of the photographs of the Fonts family in this book. She refreshed in my memory many of the stories that her sister Nancy and her father Oscar told me, and she added many others. What I am most apprehensive about as I finally finish the manuscript is that she will like this book. I hope she does. Thank you, Yeye.

There are four other family members besides Mary Lou who were alive when I was born and who I hope will read this book and like it: my uncle

Carlos (my mother's brother), and my older cousins Raquel Zita, Marita Prieto (Mara's daughters), and María Cristina (Cristy) Ansnes née Pérez (Rubén's daughter). They were all sources of stories and also served to corroborate or sharpen my memories. I owe a special debt to Cristy, who read a draft of the entire manuscript and provided me with invaluable feedback. Given my sense of "intergenerational self," I have come to greatly value the few remaining people who have known me my entire life.

Luis Costales, the grandson of Vivina, my grandmother Amparo's sister, generously shared his memories of working at the *despalillo* and of my grandfather Lisandro when I interviewed him over two days in Camajuaní in April 2018.

My colleagues and friends Esther Allen and Albert Laguna read earlier drafts of the manuscript and provided invaluable feedback and encouragement. My son Lisandro Pérez-Rey made helpful comments on an earlier draft of the prologue.

Several collections and archives were critical to my research, and the staffs of the libraries where they are housed were extremely helpful: the Beinecke Rare Book and Manuscript Library of Yale University; the Manuscripts, Archives, and Rare Books Division of the New York Public Library; the Manuscript Division of the Library of Congress; the National Archives and Records Administration in College Park, Maryland; and the Archivo Histórico Nacional in Madrid. I want to make special mention of the Cuban Heritage Collection (CHC) of the University of Miami Library, where I spent many days and benefited greatly from the assistance and support of Amanda Moreno, Martin Tsang, Gladys Gomez-Rossi, Juan Villanueva, and Dainerys Machado. I am also indebted to the CHC for accepting and processing the donation of Colonel Fonts's archive and inviting me to lecture on the Colonel's life.

Ramiro Fernández shared with me his collection of vintage photographs of Camajuaní and allowed me to include two of them in the book. Wallace (Wally) Edgecombe, an American who attended Lafayette School and a colleague of mine at the City University of New York, generously loaned me his priceless collection of the school's yearbooks. All the images were made publishable by the expert work of Dan Weisser of SugarHill Works in Harlem, who took a special interest in scanning and enhancing the documents and photographs I placed in his care. Raúl Hernández in Miami was able to draw the two maps exactly as I envisioned them. In Havana, René González Barrios generously took the time to compile and send me digital copies of several sources on the war of independence.

I started writing this book during a full-year (2017–18) sabbatical leave granted by my home institution, John Jay College of Criminal Justice (CUNY). I am also indebted to the college's Office for the Advancement of Research for awarding me a Faculty Research Award that allowed me to devote myself entirely to giving the manuscript a final push during the spring of 2022.

I am very fortunate to be married for the past twenty-six years to Liza Carbajo, whom one of her colleagues once described as "a very wise woman." I have benefited all these years from her wisdom, and I am deeply grateful for her unwavering love and companionship. When I was considering where to send this manuscript, she shared this piece of advice: "Go with who knows and appreciates you." So I sent it to New York University Press, specifically to Senior Editor Clara Platter. It was Clara and the Press who did a great job with my previous book, *Sugar, Cigars, and Revolution: The Making of Cuban New York* (2018). Not surprisingly, Liza was right. Clara embraced this second manuscript, and her enthusiastic support and guidance have been decisive in seeing me through the publication process. My thanks also to her assistant, Veronica Knutson, and to Martin Coleman for his supervision over the production process. Kristen Joseph and her team at Scribe greatly improved my original with their editing work. Luis Plascencia went above and beyond to make sure the index was accurate and comprehensive.

I have dedicated this book to all the descendants of my grandparents, especially my sons and granddaughters. I thank all of them, for they inspired me to write it.

APPENDIX

Colonel Fonts's Black Beans

This is the first time I'm writing down this recipe. I learned it hands-on by helping my mother, Nancy, cook the complete *Nochebuena* (Christmas Eve) dinner. My apprenticeship in preparing the holiday feast took place in my parents' home in Hialeah (a suburb of Miami) and started when I was in my late twenties and my mother started to need help hosting a houseful of family members who gathered every year to celebrate *Nochebuena* together. Due to her meticulous nature, Nancy always preferred to manage everything herself, but the symptoms of multiple sclerosis made it progressively more difficult for her to do so. I did not live in Miami, but I had to manage to get there by December 22, the day the preparations for *Nochebuena* would start. The first few years I was just the sous-chef, with her doing most of the work around the kitchen, but eventually I was doing all the work while she closely supervised me from her wheelchair. My apprenticeship lasted until her last Christmas, the year I was thirty-three and she was fifty-six. Every *Nochebuena* since then I have cooked for my family the entire feast, completely from scratch and from memory: black beans, white rice, a whole roast leg of pork, fried plantains, and *yuca con mojo.* Every Christmas I get to share a family tradition and remember my mother. It is a great gift.

The black bean dish is the one most laden with tradition. None of the other *Nochebuena* dishes was given a legacy. Nancy always insisted that we were preparing Colonel Fonts's beans, which is why I present the recipe here with that name, although admittedly it is impossible to know just how faithful this recipe is to the one my great-grandfather Ernesto followed in El Cerro and in Chaparra during the initial years of the twentieth century. Nor do I know if the recipe originated with him or if he borrowed it from someone else. If the Colonel ever wrote it down, that document was not in his archive. The recipe was not likely handed down directly through my grandfather Oscar, who was fourteen when his father died. But a version of these beans was served for *Nochebuena* in the house on Eighteenth Street in Miramar where my mother grew up. Perhaps Malila, Ernesto's widow, who lived there until her death, was responsible for passing on the recipe. Complicating the mystery of the origins of the recipe is that across the street from the house on Eighteenth Street lived the Valdés-Faulis, who were cousins of Oscar, descendants of Colonel Ernesto's older sister, Aurora Fonts y Sterling, who in 1881 married a lawyer named Guillermo Valdés-Fauli. Years later in the 1950s, after Oscar had moved the family to El Country, my grandmother Nancy wrote down the recipe for the black beans and entered it into a contest that Nitza Villapol, the Julia Child of Cuban television, was running on her cooking show to select from the submitted entries the dishes she was going to include in the cookbook she was compiling, *Cocina al minuto*, which became a classic reference work for Cuban cuisine. My grandmother's recipe was selected, but she chose to submit the dish with the name "Frijoles Negros a la Valdés-Fauli," and that is the way it appeared in the legendary cookbook. My mother always rued that *los frijoles del abuelo* were attributed for posterity to the Valdés-Faulis and not to the Colonel, but who knows, perhaps my grandmother knew something about the beans' provenance that my mother did not know. As the prize for submitting an accepted recipe, my grandmother received a case of cooking wine. Another possible clue to the beans' origins was provided by a friend who, after I explained to him in general terms how the beans are prepared, told me that in his family that style of black beans was referred to as "a la Menocal." Given the close association between former President Menocal and Ernesto, that opens another explanatory avenue.

Over the years both my mother and I tweaked the recipe that appeared in *Cocina al minuto*, up to now the only printed version of the recipe. The one that appears here is my latest iteration, the result of several trials and errors in which I attempted to make it more authentic by modifying it in ways that would more closely resemble the way Ernesto would have prepared it in his time. Some of those experiments worked and were incorporated, but others failed and were discarded the following year. For example, Ernesto could not have used an electric blender, because that appliance was not invented until 1922, so one year I decided to do the *sofrito* the traditional way, by finely chopping the onion and green pepper with a knife. Ernesto probably did it that way, but it did not give the beans the rich texture to which I was accustomed. Someone along the way got it right by introducing the blender and the pureed *sofrito*, and so I went back to that the next year. I also once tried roasting and peeling the red peppers instead of using canned pimientos, but there was no discernible difference in the flavor, and it was a lot more work than using the canned ones. My mother cooked the beans in a pressure cooker, an appliance that was not widely used until World War II. I went back to the way Ernesto would have cooked them, slowly over low heat for hours. That modification I kept: the beans turned out just as soft and more beans remained whole rather than smashed, compared to those coming out of the pressure cooker. Besides, I was always a bit leery of the pressure cooker, with its dancing cap rhythmically spewing steam, seemingly prepared to explode at any moment. But the most consequential modification was the simplest one. When I was cooking with my mother in the 1970s, the black beans that were available were the ones we bought in the supermarket, which were packaged and distributed by some food conglomerate. A few years ago I used organic black beans, and that made a significant difference. They taste buttery and become soft in less time than the ones I had been using. At the turn of the twentieth century, and especially in a place like Chaparra, the only beans Ernesto could have used were organic.

There are two fundamental styles for cooking black beans. One is the style in which the sauce is watery and lighter in color than the beans themselves. This is how they are usually prepared in Cuban homes and restaurants. Then there is the style that produces beans with a thicker and more uniform texture, in which bean and sauce appear as one. The Colonel's beans are in this latter style, beans that are often referred to as *cuajados* (thickened) or *dormidos* (asleep). They are purposely thickened with a reduced or dehydrated *sofrito* and by putting the beans to sleep overnight in the refrigerator the day before they are to be served.

For people who are accustomed to the more traditional watery beans, this thicker style may take some getting used to. I moved to Miami a few years after my mother died and was looking forward to having my father, who was still living in the same house in Hialeah, come over to my home for *Nochebuena* so I could serve him the same menu my mother had cooked all the years they were married, including, of course, the Colonel's beans. In the middle of the dinner, with a candidness (or curmudgeonliness) that may come with widowhood and advancing age, he suddenly said, "I never told your mother, but I never liked these beans. I prefer the ones my mother made." To which I responded, "Well, *Papi*, don't we all; I also prefer the beans my mother made."

INGREDIENTS FOR ABOUT TEN SERVINGS

1 lb. organic black beans

2 large sweet onions, peeled

2 large green bell peppers, stems and seeds removed

2 bay leaves

2 cloves garlic, peeled

1 cup olive oil

1 cup sherry cooking wine

1/4 cup apple cider vinegar

1 8 oz. can tomato sauce, preferably unsalted

1 12 oz. can whole red pimientos

1/3 cup white refined sugar

1 tsp. oregano

Salt to taste and very little, if any, pepper

The beans are to be served on day three, so the preparations start on day one (e.g., for Christmas Eve dinner on December 24, day one is December 22).

AFTERNOON OF DAY ONE: SOAK THE BEANS

Place the beans in small batches in a colander, rinse them, and pick through them to make sure there are no small stones, soil clumps, or other earthen matter. Place all the beans in a heavy stock pot, and pour enough cold water into the pot so that the beans are covered by about four inches of water. The pot should be large enough so that the water and the beans do not exceed two-thirds of the capacity of the pot. (I use the eight-quart All-Clad Stainless-Steel Stock Pot.) Slice one of the onions into rings one-quarter-inch thick and one of the green peppers into half-inch wide strips, and mix them in with the beans and water. Place the covered pot on the kitchen counter (or in the refrigerator) to soak overnight. (I usually check on the pot before I go to sleep to make sure the beans have not expanded to the point that they need more water to stay covered.)

MORNING OF DAY TWO: COOK THE BEANS

Making sure that there are at least two inches of water left covering the beans, place the pot on the stove, and bring it to a near boil before quickly turning down the heat to a healthy simmer. Add the bay leaves and an initial pinch or two of salt, and cover the pot. Simmer for at least three hours. Stir periodically to make sure there is enough water so that the beans are not at risk of sticking to the bottom. If so, add more water. After the three hours, sample a few of the beans to make sure they have no firmness; they should pretty much dissolve in your mouth. If still firm, continue cooking. There is little danger of overcooking the beans if they have enough water.

While the beans are cooking, prepare the *sofrito* by peeling the remaining onion and cutting it and the remaining green pepper into large chunks. Place the onion and pepper, the cloves of garlic, and the cup of olive oil into a blender. Blend until the ingredients liquefy into a smooth mixture. Pour the *sofrito* mixture into a twelve-inch-wide skillet at medium-low heat. When the *sofrito* starts to heat, stir it frequently, uncovered. The purpose is to cook the *sofrito* while reducing its liquid. If the mixture is splattering too vigorously, reduce the heat a bit. After about forty-five minutes, most of the natural liquid from the onion and pepper will have evaporated, and the result will be a thicker *sofrito* that will want to stick to the pan in a burnt brownish film. This is when the stirring needs to be constant and aggressive to prevent that (a stiff rubber spatula works best), continuing until the *sofrito* is close to having a purée consistency.

Once the beans are cooked, pour the *sofrito* slowly into the beans, stirring the beans as you do so to ensure an even mix. The beans will now have a thicker texture, so the heat needs to be reduced to a low simmer, and attention needs to be paid to prevent any sticking to the pot, so stir occasionally. The pot should always be covered while the beans are cooking. After about twenty minutes, to allow the *sofrito* and the beans to coalesce, add the vinegar, tomato sauce, half a cup of the sherry cooking wine, the oregano, and the pimientos, diced coarsely, along with the water in which they were packed. Adjust the salt and add ground black pepper, if desired. After allowing enough time for the beans to return to a simmer, add the sugar, stirring it in slowly. Simmer slowly for another thirty minutes, and then turn off the heat. Wait until the pot cools down before putting the beans to sleep, covered, in the refrigerator for the night.

DAY THREE: HEAT AND SERVE

About a couple of hours before they are to be served, take the beans out of the refrigerator and wake them up by stirring them a couple of times and splashing in the other half cup of the sherry. They are cold, of course, and considerably thicker than the day before, so place them on the stove over low heat, stirring them every few minutes to prevent sticking. The beans must be reheated slowly; burnt beans on the bottom will give the entire batch an unpleasant taste.

Plate by laying a bed of white, nonsticky, long-grain rice and ladling a generous serving of the beans on top.

NOTES

PROLOGUE

1 Throughout this book, I use the nouns or modifiers "American" or "Americans" to refer to people or cultural traits from the United States despite the fact that the terms have been misappropriated in a way that fails to recognize that they are applicable to the entire Americas and not just the United States. In part, the usage here is for stylistic reasons (it is usually clumsy to turn "United States" into a modifier), but it's primarily because "*americano*" or "*los americanos*" is the way Cubans themselves universally refer to people or things from the United States, especially during the period covered by this book.

2 Pérez, *Sugar, Cigars, and Revolution*.

3 Scott and Hébrard, *Freedom Papers*, 5.

4 Field, "Privilege of Family History," 602. I credit Field's work with not only influencing my thinking on the uses of family history but also leading me to other sources on the topic.

5 Ibid.

6 Field, *Growing Up*, 15.

7 García Márquez, "Solitude of Latin America."

1. FONTS

1 Gras y Elías, *Historia de los lugares*, 134.

2 Hernández Sanahuja, *Historia de Tarragona*, 69–71.

3 Martí, *Catalanes en América*, 103–4.

4 Rovira and Anguera, *Història de Torredembarra*, 57–65.

5 Santovenia, "Política colonial," 51.

6 Moreno Fraginals, *Sugarmill*, 15.

7   Ibid., 19.
8   Ibid., 25, 41, 83–85.
9   Knight, *Slave Society*, 22.
10 The genealogies of the Fonts and Aldama families can be found in Santa Cruz y Mallén, *Familias cubanas*, 1:29–30, 141–44.
11 Llaverías, *Miguel Aldama*, 6.
12 Álvarez Pedroso, *Miguel de Aldama*, 24.
13 Lobo Montalvo, *Havana*, 133.
14 Pérez, *Sugar, Cigars, and Revolution*, 78–79.
15 Santa Cruz y Mallén, *Familias cubanas*, 4:348, 382.
16 Ibid., 2:369–72.
17 Thomas, *Cuba*, 211.
18 Carlos de Borbón to Aldama, reproduced in Llaverías, *Miguel Aldama*, 16–17.
19 Aldama to Carlos de Borbón, reproduced in Llaverías, *Miguel Aldama*, 17–18. Italics for emphasis are in the Llaverías text.
20 Marrero, *Cuba*, 15:296.
21 Quiroz, "Loyalist Overkill," 266.
22 Reprinted in Soulere, *Historia de la insurrección*, 60–63.
23 Miguel de Aldama to Domingo Dulce, January 27, 1869, box 1, folio 5, Albornoz and Aldama Family Papers.
24 Zaragoza, *Insurrecciones de Cuba*, 374.
25 Miguel de Aldama to Domingo Dulce, n.d. (1869?), box 1, folio 5, Albornoz and Aldama Family Papers.
26 "New York Passenger Lists." Original source, *Passenger Lists of Vessels Arriving at New York, 1820–1897*, micropublication M237, rolls 95–580, National Archives, Washington, DC. There are many Aldamas on the manifest, and not all names are legible. The best evidence that Aldama was aboard the *Morro Castle* on May 2 is a May 20 letter from José Antonio Echeverría in Havana to José Manuel Mestre in New York, which reads, "I am sure you greeted with satisfaction the arrival of Miguel and his family." Container 61, José Ignacio Rodríguez Papers.
27 Ledger sheet, May 1, 1872, box 79, Moses Taylor Papers.
28 Abad, "Emigraciones cubanas," 176.
29 "Expediente general de deportados políticos de Cuba por medida gubernativa: Solicitud de cédula de seguridad de Carlos Fonts y Palma," Expediente 23, August 30, 1870, "Ultramar" collection, 4770.
30 Carlos Fonts y Sterling, "Signatura," Expediente 2, 1873–78, "Universidades" collection, 4026.
31 "Invoice: James Bliss, Vault Builder and Mason in General," box 1, folio 3, Albornoz and Aldama Family Papers.
32 "Message of the President to Congress," *New York Times*, June 14, 1870, 1.
33 Emilia C. de Villaverde, "La Liga de las Hijas de Cuba a los cubanos," La Liga de las Hijas de Cuba, New York, September 28, 1874, 4–5.

34 "New Buildings: The Santa Rosa Refinery," *Brooklyn Daily Eagle*, October 13, 1873; "Along Shore: A Glance at the Water Front," *Brooklyn Daily Eagle*, August 6, 1875, 3.

35 "Married by the Cardinal," *New York Times*, April 17, 1879, 5.

36 "Passengers Sailed," *New York Times*, June 25, 1880, 8; "Passengers Sailed," *New York Times*, June 24, 1881, 8.

37 "Mt. Pleasant Military Academy," Wikipedia, last accessed March 31, 2021, https://en .wikipedia.org.

38 *Catalog of Mount Pleasant Military Academy* (Sing Sing, New York: published by the academy, 1886), 8.

39 "Miguel Aldama's Remains," *New York Times*, March 27, 1888, 3.

40 Álvarez Pedroso, *Miguel de Aldama*, 130.

2. PÉREZ

1 Canet, *Atlas de Cuba*, 7; Marrero, *Cuba*, 3:64–65; Editorial Cubana, *Las Villas*, 4.

2 Martínez-Fortún y Foyo, *Anales y efemérides*, 7:8.

3 Ortiz, *Historia de una pelea*.

4 Martínez Escobar, *Historia de Remedios*, 111.

5 Ibid., 127–31.

6 Sarmiento Ramírez, *Cuba*, 78.

7 Alfonso Ballol et al., *Camino de hierro*, 13.

8 García Galló, *Biografía del tabaco habano*, 59–60.

9 Ibid, 48.

10 Rodríguez Ramos, *Siembra*, 29–104.

11 González del Valle, *Memorandum presentado*, 58.

12 Rivero Muñiz, *Tabaco*, 2:293.

13 Martínez-Fortún y Foyo, *Anales y efemérides*, 3:286.

14 Ibid., 67.

15 Ibid., 94.

16 Martínez-Fortún y Foyo, *Anales y efemérides*, 7:106.

17 Ibid., 75.

18 "Suscripción popular a favor de los familiares de las víctimas del incendio del 17 del actual," *Gaceta de La Habana* 52, no. 123 (May 25, 1890): 1006.

3. FOUR BROTHERS

1 Pérez, *Sugar, Cigars, and Revolution*, 292–99.

2 Orozco y Arascot and Fonts y Sterling, *Diccionario*.

3 On the autonomist movement, see Bizcarrondo and Elorza, *Cuba-España*.

4 Santa Cruz y Mallén, *Familias cubanas*, 7:219–41.

5 *El Sport* 2, nos. 14–17 (January 1887): 9.

6 Angulo and Mendoza. *Directorio social*, n.p.

7 Bay Sevilla, "Barriada del Cerro," 163–65.

8 Roloff y Maliofsky, *Yndice alfabético*, A-277.

9 Ibid., A-705.
10 Ferrer, *Insurgent Cuba*, 154–55.

4. COLONEL FONTS

1 Centro de Estudios Militares, *Diccionario enciclopédico*, 136.
2 Ernesto's appointments and promotions during the war are all documented in box A, collection CHC5548, documents A-2, A-4, A-5, and A-9, Ernesto Fonts y Sterling Papers.
3 Enrique del Junco y de la Cruz Muñoz to Ernesto Fonts y Sterling, June 27, 1897, box B, collection CHC5548, document B-14, Ernesto Fonts y Sterling Papers.
4 Roloff y Maliofsky, *Yndice alfabético*, B-125.
5 Ibid., B-2.
6 "The younger brother of Mr. Zafiro" to Ernesto Fonts y Sterling, March 7, 1898, box B, collection CHC5548, document B-17, Ernesto Fonts y Sterling Papers.
7 "Mr. Zafiro" to Ernesto Fonts y Sterling, n.d., box B, collection CHC5548, document B-16, Ernesto Fonts y Sterling Papers.
8 "The younger brother of Mr. Zafiro" to Ernesto Fonts y Sterling, March 7, 1898.
9 Estimate derived from the comprehensive listing of deaths in Roloff y Maliofsky, *Yndice alfabético*.
10 Pichardo, *Cartas a Francisco Carrillo*, 11.
11 Rodríguez Rodríguez, *Algunos documentos políticos*, 217.
12 Máximo Gómez to Ernesto Fonts y Sterling, June 21, 1898, box B, collection CHC5548, document B-18, Ernesto Fonts y Sterling Papers.
13 Máximo Gómez to Ernesto Fonts y Sterling, August 21, 1898, box B, collection CHC5548, document B-19, Ernesto Fonts y Sterling Papers.

5. AMPARO

1 Martínez-Fortún y Foyo, *Anales y efemérides*, 5:9.
2 Ibid., 4:171.
3 Peraza Sarausa, *Diccionario biográfico cubano*, 7:114–15.
4 Martínez-Fortún y Foyo, *Anales y efemérides*, 44:171.
5 Ibid., 4:73.
6 Ibid., 3:60.
7 Ibid., 3:252, 257.
8 "Diario del Coronel Leoncio Vidal, 1895–96," *Revista de Historia Cubana y Americana* 1, no. 3 (May 20, 1916): 107–23.
9 "Coronel Leoncio Vidal," 108–15; Martínez-Fortún y Foyo, *Anales y efemérides*, 44:207–13.
10 García del Barco y Alonso, *Camajuaní y la revolución*, 13–24.
11 Martínez-Fortún y Foyo, *Apuntes históricos de Camajuaní*, 45.
12 Martínez-Fortún y Foyo, *Anales y efemérides*, 44:211.
13 "Coronel Leoncio Vidal," 120–21.

14 This account of the attack on Santa Clara is derived primarily from García del Barco y Alonso, *Camajuaní y la revolución*, 78–83.

15 Peraza Sarausa, *Diccionario biográfico cubano*, 7:115.

16 Blanco Escolá, *General Mola*; Iribarren, *General Mola*; Maíz, *Mola, aquel hombre*; and Wilson, *Man Who Created Franco*.

17 Pérez-Reverte, *Historia de España*, 195.

6. HERE COME THE AMERICANS

1 Leonard Wood to Elihu Root, February 8, 1902, box 31, Leonard Wood Papers.

2 Hagedorn, *Leonard Wood*, 1:364–65; McCallum, *Leonard Wood*, 184–88.

3 Treasury Department of the US Military Government, Havana, to Ernesto Fonts y Sterling, January 29, 1899, box A, collection CHC5548, document A-11, Ernesto Fonts y Sterling Papers.

4 Jorgensen, *Preliminary Inventory*, 9.

5 Ladd, "Report of the Treasurer," 31.

6 Ibid., 109–10.

7 Ernesto Fonts y Sterling to Sister Isabel de los Desamparados, March 18, 1901, box 2, entry PI-145 29, Records of the Military Government of Cuba.

8 Leonard Wood to Elihu Root, February 8, 1902, box 31, Leonard Wood Papers.

9 Elihu Root to Leonard Wood, March 24, 1902, box 31, Leonard Wood Papers.

10 The description of the events of that day is from Leonard Wood's diary. "Diary, May 20th, 1900, to January 31st, 1906," box 3, Leonard Wood Papers.

11 In the translation of Estrada Palma's speech that was provided to Wood by the translators in the office of the US military government, the president's use of the words *nación soberana* in Spanish was not translated in the obvious way ("sovereign nation") but oddly as "ruling nation." English and Spanish versions of statement by Tomás Estrada Palma, May 20, 1902, box 31, Leonard Wood Papers.

12 J. D. Terrill to the Chief of the Division of Insular Affairs of the War Department, June 12, 1902, box 271, entry PI-145 15, Civil Letters Received by the Late Military Government of Cuba, 1902–3, Records of the Military Government of Cuba.

13 Statement by Tomás Estrada Palma, Leonard Wood Papers.

14 I do not have direct evidence that Ernesto was the one who notified his superiors that there would be a shortfall in the quoted amount, but it is a logical conclusion, since he was the top official of the Cuban government who was working directly with the financial accounts.

15 Tomás Estrada Palma to Leonard Wood, June 28, 1902, box 271, entry PI-145 15, Civil Letters Received by the Late Military Government of Cuba, 1902–3, Records of the Military Government of Cuba.

16 From the letterhead of the stationery used in the office's correspondence.

17 Hagedorn, *Leonard Wood*, 315.

18 "General Wood's Salary in Cuba," *New York Times*, June 7, 1902, 3.

19 "Gen. Wood Explains," *New York Times*, June 13, 1902, 1.

20 "The Thurber Incident," *New York Times*, June 13, 1902, 8.

21 "War Department Is Responsible," *New York Times*, June 13, 1902, 1.

22 Leonard Wood to Major Terrill, June 9, 1902, box 31, Leonard Wood Papers.

23 Leonard Wood to J. D. Terrill, June 10, 1902, box 274, entry PI-145 17, Civil Letters Sent by the Late Military Government of Cuba, 1902–3, Records of the Military Government of Cuba.

24 J. D. Terrill to Leonard Wood, June 18, 1902, box 206, Leonard Wood Papers.

25 Ibid.

26 Ibid.

27 J. D. Terrill to Leonard Wood, June 18, 1902, box 274, entry PI-145 15, Civil Letters Received by the Late Military Government of Cuba, 1902–3, Records of the Military Government of Cuba.

28 Frank Steinhart to Leonard Wood, June 19, 1902, box 206, Leonard Wood Papers. In this same letter, Steinhart informs Wood that the leaker of the Thurber invoices had been identified: an American named Lancashire, who was promptly dismissed by Terrill.

29 Alex Gonzalez to Leonard Wood, July [*sic*] 18, 1902, box 206, Leonard Wood Papers. Gonzalez erred in dating this letter. He wrote it on June 18, not July 18, as is evident from the chronology of the events and Wood's response on June 27.

30 Leonard Wood to Alex Gonzalez, June 27, 1902, box 31, Leonard Wood Papers.

31 Hagedorn, *Leonard Wood*, 376–77.

32 J. D. Terrill to Chief of the Division of Insular Affairs of the War Department, July 10, 1902, box 2, entry PI-145 40, Miscellaneous Letters-Endorsements, 1901–2, Records of the Military Government of Cuba.

33 J. D. Terrill to Leonard Wood, July 15, 1902, box 31, Leonard Wood Papers.

34 Frank Steinhart to Colonel H. L. Scott, July 30, 1902, box 265, entry PI-145 15, Civil Letters Received by the Late Military Government of Cuba, 1902–3, Records of the Military Government of Cuba.

35 Tomás Estrada Palma to Elihu Root, August 19, 1902, box 265, entry PI-145 15, Civil Letters Received by the Late Military Government of Cuba, 1902–3, Records of the Military Government of Cuba.

36 H. G. Squiers to John Hay, August 28, 1902, box 265, entry PI-145 15, Civil Letters Received by the Late Military Government of Cuba, 1902–3, Records of the Military Government of Cuba.

37 William Cary Sanger to Tomás Estrada Palma, August 27, 1902, box 271, entry PI-145 15, Civil Letters Received by the Late Military Government of Cuba, 1902–3, Records of the Military Government of Cuba; Leonard Wood to Elihu Root, September 8, 1902, box 31, Leonard Wood Papers; Frank Steinhart to Colonel Scott, October 6, 1902, box 271, entry PI-145 15, Civil Letters Received by the Late Military Government of Cuba, 1902–3, Records of the Military Government of Cuba.

38 "Nóminas mensuales de ausencias de empleados, abril 1904–febrero 1906," box C, collection CHC5548, document C-44, Ernesto Fonts y Sterling Papers.

39 Alicia Mendoza, conversation with the author, El Cerro, June 1979.

40 Pérez, *Platt Amendment*, 93.

41 Thomas, *Cuba*, 474.

42 Yglesia Martínez, "Organización de la república neocolonial," 70; Zanetti, *Cuba*, 61.

43 Thomas, *Cuba*, 484.

44 Rodríguez, *República de corcho*, 1:410.

45 Ibid.; Portell-Vilá, *Nueva historia*, 104.

46 Rodríguez, *República de corcho*, 1:349.

47 "President Palma to Bride," *New York Times*, February 18, 1906, 2.

48 Rodríguez, *República de corcho*, 1:349.

49 "To Accept Cuba's Gift," *New York Times*, February 3, 1906, 1; Rodríguez, *República de corcho*, 1:349.

50 Rodríguez, *República de corcho*, 1:350.

51 Secretario de la Presidencia to Ernesto Fonts y Sterling, March 29, 1906, box B, collection CHC5548, document B-37, Ernesto Fonts y Sterling Papers.

52 Yglesia Martínez, *Cuba*, 216.

53 Thomas, *Cuba*, 475.

54 Steinhart to Bacon, quoted in Pérez, *Platt Amendment*, 96.

55 Minger, "William A. Taft," 84–85.

56 Roosevelt to White, quoted in Pérez, *Platt Amendment*, 97.

57 Thomas, *Cuba*, 477.

58 Ibid., 475; Yglesia Martínez, "Organización de la república neocolonial," 73.

59 Pérez, *Platt Amendment*, 100; Yglesia Martínez, *Cuba*, 268.

60 Pérez, *Platt Amendment*, 101.

61 Rodríguez, *República de corcho*, 1:376; Pérez, *Platt Amendment*, 101–2; Yglesia Martínez, *Cuba*, 272.

62 Thomas, *Cuba*, 478.

63 Roosevelt to Foraker, quoted in Thomas, *Cuba*, 478.

64 Portell-Vilá, *Nueva historia*, 103.

65 "Sin quorum," *Diario de la Marina*, September 29, 1906, 6.

66 Minger, "William A. Taft," 85.

67 Rodríguez, *República de corcho*, 1:386; Yglesia Martínez, *Cuba*, 296.

68 F. R. McCoy to Ernesto Fonts y Sterling, October 2, 1906, box B, collection CHC5548, document B-27, Ernesto Fonts y Sterling Papers.

69 "Entrevista," *Diario de la Marina*, October 3, 1906, 4.

70 "Special Correspondence," *Louisiana Planter and Sugar Manufacturer* 47, no. 16 (October 14, 1911): 256.

71 Estrada Palma to Ernesto Fonts y Sterling, January 1, 1907, box B, collection CHC5548, document B-39, Ernesto Fonts y Sterling Papers.

72 Rodríguez, *República de corcho*, 1:453.

73 Thomas, *Cuba*, 484.

74 Pérez, *Platt Amendment*, 104–5.

75 Marquéz Sterling, *A la ingerencia extraña, la virtud doméstica*, 1.

76 Pérez, *Platt Amendment*, 107.

77 Ibid., 92.

78 Rodríguez, *República de corcho*, 2:59.

79 Malila: "Ernesto, enderézate, cada día estás más jorobado." Ernesto: "Ay Malila, si esta gente no me puede tragar jorobado, imagínate tú si me enderezo."

80 Rental receipt, September 30, 1910, box C, collection CHC5548, document C-105, Ernesto Fonts y Sterling Papers.

81 Tamayo, "Informe del Secretario," 3:39.

82 Most of the information presented here on the history of Camajuaní is derived from Martínez-Fortún y Foyo, *Apuntes históricos de Camajuaní*.

83 Gobierno Civil de Santa Clara, *Memoria, año 1901*, n.p.

84 "Certificación de matrimonio," Diócesis de Cienfuegos-Santa Clara, November 4, 1907, vol. 2, folio 106, copy created on September 11, 1986, and signed by Fr. Aguedo García Blanco, Cura Párroco, Iglesia Parroquial de Camajuaní. In accordance with Cuban norms for marriage ceremonies, Rogelio Echevarría is listed as *padrino* (godfather) on the marriage certificate.

85 Edwin, *Half a Century*, 84.

86 *Universal Tobacco Dealers Directory*.

87 Burrows and Wallace, *Gotham*, 991.

88 US Bureau of the Census, *1880 United States Federal Census*, www.ancestry.com.

89 "De Camajuaní," *Diario de la Marina*, April 1, 1913, 4.

90 "Isaac J. Bernheim Dead," *New York Times*, April 29, 1927, 21.

7. CHAPARRA

1 Santa Cruz y Mallén, *Familias cubanas* 1:148–71.

2 As an engineer with the US Navy, Aniceto drew up plans for a canal to be built across Nicaragua and commanded the Washington Navy Yard, among other positions (Ibid., 1:167).

3 Ferrer, *Cuba*, 189–90.

4 McGillivray, *Blazing Cane*, 77; Ferrer, *Cuba*, 190.

5 Ferrer, *Cuba*, 190.

6 Cuban American Sugar Company, *Annual Report, 1909–1910*, 1.

7 The earliest US investments in the region, dating back to the colonial period, were not in sugar production but in the mining of iron ore. See Pérez, "Iron Mining."

8 Hoernel, "Sugar and Social Change," 229.

9 Cuban American Sugar Company, *Annual Report, 1909–1910*, 3.

10 "En Chaparra," *Diario de la Marina*, October 21, 1911, 3.

11 There was an unconfirmed press report that said a few months into Menocal's presidency, the Treasury Secretary resigned and the president offered the job to Ernesto, who turned it down. It would have been surprising had Menocal truly offered the position to Ernesto, given the latter's value to Chaparra, but it would not have been unexpected that Ernesto would have refused it. Given his experiences during the

Estrada Palma administration, Ernesto could not have been eager to return to the Havana political game, especially with a decrease in salary (Untitled note, *Diario de la Marina*, August 22, 1913, 1).

12 Ernesto was named General Manager of the complex composed of the Chaparra, Delicias, and San Manuel *centrales*, which were managed as one property. Henceforth, references to the "Chaparra" in the text, are meant to include the entire property.

13 Ferrer, *Cuba*, 190; McGillivray, *Blazing Cane*, 95; "Inspeccionando los ingenios de Cuba," *Diario de la Marina*, March 31, 1915, 8.

14 McGillivray, *Blazing Cane*, 95.

15 Ferrer, *Cuba*, 190.

16 Canel, *Lo que ví*, 292.

17 Van Praagh, ed., *El Libro Azul de Cuba*, ix.

18 McGillivray, *Blazing Cane*, 105.

19 Canel, *Lo que ví*, 286–287.

20 Petition to Ernesto Fonts y Sterling, May 23, 1916, box C, collection CHC5548, document C-66, Ernesto Fonts y Sterling Papers.

21 Unidentified Cuban American Sugar Company executive to Ernesto Fonts y Sterling, June 21, 1917, box B, collection CHC5548, document B-33, Ernesto Fonts y Sterling Papers.

22 H. W. Wilmot to Ernesto Fonts y Sterling, August 18, 1916, box C, collection CHC5548, document C-67, Ernesto Fonts y Sterling Papers.

23 Cuban American Sugar Company, *Annual Report for the Fiscal Year Ending September 30, 1916*, 4.

24 Invoice, Thomas Nelson and Sons, July 24, 1916, box C, collection CHC5548, document C-73, Ernesto Fonts y Sterling Papers.

25 The Chaparra cocktail was recognized in 1930 by the Bartenders Club of Cuba and is even today served at the refurbished Sloppy Joe's bar in Havana.

26 McGillivray, *Blazing Cane*, 101.

27 Canel, *Lo que ví*, 289–90.

28 *Tumba la caña, / anda ligero; / corre, que viene Menocal / sonando el cuero* (Ferrer, *Cuba*, 191).

29 McGillivray, *Blazing Cane*, 102.

30 Ernesto Fonts y Sterling to Alfredo de Mariátegui y Carratalá, March 11, 1916, box C, collection CHC5548, document C-62, Ernesto Fonts y Sterling Papers.

31 Thomas, *Cuba*, 527.

32 "Resultado de los escrutinios," *Diario de la Marina*, November 3, 1916, 1.

33 "Cuba's New President," *New York Times*, November 3, 1916, 12.

34 Pérez, *Intervention, Revolution, and Politics*, 19–21.

35 Secretaría de Gobernación to Ernesto Fonts y Sterling, January 24, 1917, box C, collection CHC5548, document C-74, Ernesto Fonts y Sterling Papers.

36 Lieutenant Rodríguez to Ernesto Fonts y Sterling, February 17, 1917, box C, collection CHC5548, document C-77, Ernesto Fonts y Sterling Papers.

37 Jefe de la Oficina to Ernesto Fonts y Sterling, April 12, 1917, box C, collection CHC5548, document C-79, Ernesto Fonts y Sterling Papers.

38 McGillivray, *Blazing Cane*, 117.

39 Pérez, *Intervention, Revolution, and Politics*, 42.

40 Thomas, *Cuba*, 531.

41 Mario G. Menocal to Ernesto Fonts y Sterling, April 17, 1917, box B, collection CHC5548, document B-29, Ernesto Fonts y Sterling Papers.

42 Cuban American Sugar Company, *Annual Report for the Fiscal Year Ending September 30, 1917*, 3.

43 Carlos Fonts y Sterling to Ernesto Fonts y Sterling, May 22, 1917, box B, collection CHC5548, document B-31, Ernesto Fonts y Sterling Papers.

44 Chaparra company official to Ernesto Fonts Sterling, June 21, 1917, box B, collection CHC5548, document B-33, Ernesto Fonts y Sterling Papers. The lengthy letter was handwritten on the stationery of the Hotel Van Rensselaer in New York, where its author was staying during a visit to company offices, a trip that immediately followed his meeting with Menocal in Havana. The signature is illegible, but it is clear from the contents that he was the legal counsel in Chaparra.

45 Ibid.

46 Ibid. The underlining is in the original document.

47 Ernesto Fonts y Sterling to J. H. Land, February 24, 1918, box C, collection CHC5548, document C-98, Ernesto Fonts y Sterling Papers.

48 Suzanne Despres, "Habaneras," *Diario de la Marina*, April 18, 1918, 5.

49 Box B, collection CHC5548, document B-41, Ernesto Fonts y Sterling Papers, is a collection of newspaper clippings on Ernesto's death, funeral, and burial, as well as obituaries published upon his death. They are not cited here because they were clipped and inserted in the archive without citations. See also "El Coronel Ernesto Fonts," *Diario de la Marina*, May 21, 1918, 1, 5; "Un Justo," *Diario de la Marina*, May 22, 1918, 16; Emilio Iglesia, "Ernesto Fonts y Sterling," *Revista de la Víbora* 5, no. 5 (May 1918), 1–2; "La república de luto," *La Nación*, May 21, 1918, 1; and "Duelos de la Patria," *La Discusión*, May 21, 1918, 4.

50 "El senado," *Diario de la Marina*, May 22, 1918, 10; "En la cámara," *Diario de la Marina*, May 25, 1918, 20.

51 "El entierro del Cnel. Ernesto Fonts y Sterling," *Diario de la Marina*, May 22, 1918, 1.

52 "Ernesto Fonts y Sterling," *La Nación*, May 21, 1918, 4 (unsigned editorial, attributed to Manuel Márquez Sterling, director of the newspaper).

8. GENERAL CIGAR

1 Maysilles, "Remembrance," 39.

2 General Cigar Company, *Annual Statement 1921*, n.p. After being sold several times, General Cigar is currently owned by the Scandinavian Tobacco Group. General Cigar's premium brands, of which Macanudo is the best-known, are manufactured outside the US, in the Dominican Republic, Honduras, Nicaragua, and Jamaica, using exclusively leaves from Latin America and Asia.

3 Lisandro Pérez Moreno personal notebook, 1938–49.

4 Ibid.

5 Luis Costales, interview with the author, Camajuaní, April 2018.

6 The operational details presented here on the process my grandfather Lisandro followed for purchasing and processing tobacco leaves are drawn primarily from a text that my father, upon my request, wrote around 1995. He typed it in English, anticipating that I would eventually use it in my research. It was lengthier and more detailed than what I anticipated, so I am summarizing here. I have verified and complemented his account with what I learned from a two-day interview in Camajuaní in April 2018 with Luis Costales, grandson of Vivina, a sister of my grandmother Amparo. Luis was a lifelong employee of the *despalillo* in Camajuaní. I have also consulted the following sources: Casado, *Nuestro tabaco*; García Galló, *Biografía del tabaco habano*; Perdomo, *Léxico tabacalero cubano*; Rivero Muñiz, *Tabaco* (2 vols.); and Rodríguez Ramos, *Siembra*.

7 Hudson, *Bankers and Empire*, 188.

8 "Don Lisandro Pérez Moreno," *El Caribe* (Camajuaní), December 17, 1937, 1.

9. OSCAR AND NANCY

1 *Gaceta Oficial* 17, no. 129 (June 1, 1918), 8161.

2 The Walton is now a condominium building that retains its original name.

3 US Bureau of the Census. "1920 United States Federal Census," 2010, www.ancestry.com.

4 "New York, US, Arriving Passenger and Crew Lists (including Castle Garden and Ellis Island), 1820–1957," 2010, www.ancestry.com. The ages of the Boullosa sisters that appear on the ship manifest are slightly incorrect and have been corrected on the basis of their confirmed birth dates.

5 Juan Boullosa, "Certificación de Partida Bautismal: Iglesia de Nuestra Señora de la Caridad de la Ciudad, provincia y archidiócesis de La Habana," vol. 37, folio 393, no. 566, copy issued on August 19, 1960.

6 The enrollment of the Boullosa sisters in St. Cecilia was confirmed by an email message to the author from Bridget Nolan Thomas, director of alumnae relations, St. Cecilia Academy, April 12, 2017.

10. LIFE IN HAVANA

1 Rosa Marina Pérez, "Inscripción de Nacimiento," República de Cuba, Secretaría de Sanidad y Beneficencia, vol. 26, folio 499, issued September 19, 1910. Original in possession of the author.

2 Martínez, *Carlos Enríquez*, 25–29.

3 Lisandro Pérez Moreno personal notebook, 1938–49.

4 Since my father had spent several of his childhood years at the house in La Víbora, we visited it during his return trip to Cuba in 2000. It was then that he realized the similarities between that house and the one on G Street and concluded that it had been the model that his father had used to build the latter.

5 República de Cuba, *Censo de 1943*, 811, 883.

6 Pérez, *Religiosas del Sagrado Corazón en Cuba*, 27–33.
7 Ibid.
8 US Bureau of the Census, *Mortality Statistics 1931*, 150.
9 "Florida, US, Arriving and Departing Passenger and Crew Lists, 1898–1963," 2006, www.ancestry.com.

11. TANO

1 See, for example, Chia Garzón, *Monopolio del jabón*, and Pino Santos, *Asalto a Cuba*.
2 John Drebinger, "Giants Win Twice, 1st in 18 innings," *New York Times*, July 3, 1933, 7.
3 "La Salle Defeats St. Ann's, 23 to 20," *New York Times*, January 19, 1939, 17.
4 "The Portfolio: Commencement Issue, Woodmere Academy," May 1938, 6. In the author's possession.
5 "Ocean Travelers," *New York Times*, June 17, 1938, 18.
6 Persons with mixed African and Chinese ancestry were common in Cuba, as the large Chinese immigrations of both the nineteenth and early twentieth centuries were composed almost exclusively of males for whom Afro-Cuban women represented a pool of potential marriage partners at their same socioeconomic level.
7 All Camajuaní, as well as my father's entire family, knew about the fatal episode involving Isabel Rubio. I suspect my mother never learned of it, since Nancy's sister Mary Lou had no knowledge of it until I recently recounted it to her, and she is sure that her sister would have told her had she known. I only learned of it after my father's death. This account was derived from two lengthy interviews: one with my uncle Sergio in Miami in August 2003, and the other with Luis Costales, a cousin of my father on Amparo's side, whom I interviewed in Camajuaní in April 2018. The two interviews yielded remarkably similar details of the episode. The fatalities were also reported in the local press (Martínez-Fortún y Foyo, *Anales y efemérides*, 16:44).

12. BIRTH AND DEATHS

1 *Diario de la Marina*, August 14, 1949, 10.

13. AN (AMERICAN) CHILDHOOD

1 "Cuban Lawyer a Suicide," *New York Times*, January 5, 1931, 16.

14. NEW YEAR, NEW CUBA

1 Goode, *Crown Jewel*, 17, 24.

15. STAMPS

1 "Son ustedes los que tienen que hacer la Revolución," *Diario de la Marina*, September 15, 1959, 10.
2 *Noticias de Hoy* 22, no. 54 (March 6, 1960), 7; Brenner and Eisner, *Cuba Libre*, 107.

EPILOGUE

Epigraph: Keith H. Basso, *Wisdom Sits in Places: Landscape and Language among the Western Apache*, xiii.

1 Fivush, Bohanek, and Duke, "Intergenerational Self"; and Bruce Feiler, "The Stories That Bind Us," *New York Times*, March 17, 2013, ST1, both quoted in Field, *Growing Up*, x.

2 Kela left Cuba for Puerto Rico in 1961 with all the nuns in the Sacred Heart convent when the school was nationalized and the order expelled. She was one of two Sacred Heart sisters who returned to Cuba in 1972 to reestablish the presence of the order on the island, doing community religious work first in Santiago de Cuba and later in Havana.

BIBLIOGRAPHY

ARCHIVES AND MANUSCRIPT COLLECTIONS

Carrillo de Albornoz and Aldama Family Papers. Beinecke Rare Book and Manuscript Library, Yale University, New Haven, CT.

Ernesto Fonts y Sterling Papers. Cuban Heritage Collection. University of Miami Libraries, Coral Gables, FL.

José Ignacio Rodríguez Papers. Manuscript Division. Library of Congress, Washington, DC.

Leonard Wood Papers. Manuscript Division. Library of Congress, Washington, DC.

Lisandro Pérez Moreno personal notebook, 1938–49. In the author's possession.

Moses Taylor Papers. Manuscripts, Archives, and Rare Books Division. New York Public Library, New York, NY.

Records of the Military Government of Cuba, 1898–1902. Record Group 140. National Archives and Records Administration, College Park, MD.

"Ultramar" and "Universidades" collections. Archivo Histórico Nacional, Madrid, Spain.

DATA SETS FROM ANCESTRY.COM

"Florida, US, Arriving and Departing Passenger and Crew Lists, 1898–1963."

"New York, US, Arriving Passenger and Crew Lists (including Castle Garden and Ellis Island), 1820–1957."

"New York Passenger Lists, 1851–1891."

"US Arriving and Departing Passengers and Crew Lists, 1898–1963."

"US Arriving Passengers and Crew Lists, New York, 1820–1957."

US Bureau of the Census. "1880 United States Federal Census." New York City.

US Bureau of the Census. "1920 United States Federal Census." New York City.

NEWSPAPERS AND OTHER SERIALS

Brooklyn Daily Eagle
Cuba y América
Diario de la Marina
El Caribe
Gaceta de La Habana
Gaceta Oficial
La Discusión
La Nación
Louisiana Planter and Sugar Manufacturer
New York Times
Noticias de Hoy
Revista de Historia Cubana y Americana
Revista de la Víbora

BOOKS AND JOURNAL ARTICLES

Abad, Diana. "Las emigraciones cubanas en la Guerra de los Diez Años." *Santiago* 53 (1984): 143–84.

Alfonso Ballol, Berta, Mercedes Herrera Sorzano, Eduardo Moyano, Jesús Sanz Fernández, and Martín Socarrás Matos. *El camino de hierro de La Habana a Güines: Primer ferrocarril de Iberoamérica*. Madrid: Fundación de los Ferrocarriles Españoles, 1987.

Álvarez Pedroso, Antonio. *Miguel de Aldama*. Havana: Academia de la Historia de Cuba, 1948.

Angulo, Lorenzo, and Miguel Angel Mendoza, eds. *Directorio social de Cuba, Habana, año 1919*. Havana: Editorial Directorio Social de Cuba, 1920.

Arbelo, Manuel. *Recuerdos de la última guerra por la independencia de Cuba, 1898 a 1898*. Havana: Imp. Tipografía Moderna, 1918.

Bay Sevilla, Luis. "La barriada del Cerro: Domínguez 4." *Arquitectura* 13, no. 142 (May 1945): 163–65.

Bizcarrondo, Marta, and Antonio Elorza. *Cuba-España: El dilema autonomista, 1878–1898*. Madrid: Editorial Colibrí, 2001.

Blanco Escolá, Carlos. *General Mola: El ególatra que provocó la guerra civil*. Madrid: La Esfera de los Libros, 2002.

Brenner, Philip, and Peter Eisner. *Cuba Libre: A 500-Year Quest for Independence*. Lanham, MD: Rowman & Littlefield, 2018.

Burrows, Edwin G., and Mike Wallace. *Gotham: A History of New York City to 1898*. New York: Oxford University Press, 1999.

Canel, Eva. *Lo que ví en Cuba (a través de la isla)*. Havana: Imprenta y Papelería La Universal, 1916.

Canet, Gerardo. *Atlas de Cuba*. Cambridge, MA: Harvard University Press, 1949.

Casado, Ricardo A. *Nuestro tabaco: El habano sin igual*. Havana: Ricardo A. Casado, 1939.

Casey, Matthew. *Empire's Guestworkers: Haitian Migrants in Cuba during the Age of US Occupation*. Cambridge: Cambridge University Press, 2017.

Centro de Estudios Militares. *Diccionario enciclopédico de historia militar de Cuba*. Vol. 1, pt. 1. Havana: Ediciones Verde Olivo, 2001.

Chia Garzón, Jesús A. *El monopolio del jabón y el perfume en Cuba*. Havana: Editorial de Ciencias Sociales, 1977.

Collazo, Enrique. *La revolución de agosto de 1906*. Havana: Casa Editorial C. Martínez y Ca., 1907.

Cuban American Sugar Company. *Annual Reports*. New York: Cuban American Sugar Company, 1909–17.

Cuban Information Archives. "Anglo-American Directory of Cuba 1960: Province of Havana." Accessed February 6, 2023. www.cuban-exile.com.

Dolz y Arango, Ricardo. *El proceso electoral de 1916*. Havana: Imp. y Papelería La Universal, de Ruiz y Ca., 1917.

Editorial Cubana, ed. *Las Villas: Album-resumen ilustrado*. 2nd ed. Havana: Imprenta La Milagrosa, 1941.

Ferrer, Ada. *Cuba: An American History*. New York: Scribner, 2021.

———. *Insurgent Cuba: Race, Nation, and Revolution, 1868–1898*. Chapel Hill: University of North Carolina Press, 1999.

Field, Kendra Taira. *Growing Up with the Country: Family, Race, and Nation after the Civil War*. New Haven: Yale University Press, 2018.

———. "The Privilege of Family History." *American Historical Review* 127, no. 2 (June 2022): 600–633.

Fivush, Robyn, Jennifer G. Bohanek, and Marshall Duke. "The Intergenerational Self: Subject Perspective and Family History." In *Self-Continuity: Individual and Collective Perspectives*, edited by Fabio Sani, 131–41. New York: Psychology Press, 2008.

García del Barco y Alonso, José. *Camajuaní y la revolución del 95*. Havana: Imprenta Siglo XX, 1928.

García Galló, Gaspar Jorge. *Biografía del tabaco habano*. Havana: Comisión Nacional del Tabaco Habano, 1961.

García Márquez, Gabriel. "The Solitude of Latin America." Nobel Lecture. The Nobel Prize, December 9, 1982. www.nobelprize.org.

General Cigar Company. *Annual Statement 1921*. New York: General Cigar Company, 1921.

Gobierno Civil de Santa Clara. *Memoria, año 1901*. Villaclara, Cuba: Imprenta Iris, 1902.

González del Valle, Angel. *Memorandum presentado a la Comisión Nacional de Propaganda y Defensa del Tabaco Habano*. Havana: Imprenta el Siglo XX, 1929.

Goode, Linda, ed. *The Crown Jewel: Lake Wales High School Yearbook 1959*. Accessed January 4, 2021. www.classmates.com.

Gras y Elías, Francisco. *Historia de los lugares, villas y ciudades de la Provincia de Tarragona*. Barcelona: Tipografía de Julián Doria, 1907.

Hagedorn, Hermann. *Leonard Wood: A Biography*. 2 vols. New York: Harper & Brothers, 1931.

Hernández Sanahuja, Buenaventura. *Historia de Tarragona desde los más remotos tiempos hasta la época de la restauración cristiana*. Vol. 1, edited by Emilio Morera Llauradó. Tarragona: Est. Tip. de Adolfo Alegret, 1892.

Hoernel, Robert B. "Sugar and Social Change in Oriente, Cuba, 1898–1946." *Journal of Latin American Studies* 8, no. 2 (November 1976): 215–49.

Hudson, Peter James. *Bankers and Empire: How Wall Street Colonized the Caribbean.* Chicago: University of Chicago Press, 2017.

Iglesias, Marcos A. *Los caminos de hierro de Yaguajay.* Ontario, Canada: M & T, 2003.

Iribarren, José María. *El General Mola.* 3rd ed. Madrid: Editorial Bullón, 1963.

Jorgensen, Margaret, comp. *Preliminary Inventory of the Records of the Military Government of Cuba.* Washington, DC: National Archives, 1962.

Knight, Franklin. *Slave Society in Cuba during the Nineteenth Century.* Madison: University of Wisconsin Press, 1970.

Ladd, Eugene F. "Report of the Treasurer of the Island of Cuba." In *Annual Reports of the War Department for the Fiscal Year Ended June 30, 1900. Part 11: Report of the Military Governor of Cuba On Civil Affairs.* Vol. 1, pt. 3. Washington, DC: US Government Printing Office, 1901.

Llaverías, Joaquín. *Miguel Aldama, o la dignidad patriótica.* Havana: Imprenta Molina, 1937.

Lobo Montalvo, María Luisa. *Havana: History and Architecture of a Romantic City.* New York: Monacelli, 2000.

Maíz, B. Félix. *Mola, aquel hombre: Diario de la conspiración 1936.* Barcelona: Editorial Planeta, 1976.

Márquez Sterling, Carlos. *A la ingerencia extraña, la virtud doméstica: Biografía de Manuel Márquez Sterling.* Miami, FL: Ediciones Universal, 1986.

Marrero, Leví. *Cuba: Economía y sociedad.* Vol. 3, *Siglo XVII, parte 1.* San Juan, PR: Editorial San Juan, 1984.

———. *Cuba: Economía y sociedad.* Vol. 15, *Azúcar, ilustración y conciencia (1763–1868).* Madrid: Editorial Playor, 1992.

Martell Álvarez, Raúl. *Gustav Bock: Los monopolios tabacaleros en Cuba.* Havana: Ediciones Cubanas Artex, 2017.

Martí, Carlos. *Los catalanes en América: Cuba.* Barcelona: Editorial Minerva, 1920.

Martínez, Juan A. *Carlos Enríquez: The Painter of Cuban Ballads.* Coral Gables, FL: Cernuda Arte, 2010.

Martínez Escobar, Manuel. *Historia de Remedios.* Havana: Jesús Montero, 1944.

Martínez-Fortún y Foyo, José A. *Anales y efemérides de San Juan de los Remedios y su jurisdicción.* Vols. 1–44. Havana: Pérez, Sierra y Comp., 1930–45.

———. *Apuntes históricos de Camajuaní.* Havana, 1943. Mimeograph.

Martínez-Fortún y Foyo, José A., and Humberto Arnáez y Rodríguez. *Diccionario biográfico Remediano.* Vol. 1. Havana: Imprenta el Siglo XX, 1960.

Maysilles, Jean. "A Remembrance of General Cigar Company in Lancaster County." *Journal of the Lancaster County Historical Society* 96, no. 2 (Spring 1995): 39–47.

McCallum, Jack. *Leonard Wood: Rough Rider, Surgeon, Architect of American Imperialism.* New York: New York University Press, 2006.

McGillivray, Gillian. *Blazing Cane: Sugar Communities, Class, and State Formation in Cuba.* Durham, NC: Duke University Press, 2009.

Minger, Ralph Eldin. "William H. Taft and the United States Intervention in Cuba in 1906." *Hispanic American Historical Review* 41, no. 1 (February 1961): 75–89.

Moreno Fraginals, Manuel. *The Sugarmill: The Socioeconomic Complex of Sugar in Cuba.* Translated by Cedric Belfrage. New York: Monthly Review Press, 1976.

Orozco y Arascot, Anastacio de and Carlos Fonts y Sterling. *Diccionario en las materias contenidas en la ley hipotecaria para las islas de Cuba y Puerto Rico.* Vol. 1. Havana: Gobierno y Capitania General por S. M., 1880.

Ortiz, Fernando. *Historia de una pelea cubana contra los demonios.* Havana: Editorial de Ciencias Sociales, 1975.

Padula, Alfred L., Jr. "The Fall of the Bourgeoisie: Cuba, 1959–1961." PhD diss., University of New Mexico, 1974.

Peraza Sarausa, Fermín. *Diccionario biográfico cubano.* Vol. 7. Gainesville, FL: Fermín Peraza Sarausa, 1967.

Perdomo, José E. *Léxico tabacalero cubano.* Miami: Ediciones Universal, 1998.

Pérez, Lisandro. "Iron Mining and Socio-demographic Change in Eastern Cuba, 1884–1940." *Journal of Latin American Studies* 14, no. 2 (November 1982): 381–405.

———. *Sugar, Cigars, and Revolution: The Making of Cuban New York.* New York: New York University Press, 2018.

Pérez, Louis A., Jr. *Cuba under the Platt Amendment, 1902–1934.* Pittsburgh, PA: University of Pittsburgh Press, 1986.

———. *Intervention, Revolution, and Politics in Cuba, 1913–1921.* Pittsburgh, PA: University of Pittsburgh Press, 1978.

Pérez, Raquel. *Religiosas del Sagrado Corazón en Cuba.* San Juan, PR: Gráfica Metropolitana, 1997.

Pérez Linares, Ramón. *Tabaco y desafíos laborales en la región central de Cuba (1940–1958): La agro-manufactura tabacalera y el movimiento obrero.* Berlin: Editorial Académica Española, 2011.

Pérez-Reverte, Arturo. *Una historia de España.* Barcelona: Alfaguara, 2019.

Pichardo, Hortensia. *Cartas a Francisco Carrillo.* Havana: Instituto Cubano del Libro, 1971.

Pino Santos, Oscar. *El asalto a Cuba por la oligarquía financiera yanki.* Havana: Casa de las Américas, 1973.

Portell-Vilá, Herminio. *Nueva historia de la República de Cuba (1898–1979).* Miami: La Moderna Poesía, 1996.

Quiroz, Alfonso W. "Loyalist Overkill: The Socioeconomic Costs of 'Repressing' the Separatist Insurrection in Cuba, 1868–1878." *Hispanic American Historical Review* 78, no. 2 (1998).

República de Cuba. *Censo de 1943.* Havana: P. Fernández y Compañía, 1945.

Rivero Muñíz, José. *Tabaco: Su historia en Cuba.* Vol. 1, *Desde su descubrimiento en 1492, hasta la implantación de la segunda factoría de tabacos de La Habana en 1761.* Havana: Instituto de Historia, 1964.

———. *Tabaco: Su historia en Cuba.* Vol. 2, *Desde los inicios de la segunda factoría de tabacos de La Habana hasta mediados del siglo XX.* Havana: Instituto de Historia, 1965.

Rodríguez, Rolando. *República de corcho*. 2 vols. Havana: Editorial de Ciencias Sociales, 2012.

Rodríguez Ramos, Manuel. *Siembra, fabricación é historia del tabaco, con el manual del tabaquero*. Havana: Librería é Imprenta Monte Núm. 17, 1905.

Rodríguez Rodríguez, Amalia. *Algunos documentos políticos de Máximo Gómez*. Havana: Biblioteca Nacional José Martí, 1962.

Roloff y Maliofsky, Carlos, comp. *Yndice alfabético y defunciones del Ejército Libertador de Cuba*. Havana: Imprenta de Rambla y Bouza, 1901.

Rovira, Salvador-J., and Pere Anguera. *Història de Torredembarra segles XVIII–XX*. Torredembarra, Spain: Ajuntament de Torredembarra, 1984.

Santa Cruz y Mallén, Francisco Javier de. *Historia de familias cubanas*. Vols. 1–6. Havana: Editorial Hercules, 1940–50.

———. *Historia de familias cubanas*. Vols. 7–9. Miami: Ediciones Universal, 1985–88.

Santovenia, Emeterio. "Política colonial." In *Historia de la nación cubana*. Vol. 2 of *Guerras coloniales, conflictos y progresos, desde 1697 hasta 1790*, edited by Ramiro Guerra y Sánchez, José M. Pérez Cabrera, Juan J. Remos, and Emeterio S. Santovenia, 12–63. Havana: Editorial Historia de la Nación Cubana, 1952.

Sarmiento Ramírez, Ismael. *Cuba: Entre la opulencia y la pobreza*. Madrid: Agualarga Editores, n.d.

Scott, Rebecca J., and Jean M. Hébrard. *Freedom Papers: An Atlantic Odyssey in the Age of Emancipation*. Cambridge, MA: Harvard University Press, 2012.

Soulere, Emilio A. *Historia de la insurrección de Cuba, 1869–1879*. Vol. 1. Barcelona: Establecimiento Tipográfico-Editorial de Juan Pons, 1879.

Tamayo, Diego. "Informe del Secretario de Estado y Gobernación." In *Civil Report of the Military Governor of Cuba, 1899–1900*. Vol. 3. Washington, DC: US Government Printing Office, 1901.

Tejera, Eduardo J. *Historia política y económica de Cuba (1800–1961): Una república en formación*. Madrid: Editorial Dykinson, 2019.

Thomas, Hugh. *Cuba, or The Pursuit of Freedom*. Rev. ed. New York: Da Capo, 1998.

Universal Tobacco Dealers Directory for the Year 1867. New York: Barrett, 1867.

US Bureau of the Census. *Mortality Statistics 1931*. Washington, DC: US Government Printing Office, 1935.

US War Department. *Annual Reports for the Fiscal Year Ended June 30, 1900. Part 11: Report of the Military Governor of Cuba on Civil Affairs*. Vol. 1, pt. 3. Washington, DC: US Government Printing Office, 1901.

Wheeler, Joseph Lewis. *Report of a Survey Preliminary to the Establishment of the Ramon Guiteras Public Library at Matanzas, Cuba, Made March 1949*. Providence, RI: Industrial Trust Comp., 1949.

Wilson, Hugh R. *The Man Who Created Franco: General Emilio Mola*. Devon, UK: Arthur H. Stockwell, 1972.

Yglesia Martínez, Teresita. *Cuba: Primera república, segunda ocupación*. Havana: Editorial de Ciencias Sociales, 1976.

————. "Organización de la república neocolonial." In *La neocolonia: Organización y crisis desde 1899 hasta 1940*, edited by Instituto de Historia de Cuba, 46–98. Havana: Editorial Política, 1998.

Zanetti Lecuona, Oscar. *Cuba: El largo siglo XX*. Santo Domingo, Dominican Republic: Archivo General de la Nación, 2021.

Zanetti Lecuona, Oscar, and Alejandro García Álvarez. *Caminos para el azúcar*. Havana: Editorial de Ciencias Sociales, 1987.

Zaragoza, Justo. *Las insurrecciones de Cuba: Apuntes para la historia política de esta isla en el presente siglo*. Vol. 2. Madrid: Imprenta de Miguel G. Hernández, 1873.

INDEX

Page numbers in *italics* refer to figures.

Fonts y Sterling, Ernesto (*continued*)
reported shortfall in US funds to Cuba,
79–80; resigned, along with Estrada
Palma and cabinet, 92; resigned as
General Manager of Chaparra, 121;
returned to Cuba before graduating from
military academy, 35; roasted *jutías* (West
Indies rodents), 50; sent to New York
under guardianship of Aldama y Alfonso,
Miguel de, 33–34; signatory to the 1897
constitution, 51; thrown off a horse and
injured his spine, 118; Treasurer for Las
Villas, 51; Treasurer of the National Bank
of Cuba, 96; Treasury Secretary in Estrada Palma's second term, 89; Treasury
Secretary in the Cuban government-in-
arms, 54; Undersecretary of the Cuban
Treasury, 51
Fonts y Sterling, Oscar, 25, 227; did not
join the war for independence, 44;
entrenched in Havana's elite financial
and social circles, 46; on governing
board of the National Bank of Cuba, 46;
married a woman from an established
family in Cuba, 46; owned elegant house
in El Cerro, 46; practice law in Havana
during war for independence, 44; pro-
independence actors met at his house at
El Cerro, 47; suicide, 228; supportive of
independence war, 56; Vice President of
the Automóvil Club of Cuba, 46
Fonts y Sterling, Raúl, 25, 46
Franco, Francisco (Gen.), 65, 295n16
(chap. 5)

García-Menocal y Deop, Mario (Gen./
President), 91, 106; administered the
Chaparra Sugar Company, 107; admonished Fonts y Sterling, Ernesto, for damages at Chaparra, 119–20; agent of US
sugar interests in Cuba, 106–7; Chaparra
employed three thousand workers, 110;

Chaparra Sugar Company renamed
the Cuban American Sugar Company,
107; Chinese labor recruited, 111; corporation owned private port facilities, 109;
Cuban American Sugar Company held
over 460,000 acres, 112; deployed troops
to protect Chaparra, 118; descendant of
aristocratic family in Spain, 106; did not
tolerate worker discontent, 115; elected
President in 1912, 109; engineering degree
from Cornell University, 106; established
the Conservative Party, 108; favored
by the US State Department for second
term, 119; granted pension for Acosta
y de la Cruz Muñoz, María Luisa, and
sons, 143–44; hired Fonts y Sterling,
Ernesto, to administer the Delicias
central (sugar factory), 108; interfered
with the 1916 elections to remain in
power, 117; member of Conservative
Party, 164; named to board of directors
of the Cuban American Sugar Company,
107; one of the largest US investments
in Cuba, 112; promoted to General, 106;
ran against Gómez, José Miguel, for
President but lost, 108; recommended
the purchase of the Chaparra sugar mill,
107; recruited cane cutters from Caribbean islands, 111; security in Chaparra,
115; selected Fonts y Sterling, Ernesto, as
the General Manager of Chaparra, 109;
sought a conciliation between Liberals
and Moderates, 91, 108
García-Menocal y Martín, Aniceto, 106
General Cigar Company: based in New
York, 127; Cuban subsidiary, General
Cigar Company of Cuba, Ltd., 131;
expanded to include Cuban tobacco, 128;
fifteen tobacco houses and a warehouse,
132; known previously as United Cigar
Manufacturers Company, 128; most important asset in purchase of Echevarría

ABOUT THE AUTHOR

Aside from being the son of Tano and Nancy and the grandson of Lisandro, Amparo, Oscar, and Nancy, LISANDRO PÉREZ is a professor of Latin American and Latinx Studies at John Jay College, City University of New York. He received a PhD degree in sociology and Latin American studies from the University of Florida. Pérez has served as editor of the journal *Cuban Studies* and co-authored *The Legacy of Exile: Cubans in the United States* (Allyn & Bacon, 2003). He has published in the *Latin American Research Review, International Migration Review, Journal of Latin American Studies, Cuban Studies*, and the *Annals of the American Academy of Political and Social Science*, among other journals. His 2018 book, *Sugar, Cigars, and Revolution: The Making of Cuban New York* (NYU Press), won the Herbert H. Lehman Prize for Distinguished Scholarship in New York history, awarded by the New York Academy of History. A Spanish edition of the book was published in 2020 by Casa de las Américas, a leading Cuban cultural institution. In 2023, he received the Prize for Outstanding Scholarly Contributions to Cuban Studies, awarded by the Cuba Section of the Latin American Studies Association.